50

reasons people give
for believing in a god

CRITICAL ACCLAIM FOR
50 REASONS PEOPLE GIVE FOR BELIEVING IN A GOD

"There may be 50 ways to leave your lover, but now Guy Harrison has given us 50 ways to believe in God, or not if you care to read this engaging and enlightening book in light of what it says about the cultural and psychological power of belief. If the number one predictor of which God someone believes in is what culture and time period they happened to have been born in, what does that say about the actual existence (or not) of a deity? Read this book to explore the many and diverse reasons for belief."

—Michael Shermer
Publisher of *Skeptic* magazine,
monthly columnist for *Scientific American*,
and author of *Why Darwin Matters*

"Guy P. Harrison does a splendid job of critically examining the many reasons people offer in support of their religious beliefs. He shares the exhilaration of moving beyond religion, but Harrison doesn't bully or condescend. Rather, he approaches the reader gently. Reading Harrison's book is like having an amiable chat with a wise old friend."

—Cameron M. Smith and Charles Sullivan
Authors of *The Top 10 Myths about Evolution*

"Religion is as universal as language, which hints at a biological basis. Why did our ancestors evolve an attraction to the supernatural? The fundamental question is not whether this attraction is rational or not—which is the subject of a dozen recent provocative books—but what exactly faith delivers to those who possess it. The present book treats this question respectfully, listening to the answer of the believers themselves, which seems an excellent place to start."

—Frans de Waal
Leading primatologist, author of *Our Inner Ape*

50

reasons people give
for believing in a god

Guy P. Harrison

Visit www.guyharrison.info for essays,
book reviews, and more by Guy P. Harrison.

Prometheus Books

59 John Glenn Drive
Amherst, New York 14228-2119

Published 2008 by Prometheus Books

Inquiries should be addressed to
Prometheus Books
59 John Glenn Drive
Amherst, New York 14228–2119
VOICE: 716–691–0133, ext. 210
FAX: 716–691–0137
WWW.PROMETHEUSBOOKS.COM

12 11 10 09   5 4 3 2

Library of Congress Cataloging-in-Publication Data

Harrison, Guy P.
    50 reasons people give for believing in a God / by Guy P. Harrison
        p. cm.
    Includes bibliographical references.
    ISBN 978–1–59102–567–2
    1. Faith—Miscellanea. I. Title. II. Title: Fifty reasons people give for believing in a God

BL626.3.H37 2008
212—dc22

2007051814

Printed in the United States on acid-free paper

For Natasha, Jared, and Marissa.
May your minds be curious and free forever.

Acknowledgments

I thank editors Steven L. Mitchell and Jacinta Meyers, and Prometheus Books for helping to make this book a reality. I am deeply grateful to my wife, Sheree, for her consistent encouragement and my son, Jared, for his helpful advice. I also thank Andrea Roach for her invaluable comments and criticism. My greatest debt of all, however, is to the many people around the world who openly shared with me their reasons for believing.

Contents

ACKNOWLEDGMENTS 7

INTRODUCTION 13

1. My god is obvious. 17

2. Almost everybody on Earth is religious. 23

3. Faith is a good thing. 27

4. Archaeological discoveries prove that my god exists. 37

5. Only my god can make me feel significant. 45

6. Atheism is just another religion. 49

7. Evolution is bad. 57

8. Our world is too beautiful to be an accident. 65

9. My god created the universe. 71

10. Believing in my god makes me happy. 77

11. Better safe than sorry. 85

12. A sacred book proves my god is real.   91

13. Divine justice proves my god is real.   101

14. My god answers prayers.   107

15. I would rather worship my god than the devil.   117

16. My god heals sick people.   123

17. Anything is better than being an atheist.   131

18. My god made the human body.   139

19. My god sacrificed his only son for me.   147

20. Atheists are jerks who think they know everything.   153

21. I don't lose anything by believing in my god.   161

22. I didn't come from a monkey.   169

23. I don't want to go to hell.   175

24. I feel my god when I pray.   179

25. I need my god to protect me.   183

26. I want eternal life.   191

27. Without my god we would have no sense of
    right and wrong.   197

28. My god makes me feel like I am part of something
    bigger than myself.   207

29. My religion makes more sense than all the others. 213

30. My god changes lives. 221

31. Intelligent design proves my god is real. 225

32. Millions of people can't be wrong about my religion. 231

33. Miracles prove my god is real. 235

34. Religion is beautiful. 241

35. Some very smart people believe in my god. 247

36. Ancient prophecies prove my god exists. 251

37. No one has ever disproved the existence of my god. 263

38. People have gone to heaven and returned. 267

39. Religion brings people together. 273

40. My god inspires people. 281

41. Science can't explain everything. 287

42. Society would fall apart without religion. 295

43. My religion is so old, it must be true. 303

44. Someone I trust told me that my god is real. 309

45. Atheism is a negative and empty philosophy. 315

12 CONTENTS

46. Believing in a god doesn't hurt anyone.   325

47. The earth is perfectly tuned to support life.   331

48. Believing is natural so my god must be real.   337

49. The end is near.   343

50. I am afraid of not believing.   349

Introduction

Gods are fragile things; they may be killed by a whiff of science or a dose of common sense.
—Chapman Cohen

No gods were harmed in the writing of this book.
—Guy P. Harrison

I have asked many believers in many countries over several years a basic question: Why do you believe in your god or gods? This book is a response to the fifty most common answers I heard to that question. Many people gave me virtually identical reasons for belief, despite being adherents of contradictory religions. I learned that the gods may be very different and the faithful may sometimes hate and kill one another, but believers are remarkably synchronized on why they believe.

I also discovered that if you ask believers on the streets of Jerusalem, Cairo, Paris, Nairobi, New Delhi, Athens, Suva, New York City, and Port Moresby why they believe in their gods, the answers you hear are significantly different from the noise coming from theologians and religious philosophers. Most of the Christians I have encountered around the world, for example, don't give much thought to the works of St. Thomas Aquinas or C. S. Lewis. They will tell anyone who asks, however, that they believe Jesus is a real god because the Bible says so or because they feel his presence when they pray. Out in the real world I found that believers have little interest in convoluted arguments for gods that involve imagining perfection, irreducible complexity, or the laws of thermodynamics. Unlike professional creationists and apologists, most of the believers I talk with do not feel the need to cite long lists of questionable evidence to attempt to prove that their god is real. They "know" their gods are real because they have "faith" that they are. They believe because they think that they must in order to be a good person. They believe because the world is "perfect" or at least "beautiful." They believe in a god because it is the only way they have ever known.

This book is not an attempt to prove the nonexistence of gods. Nor is it an attack on anyone's entire religion. This is a respectful reply to the friendly people around the world who shared with me their reasons for believing in a god or gods, nothing more. Too many books that attempt to challenge belief in gods are interpreted by believers as combative and arrogant. I have made a sincere effort to prevent believers from feeling that way about this book. There is no name calling or condescending tone here. I do not think that I am smarter than believers, nor do I agree with anyone who feels that believers' minds are hopelessly closed. My fifty replies to common justifications for belief can be read as friendly chats designed to do nothing more than stimulate critical thinking. I am not interested in winning debates or insulting anyone. I only want to encourage readers to think more deeply about why they believe in a god.

Readers will notice that I do not limit the scope of this book to the religions that are currently popular in the West. In my view all gods are equal, regardless of how many people believe in them at this moment in history. My skepticism for Ra and Apollo, for example, is no more or less than my skepticism for Jesus and Allah. Throughout this book I usually will write of gods in the plural rather than singular. This may feel awkward to readers who are used to only hearing and talking about one god. The fact is, however, there are many thousands of other gods that people have confidently claimed to be real throughout history. Failure to acknowledge this important truth would be historically ignorant and culturally prejudiced. Fairness and logic demand that we respect the indigenous tribal believer who sees many gods in the forest and the ancient Greek who saw several gods atop a mountain as much as we do the contemporary monotheist who sees one god in the sky.

Many people think that religious belief should be above challenge or somehow out of bounds. I disagree. There is a lot of good to be found in the world's religions. I would never deny that. However, the dark side of religion cannot be overlooked. When claims for the existence of gods negatively impact world peace, the education of children, the development of new medical cures, safety and justice for women, and the progress of science, they must be challenged.

Chapter 1

My god is obvious.

If God has spoken, why is the world not convinced?
—Percy Bysshe Shelley

Perhaps the most common reason that people give for believing in a god is the claim that their god is obviously real. The god's existence is so plain to see that even listening to counterarguments or entertaining doubt is a waste of time. Probably the majority of the world's believers have no interest in investigating or debating the existence of their god for this reason. They see no possibility that they could be wrong about this because it is just so darn obvious that they are right. After all, their god is everywhere. Their god made everything. Their god answers prayers. Their god runs the universe. Nothing could be clearer than their god's existence, they say. Many believers find the mere suggestion that their god might not exist to be laughable.

Obvious or not, belief in gods deserves to be challenged. Believers owe it to the world and our collective future to at least hear and consider basic questions about gods. These claims can't be given a pass because they are connected to some of humankind's most divisive and dangerous behavior. If a significant portion of our species insists on discriminating, hating, killing, and slowing scientific progress in the name of gods, then don't we owe it to ourselves to at least try and confirm whether or not these gods are even real in the first place?

I have found that most believers are highly skeptical people. I have

17

talked with Muslims who are world-class skeptics on the subject of Christianity. They know how to punch holes in virtually every claim that religion makes. Many Christians I have encountered are brutally analytical and filled with doubt when it comes to the claims of Islam. They can dismantle every Muslim argument very effectively. I have read the Koran and it is not obvious to me that it is a perfect book that was inspired by a god. Christians feel the same way about it. They agree with me that Muslims should be more skeptical about Muhammad's claims and demand evidence. But I also have read the Bible and it is not obvious to me that it is a perfect book that was inspired by a god either. Muslims agree with me because it's not obvious to them either. They also agree with me that Christians should be more skeptical about the Bible and demand evidence. Of course all this skepticism vanishes when the spotlight turns to their own religion. The truth is, just about everybody is a skeptic—except when it comes to their own "obviously true" belief. Unfortunately, this is the one religion that they need to challenge most of all. It makes no sense for a believer to arbitrarily exempt one religion out of thousands. All religions deserve equal scrutiny, even if it is the one that mom and dad told you was true when you were a child.

The breakdown of who believes in which god and how they must be worshipped should trouble religious people, or at least make them curious. Why is it, for example, that the "obvious" god of more than one billion Muslims is unrecognizable to the five billion non-Muslims who are alive today? About five-sixths of the human population does not think he is really there. Nothing is more obvious to Christians than Jesus. So why do more than four billion people not believe he is a god? Some one billion Hindus think their gods are obviously real. But five billion of their fellow humans do not see it that way. This misalignment of belief demolishes claims that anyone's god is obvious. Wouldn't an obvious god be able to convince at least a majority if not all of the world's people that he or she exists?

Believers who say that their god is obviously real should explain what they mean. A tree standing in front of you is obviously real. A shoe on your foot is obviously real. How is an invisible and silent god (at least to most of us) obviously real? It shouldn't be too hard to convince others if the god truly is obvious. Of course, believers already put a tremendous amount of effort into trying to show others "glaringly obvious" gods. Everything from songs and comic books to missionaries and military invasions have been used to try and get people to see an "obvious" god. For some reason, however, the results have been mixed. Today, after two thousand years of Christianity and fourteen hundred years of Islam, for example, half the world's population still thinks those two religions have it all wrong. How can this be explained if Jesus and Allah are obvious?

Any god that is obviously real should be recognizable to anyone, even atheists. I don't think most atheists would deny the obvious. I cannot speak for all nonbelievers but certainly I know that I am open to the possibility that gods exist. I would never close my eyes or my mind to good evidence or strong arguments. I am a curious person and want to know as much as I can about everything. I would never deny scientific confirmation of a god. If the African god Fidi Mukullu descends upon Times Square tomorrow, I would be glued to the TV and Web to find out every detail about the historic event. I would be excited, not upset. My first impulse would be to try and get an interview with him to learn everything I could about what it's like to be a god. I certainly wouldn't cling to atheism. I am a passionate fan of science and enjoy learning about the latest microbes found at the bottom of a deep sea or the weird behavior of atoms. I couldn't turn away from any unusual discovery—including a god—if I tried. If the world's scientific community presented overwhelming evidence that Fidi Mukullu or any other god was real, I would not hang my head in shame for having been an atheist. I would be grateful to know something new and important. If any gods are real I sincerely want to know them.

The problem is that what may seem obvious to many believers is far from obvious to nonbelievers. Stories in sacred books have not convinced most people that one god or another is real. Merely pointing out the complexity of the universe has not been enough either. At this point in time it looks doubtful that anyone will ever come up with something that will show that a god is undeniably real. For centuries, brilliant theologians, monks, imams, authors, and even many scientists have taken their best shot at showing the entire world that their god was real. But none of them came close to succeeding. Today a high school student with a fair understanding of religious claims and a good science education can defeat, or at least cast crippling doubt on, every argument for a god ever posed by the greatest religious minds of history. This is not to say that Thomas Aquinas, Martin Luther, C. S. Lewis, Jonathan Edwards, and all the others were dumber than a high school kid. It just shows that there is a severe lack of ammunition when it comes to defending the claim that gods are real.

Still, a believer might say, *someone* is up there. Maybe we got the name wrong and maybe organized religions have corrupted the stories, but a god must have created everything. A god must be making the world go round. This much is obvious, they say. However, even a claim as vague as this is not obvious to everyone. There are many people all over the world who do not believe in any gods. According to sociologist Phil Zuckerman, between five hundred million and seven hundred fifty million people currently have no belief in any gods (Zuckerman 2005). This is a huge number. And it is even more impressive than it appears at first glance because Zuckerman only included what he calls "organic atheism" in his calculations. Organic atheists, he says, are true nonbelievers who are living in relatively free societies and able to believe or not believe without fear of severe punishment from an oppressive government.

So who are these five hundred to seven hundred fifty million infidels without a god in their lives? Are they the misfits and maniacs of the world? Are these the people who fill the world's prisons? It doesn't seem so. Zuckerman's research shows that these nonbelievers mostly come from the safest, healthiest, most educated, most charitable, most technologically advanced, and most crime-free nations on Earth. Countries with high percentages of nonbelievers include global bright spots such as Sweden, Denmark, Norway, Japan, Canada, and France. These people are not the world's idiots. If a god was obviously real, it's likely that they would be bright enough to recognize it and honest enough to admit it.

A more specific group of people worth considering are scientists. Why do so many scientists fail to see these "obvious" gods whom believers keep talking about? Despite the fact that the United States is a highly religious society, almost all elite American scientists are non-believers. Researchers Edward J. Larson and Larry Witham revealed this with a study of members of the National Academy of Sciences in 1998. They found that only 7 percent of these accomplished scientists believed in a god. A full 93 percent indicated that no god is obvious to them (American Atheists 1999). But how can this be? The ability of modern scientists to detect and observe objects and phenomenon both far and near is astonishing. Scientists are able to study viruses, molecules, atoms, even parts of atoms. Scientists are able to see far beyond our solar system and our galaxy. They can even see back in time with deep-space imaging. But despite all of these abilities, no one has ever had any success at discovering so much as the slightest trace of a god. After all of this searching, listening, and looking, we still have nothing but weak arguments and unreliable eyewitness accounts to support the existence of gods. I'm not sure how anyone who thinks their god is obvious can explain what is going on in the minds of these nonbelieving scientists. We can safely assume that these are very smart people. That's why they ended up being elite scientists. If an obviously real god created the universe, the earth and all life on it, wouldn't you think that America's best astronomers, geologists, and biologists would be the first people in line to worship that god? Wouldn't you think that smart professionals who have dedicated their lives to exploring, discovering, experimenting, and thinking about life and the universe would be the first to detect a god? How can it be that so many of the brightest people on earth have not yet come across a compelling reason to believe in a god? At the very least it means the existence of gods is far from obvious.

CHAPTER 1 BIBLIOGRAPHY AND RECOMMENDED READING

American Atheists. "God and the Scientists: A New Debate, an Old Question." August 26, 1999, www.atheists.org/flash.line/atheism6.htm.

Dennett, Daniel C. *Breaking the Spell: Religion as a Natural Phenomenon.* New York: Viking Adult, 2006.

Mythology: Gods, Goddesses and Heroes from Around the World. London: Kingfisher Publications, 2001.

Zuckerman, Phil. "Atheism: Contemporary Rates and Patterns." In *The Cambridge Companion to Atheism*, ed. Michael Martin, 47–65. Cambridge: Cambridge University Press, 2005.

Chapter 2

Almost everybody on Earth is religious.

Do you ever ask yourself: What if I'm wrong?
—Daniel C. Dennett

Belief in gods is old and widespread. Our fascination with spirits, ghosts, and gods surely predates civilization. Today, more than two hundred years after the Enlightenment and within sight of a possible Star Trek–like future, there remains some attraction to gods in every society. Belief in gods seems to be nearly as much a part of being human as music and language are. Was our tendency toward belief carved into our minds by evolution because it fostered tribal unity during prehistory? Or could it simply be an odd idea that stuck, gained momentum, and never looked back? We cannot yet say with certainty. One thing is clear: belief is popular. So popular, in fact, that many people find confirmation for their god in numbers alone.

More than 80 percent of the world's people claim to have some sort of religious identification or belief in a god. It is likely that this percentage has been even higher throughout most of our past. Many believers take note of the overwhelming majority of religious people around the world and conclude that there must be something to it. All this praying and prostrating that is going on day and night could not possibly be in vain, they say. Five billion believers can't be wrong, right? Some believers stretch this idea even further,

23

declaring that "if almost everyone in the world is religious, then *my* god must be real."

There are problems with this attempt to justify belief, however. First of all, every believer around the world, regardless of what religion he or she follows, is operating without overwhelming evidence or arguments for any of the supernatural claims they may be making. The weight of believers alone is not enough to tip the scales. Only the weight of evidence can do that. Imagine, for example, if a couple of billion people believed that elves were real but none of them had any evidence or good arguments to support their belief. Obviously it would be intellectually lax to conclude that a high number of elf-believers alone meant that elves were real. It would make the case no better than if there was only one elf-believer. When it comes to claims for the existence of elves or gods, count the evidence, not the believers.

It is important to keep in mind that all the world's believers are not continually discovering the same gods on their own generation after generation. Virtually every believer today believes in the same god or gods that their parents taught him or her to believe in. Religious beliefs are learned not discovered. They don't thrive for centuries on their own. It is likely that the sharing of belief from adults to children is the primary means of survival for religions. This brings into question the significance of large numbers of religious people. A high number of believers in the present shows only that a high number of believers in the past taught religious belief to their children and nothing more. It is far from proof that gods are real.

The need for parents and other adults to make an effort to get children to believe in various gods raises questions. If the human brain is hardwired for belief in gods, as some scientists think it is, then why should there be this need for so much instruction, encouragement, and even coercion in many cases for belief to survive? Furthermore, if one particular belief is valid, then why do people have to be taught about it and consistently encouraged to accept it? If a god or gods were real one might think it would take root naturally, without the need for so many Sunday schools, madrassas (Islamic schools), books, movies, and marketing campaigns. So much money, time, and effort are invested into teaching children to believe in gods that it leads one to wonder if belief might vanish overnight if it was left up to gods rather than people. Isn't it interesting that most adult believers so easily dismiss every religion except the one they were encouraged to believe in childhood? Many believers are not too shy to admit that they view other religions as unproven and maybe even a bit silly. And this is despite the fact that these religions have no more or less evidence than their own. What would happen if most people grew up without any belief system imposed on them? Would they see all religions as unproven and maybe even a bit silly?

Another problem with the "everybody is religious" justification for belief is that "religious" is a loose term that applies to many different beliefs. The extraordinary diversity of belief does not make for a unified front for all religions. Nor does it make a good argument for any one of them. The world's believers are not in agreement on even the most basic points. There is no consensus on which gods are real or how these gods want us to worship them. Nobody can even agree on what the gods want us to eat or how they want us to dress. Disagreement and disunity is the rule for the world's believers. A high number of religious people says our species is fond of religion and nothing more. One cannot find evidence for a god in billions of believers alone. How, for example, does a modern-day worshiper of pagan gods in Greece reinforce the claims of a Mormon in America? How exactly do a billion Hindus complement the religious claims of 1.5 billion Muslims when the two are in complete disagreement on the basic claims of their respective belief systems? Finally, some religious people—including many Buddhists and Taoists, for example—do not believe in any gods at all. Therefore, they should not be lumped in with Christians, Muslims, Hindus, and others who do.

Various religious groups make claims that are vastly different from each other and, in most cases, irreconcilable. It is impossible to unite them all under the banner of religion and declare that collectively they prove gods are real. If anything, all of these opposing beliefs cancel each other out and only show how prone humans are to believing in unproven gods. Let's say, for example, that we decide Allah is the one real god and Islam is the only true religion. That would mean about four billion non-Muslim religious people have made a big mistake. They believe in the wrong gods and follow the wrong religions. The mere presence of these billions of misguided believers would be a strong indication that there is something about the human mind or human culture that makes us vulnerable to believing in gods that do no exist. Once we accept that, however, we would need go back and rethink Allah's existence too, because if the majority of believers can confidently believe in gods that were never there, then the minority of Muslims might be mistaken too. Look around our world today and you will see most people not just believing, but believing in many different gods. Look back across history and it becomes impossible to count the religions and the gods. Is this really validation for claims that any particular god is real? Or could it simply be an indication that we have always been very good at inventing gods?

CHAPTER 2 BIBLIOGRAPHY AND RECOMMENDED READING

Hitchcock, Susan Tyler, and John L. Esposito. *Geography of Religion.* Washington, DC: National Geographic, 2006.
Joshi, S. T., ed., *Atheism: A Reader.* Amherst, NY: Prometheus Books, 2000.

Chapter 3

Faith is a good thing.

I do not feel obliged to believe that the same God who has endowed us with sense, reason, and intellect has intended us to forgo their use.

—Galileo Galilei

Faith is believing what you know ain't so.

—Mark Twain

While some believers attempt to produce evidence to support claims of their god's existence, others simply declare that "faith" is enough and leave it at that. In this context, faith is belief in a god that is secure and unconcerned with logic or reason. It is important to separate "faith" that a god exists from the kind of "faith" one has in a friend or family member. The latter describes a form of trust that is based on past experiences and loyalties to people who obviously exist. Faith in a god's existence also is very different from having faith that the sun will rise tomorrow morning. The latter is a prediction based on previous observations and knowledge about the solar system. Some believers merge or seamlessly switch back and forth between these meanings during conversations about their god. But they are not the same. Yes, I have faith in many things too, but not in the existence of gods because there is nothing to base that faith on. I have faith in my children, for example, meaning I think they are good

27

kids and will do the right thing in most situations. But I don't have faith that they exist because I don't need to. I *know* that they exist because I have seen them, heard them, and felt the bitter sting of their little kicks and punches when we played Roman gladiators.

Many believers are not shy about declaring that they "know" their god is real simply because they believe it so strongly. According to them, faith means believing in a god even though there is no reason to believe in a god. It sounds silly when put like that but that's what faith is. It is believing without reason. Despite the hype, this is not a very good justification for believing in a god or anything else.

A big problem with faith is figuring out where one should apply it. How does a believer justify picking one god over another if faith works for the existence of any god? Why, for example, is faith in the existence of Allah or Ganesha more or less valid than faith in the existence of Jesus? Faith that a god is real has nothing to do with evidence or reason, therefore it can be directed with equal force toward any god. Yet for some reason Muslims I have spoken to about this have little or no respect for the faith that confirms the reality of Jesus as a god to Christians. To Muslims this is a mistake, an error in judgment. Faith is not a good enough answer for them. But then Christians tell me that the faith Muslims have in Allah's existence is not the same as their faith. How they know this is a mystery.

There are people in the world today who believe that fairies are real. Don't laugh. According to the *Skeptic's Dictionary*, belief in fairies "seems common in rural peoples around the world" (Carroll 2003, 136–37). Many of these people probably base their conclusion about fairies on faith. It must be faith because, to my knowledge, no one has produced any genuine fairy fossils or little fairy footprints. Who needs evidence or good reasons to believe when you have faith? Probably most believers in a god—I hope—would agree with me that fairies are not real. But how did they come to the conclusion that there are no little winged people buzzing around in gardens? How can faithful god-believers so easily dismiss the faith of fairy-believers? Is fairy faith significantly different from god faith? If it is, how so?

Having lived most of my life in societies that are dominated by Christian believers, I have heard many times that I "just need to have faith" that Jesus is real. Believers have told me that all I have to do is stop all my obsessing about evidence and "just believe" that he is real. But if faith works for Jesus, why won't it work for fairies, and Odin too? Shouldn't every person who defends faith as a legitimate reason to conclude that their god is real also respect faith when it comes to the existence of thousands of other gods? What's the difference? But if one can have faith in the existence of just about anything, then faith would seem to be of no value at all for getting to the truth.

Probably nothing frustrates nonbelievers more than the concept of faith. To many atheists, the believer's reliance on faith seems like a complete surrender of the mind or at least a stubborn reluctance to think. Nonbelievers may scoff at faith but they should never underestimate it. Faith can be like an impenetrable wall that stands firm against any and all challenges from skeptics. No matter how thoroughly devastating arguments against belief may be, faith usually prevails. It is obvious why this is the case. Arguments based on reason and reality are not likely to have much of an impact on a concept that has nothing to do with reason and reality. Atheists who hope to encourage critical thinking about belief should probably forget arguing directly against faith. Faith doesn't lose debates because it doesn't play by those rules. It is perhaps more productive to simply encourage believers to think more about the concept of faith itself. It is more likely that believers will challenge their concept of faith first and maybe the existence of their god later. It is not impossible for believers to recognize that faith is an empty justification for belief. After all, most god-believers already reject fairy-faith and the faith that props up all those rival gods, remember? Most believers recognize how intellectually feeble faith is when they see it applied to anything other than their god.

If it sinks in that faith is belief without a reason, some religious people may see that relying on it as a primary justification for belief in a god is just not good enough. Believers might also consider that retreating to the faith defense looks a lot like admitting that they can't make a good case for believing in their god. Isn't this what believers who stress faith above reason and evidence are really saying? Isn't it a sort of confession that their belief is based on nothing substantial? Philosopher Daniel C. Dennett thinks so. He suspects that the constant talk we hear about faith reveals deep insecurities among believers. In his book, *Breaking the Spell*, Dennett compares the attitudes of people in contrasting belief systems:

> Those who practice a folk religion don't think of themselves as practicing a religion at all. Their "religious" practices are a seamless part of their practical lives, alongside their hunting and gathering or tilling and harvesting. And one way to tell that they really believe in the deities to which they make their sacrifices is that they aren't forever talking about how much they believe in their deities—any more than you or I go around assuring each that we believe in germs and atoms. Where there is no ambient doubt to speak of, there is no need to speak of faith. (Dennett 2006, 160–61)

It fascinates me that believers have made faith in a god's existence into an admired and respected concept. Some people brag endlessly about their great faith in a god, never once considering that giving up on their mind's ability to weigh evidence and analyze arguments may not be such a good thing. I cannot imagine how it can ever be right to default to faith when considering an unusual claim. For example, I have an interest in space exploration and in SETI, the Search for Extraterrestrial Intelligence. While I do not know if there is life somewhere else in the universe, I think that there is a very good chance there is. I also think that at least a few planets out there probably have intelligent life on them. I hope that we discover extraterrestrial life in my lifetime. It would be a tremendously exciting moment in history and could shed a lot more light on our own origins and evolution. If we make contact with intelligent life—assuming they don't exterminate us—I would be so excited that I probably wouldn't sleep for a week.

Eager and hopeful as I may be about alien life, however, I could never take the leap of faith and pretend that I know for a fact that it exists. It just wouldn't feel right. I would know deep down that I was lying. I would be counterfeiting my hope, pretending to know something that I did not. I might be able to talk for hours about my "strong faith" in extraterrestrial civilizations, but I am pretty sure that I would feel guilty about it later. Faith sounds a lot like cheating. It's jumping ahead to the conclusion before you have a right to, before it has been earned by discovery and thinking. Maybe gods really do exist, but shouldn't we wait until we discover convincing evidence before we say we know?

Dan Barker, a Christian preacher who became an atheist, once pushed the concept of faith to thousands of believers. Today, however, he finds it difficult to believe that it used to make sense to him. Barker's personal journey to religion and back is fascinating. He was a devout believer who dedicated his life to converting others to Christianity and strengthening their belief in Jesus. Faith worked well for him until he started questioning it. But once he admitted that it was a hollow justification for belief in a god, he had no choice but to let go.

"Faith is a cop out," Barker writes in his book, *Losing Faith in Faith*:

> If the only way you can accept an assertion is by faith, then you are conceding that it can't be taken on its own merits. It is intellectual bankruptcy. With faith, you don't have to put any work into proving your case. You can "just believe."
>
> Truth does not have to be believed. Scientists do not join hands every Sunday, singing, "Yes, Gravity is real! I will have faith! I believe in my heart that what goes up must come down, down, down. Amen!" If they did, we would think they were pretty insecure about it. (Barker 1992, 102)

Dennett and Barker are right on the mark. The prominence of the faith concept betrays the believers' own doubts about their gods. But not only is faith intellectually lazy for the individual, it might also be harmful to society. It cannot be a good idea in modern times for millions of people to think it is okay to make decisions based on faith rather than reason. If anything, faith—accepting claims without evidence—should be strongly discouraged. I don't want my hospital staff, police department, fire service, and government representatives making decisions based on faith. I want them to base their decisions on something more substantial, such as logic, data, facts, past experience, and science. Don't you?

To better understand the weakness of the faith concept, imagine if atheists tried using faith to support the idea that gods do not exist. How would that sound to the ears of believers? Barker writes:

> Suppose an atheist, refusing to look at any religious claims, were to say, "You must have faith that there is no God. If you believe in your heart that nothing transcends nature and that humanity is the highest judge of morality, then you will know that atheism is true." Wouldn't the Christians [and followers of other religions] snicker? (Barker 1992, 102–103)

Believers who are reluctant to let go of the faith concept might consider that there is no logical end to it. Faith doesn't stop at fairies and rival gods. Once it is accepted as a means of determining what is real and what is not, it can creep into many other areas of life. If, for example, one sees no problem with having faith that an undetectable god is real, why should that person refuse to have faith in astrology or psychic readings too? What is the difference? In fact, it might be easier. After all, unlike gods, one can actually see stars and psychics. There is no credible evidence that an alien spaceship has ever visited the Earth but faith can make it so, if only in our minds. Just have faith and—eureka!—we are not alone. The UFOs are here. Where does it end? Sadly, of course, for some people there is no limit to the application of faith and they really do believe virtually every wild claim that comes along. Billions of dollars are made off such people by armies of heartless quacks and con artists.

I am reluctant to quote Richard Dawkins, the prominent scientist, author, and atheist activist. I know that the mere mention of his name sends irritating shivers up the spines of some believers. But he is too brilliant and too relevant to leave out of any discussion about faith. In his book, *The God Delusion*, Dawkins argues that religion should never be imposed on young children because they may not yet be capable of sufficiently high levels of critical thinking. He especially despises use of the faith concept to convince children that gods are real and ancient holy books true.

> Faith is an evil precisely because it requires no justification and brooks no argument. Teaching children that unquestioned faith is a virtue primes them—given certain other ingredients that are not hard to come by—to grow up into potentially lethal weapons for future jihads or crusades. Immunized against fear by the promise of a martyr's paradise, the authentic faith-head deserves a high place in the history of armaments, alongside the longbow, the warhorse, the tank and cluster bomb. If children were taught to question and think through their beliefs, instead of being taught the superior virtue of faith without question, it is a good bet that there would be no suicide bombers. Suicide bombers do what they do because they really believe what they were taught in their religious schools: that duty to God exceeds all other priorities, and that martyrdom in his service will be rewarded in the gardens of Paradise. And they were taught *that* lesson not necessarily by extremist fanatics but by decent, gentle, mainstream religious instructors, who lined them up in their madrassas, sitting in rows, rhythmically nodding their innocent little heads up and down while they learned every word of the holy book like demented parrots. Faith can be very very dangerous, and deliberately to implant it into the vulnerable mind of an innocent child is a grievous wrong. (Dawkins 2006, 308)

Dawkins is right, of course, but it has been my experience that most believers do not recognize any link between themselves and believers who would kill innocent people in the name of a god. They dismiss such people as "fanatics" or "extremists" and deny that they share the common foundation of the faith concept. But, of course, they do. If faith is the willing abandonment of reason, then it's not much of a stretch to imagine people doing just about anything in faith's name. History shows how easy it is to lead faithful people down terrible paths. But consider how difficult it would be to recruit me or most other nonblievers to become assassins, crusaders, or suicide bombers for a god. It just wouldn't work because someone first would have to show convincing evidence of an afterlife in heaven as well as prove that the particular god exists in the first place. Imagine if all those men who hijacked those planes the morning of September 11, 2001, had rethought their worldview the night before. What if they had decided to question their faith in the god who they saw as the ultimate justification for their mission? What if they had rejected faith and instead asked for evidence?

While it may seem unlikely for a believer who is firmly entrenched in faith to ever readjust their view and begin to ask for evidence, it is not impossible. Millions of people around the world have turned away from believing in gods. They were led to believe in a god by their parents and their society but eventually found the courage to think their way free of faith. It may take some time but it does happen. Once believers take an honest look at faith, there is a chance that they will see that it makes no sense. Believing in what there is no reason to believe is simply not a justifiable position, especially for anyone who thinks highly of truth and reality.

Author Michael Shermer was once a born-again Christian. Empowered by faith, he was confident that he knew the ultimate truth of the universe. Today, however, he is a nonbeliever who preaches science and reason. He founded the Skeptics Society, publishes the excellent magazine *Skeptic*, and has written several popular science books. In *The Science of Good and Evil* Shermer describes his journey from believer to nonbeliever:

> I have been asked countless times how and why I lost my faith. Although my conversion to Christianity was sudden and dramatic . . . my "de-conversion" was gradual and evolutionary. The scales did not suddenly fall from my eyes . . . Rather there was a

slow but systematic displacement of one worldview and way of thinking by another: Genesis and Exodus myths by cosmology and evolution theories; faith by reason; final truths by provisional probabilities; trust by verification; authority by empiricism; and religious supernaturalism by scientific naturalism. (Shermer 2004, 231–32)

Faith cannot be argued away if a believer will not first consider its underlying weakness. Faith is unlikely to be defeated by an essay, a book, or a debate. As with Shermer's deconversion, faith is best eroded from within. Scientific facts and reasoned arguments from outside sources can help, of course, but the real battle is fought in the heart of the believer. They must decide to let go of faith all by themselves. Nobody can do it for them.

CHAPTER 3 BIBLIOGRAPHY AND RECOMMENDED READING

Barker, Dan. *Losing Faith in Faith: From Preacher to Atheist.* Madison, WI: Freedom From Religion Foundation, 1992.

Carroll, Robert Todd. *The Skeptic's Dictionary: A Collection of Strange Beliefs, Amusing Deceptions, and Dangerous Delusions.* New York: Wiley, 2003.

Dawkins, Richard. *The God Delusion.* New York: Houghton Mifflin, 2006.

Dennett, Daniel C. *Breaking the Spell: Religion as a Natural Phenomenon.* New York: Viking, 2006.

Juergensmeyer, Mark. *Terror in the Mind of God: The Global Rise of Religious Violence.* Berkeley: University of California Press, 2003. Think faith is a good thing? Read this book and think again.

Mills, David. *Atheist Universe: Why God Didn't Have a Thing to Do with It.* Philadelphia, PA: Xlibris, 2003.

Shermer, Michael. *The Science of Good and Evil.* New York: Times Books, 2004.

Chapter 4

Archaeological discoveries prove that my god exists.

Archaeology testifies to this event.
—From an article about the destruction of
Sodom and Gomorrah
in a Jehovah's Witness booklet.

Archaeology and paleontology have always fascinated me. I can remember as a young child carefully excavating old Coke bottles and fish skeletons from muddy riverbanks in Florida while my father fished nearby. I always made sure to extract my treasures up from the earth with delicate precision, just like the real archaeologists I saw in television documentaries. It's an exciting process to find, then hold an artifact in your hand and try to imagine it as it was before time claimed it. As an adult I was able to relive those childhood memories by volunteering with an archaeological project in the Caribbean. Touching an object that was last held by people who lived centuries ago is the closest thing to time travel. It's a real thrill. But archaeology is no mere hobby. It's an invaluable science that offers a way for us to learn about our past. If we only had historical documents to go by, we would know much less about who we are and where we came from. In many cases, only archaeology can dig up the truth. So when somebody has archaeological evidence to support her or his claims, I tend to listen up. Unfortunately, I have learned over the years that archaeology's good name has been hijacked by some believers who bend the truth.

Some believers claim that archaeology has proven their god's existence. That's a bold claim but they do make it. This is great that some believers are willing to let science have a say on the issue of their god's existence. The problem for them, however, is that archaeology offers no evidence for the existence of any gods. Many thousands of excavations have been conducted all over the world and not one single artifact has ever been found that is direct evidence of even one god. The only thing that archaeologists keep finding is evidence that humans believe in gods.

"Biblical archaeology" is an industry unto itself today, generating professional societies, clubs, books, magazines, Web sites, documentaries, and even archaeology-themed tours to the Holy Land. Searching for one's god in the sands of the ancient past, it seems, is irresistible to many believers. The truth is, however, most of the world's professional archaeologists don't think much of anyone in their field who tries to match evidence to a forgone conclusion that is not open to revision. Archaeology is a science and as such it has an obligation to accept the evidence no matter if it supports something in a holy book or not. I'm not suggesting that all religion-motivated archaeologists are unethical or incompetent but there can be problems when one sincerely believes that they are digging for a god.

Despite the glaring absence of a single discovery to substantiate the existence of any gods, some believers insist that archaeology has confirmed their claims. I once interviewed a Mormon for a feature article on his religion, for example, and he said he believed the claims made by Joseph Smith were all true, based largely on archaeological evidence. For those who don't know, Smith is the founder of the Mormon religion, also known as the Church of Latter-day Saints of Jesus Christ. While living in the state of New York in the early 1820s, Smith said he was led by an angel named Moroni to "golden tablets." He said he translated the tablets with a "seer stone" (crystal) and looking through his hat. The translation became the Book of Mormon, the central document for the religion that now has some ten million members. The tablets have never been found.

Although the story of Joseph Smith seems unlikely, my interview subject confidently told me that he believes it without hesitation. He explained that he does not need to rely upon faith to believe in the cave, the golden tablets, and the Book of Mormon because archaeological discoveries have confirmed it to all be true. The fact is, however, no archaeologist has ever found anything that confirms any of the supernatural claims in the Book of Mormon. Many Muslims, Catholics, Protestants, Jews, and Hindus make the same claims about their beliefs. It would seem that archaeology has discovered gods many times over. But has it really?

Believers who claim that archaeology has revealed hard evidence for the existence of their god are mistaken. No archaeological discovery has ever proven anything supernatural. There has never been any find made anywhere that ever provided evidence for the existence of one god, one miracle, one angel, one genie, or one demon. It's true, despite all the hype and all the claims by believers, not one artifact among millions discovered to date points to the existence of a god. So what are all these believers talking about? I don't think they are lying and I don't think they are stupid. More likely they have been misled by overly eager people who are desperate to show the world that their religion is the true one. In the cases that are not outright frauds what generally happens is that somebody will find a site or artifact that loosely corresponds with a story within a belief system but still offers no evidence of a god or anything supernatural. Then a misleading news report, written by a biased or incompetent journalist, is published exaggerating the significance of the find. Believers, perhaps short on skeptical skill to begin with, gobble it up enthusiastically and proceed to repeat the bogus claim to anyone who will listen.

I often end "archaeology proves my god" conversations with believers simply by asking them to name the most impressive archaeological discovery that proves their god is real. Silence usually follows. Some Jews and Christians will say the Dead Sea Scrolls. But I have seen the Dead Sea Scrolls on display at the Israel Museum in Jerusalem. To me they look like documents that were produced by people, not gods. They do not float in the air or glow magically. They are words on parchment, nothing supernatural about them from what I could see. So then I ask believers how ancient writings prove anything other than ancient people knew how to write. Believers usually respond to that with the claim that they contain prophecies that came true. Of course that doesn't lead anywhere either. (Chapter 36 addresses prophecies.) The bottom line is that if there was just one example of archaeological evidence that confirmed the existence of a god beyond a reasonable doubt, don't you think you would have heard about it? Wouldn't it be a big deal and stick around longer than one news cycle? Wouldn't the archaeologist who found it be a household name? But none of this has happened because archaeology so far has nothing to say on the question of whether or not gods exist.

Unfortunately, some believers can be stubborn about their "evidence." For them, more reasonable and down-to-earth explanations are not enough to change their minds. This is what we see with the case of the Shroud of Turin, cited by many believers as proof that Jesus was a god. This fourteen-foot burial cloth contains the haunting image of a man's face that is seemingly burned into its fabric. It is housed today in Turin, Italy, at the cathedral of St. John the Baptist. This cloth was not dug up by archaeologists but archaeological techniques have been used to analyze it.

Is the Shroud really evidence of a god? Skeptics say no. Radiocarbon dating places the cloth's origins in the Middle Ages, not two thousand years ago when Jesus was believed to have been executed. They also suggest that a more likely explanation is that the cloth was a forgery created to excite the faithful and extract money from pilgrims, a common practice in Europe at that time. The important point about the Shroud of Turin controversy is that some believers see it as archaeological proof that Jesus was a god. They cite it as if science has confirmed the claim. But clearly the Shroud is not proof of anything at this time.

A common error some believers make when it comes to archaeology is to overreach with an artifact's significance. It would take a very special find to prove a god is real. For example, if the Shroud of Turin had Jesus's name embroidered on it, had been found in a Jerusalem tomb that was sealed for two thousand years, and radiocarbon dating confirmed its age, it still would not prove that Jesus was a god! It would be like discovering golden tablets in a cave in New York today. Even if they were shown to be authentic and somehow linked to Joseph Smith, it would not prove that any supernatural claims inscribed on them are true. Believers who like to stretch archaeological artifacts to obtain maximum mileage for their religion might ask themselves why the spectacular and numerous archaeological discoveries made in Egypt fail to convince them that the pharaohs were gods as was claimed during their reign. A 450-foot pyramid that once entombed a god is at least as impressive as a burial cloth with a facial imprint, isn't it? I've been deep inside the Great Pyramid of Khufu, spent days walking around Karnak and breathed the musty air inside several royal tombs. Impressive? Yes. Evidence that gods, not men, ruled ancient Egypt? Not even close.

There are many examples of exaggerated evidence. The ancient cities of Sodom and Gomorrah may have burned to the ground but this alone does not confirm that a god lit the fire as some say. Archaeologists may have found remains of what were once the walls around a community named Jericho. So what? The confirmed existence of a place that is mentioned in an ancient story does not mean the magical claims within the story are true. Stones that were once part of a wall are not evidence that anything supernatural ever happened there. After all, there are stories of gods running around ancient Greece too. Do archaeological excavations of places named in those stories prove that Zeus and Athena are real? Of course not. When people write down their myths it's not unusual for them to use familiar settings—real places. But this is not a reason to conclude that the entire story is true.

The idea that archaeology supports religious claims reminds me of those "Lost City of Atlantis Found" reports that show up in the news on a regular basis. It seems like every year some guy with scuba gear and a lot of time on his hands announces that he has discovered Atlantis. I agree that the discovery of an ancient city built by Poseidon and inhabited by a race of magical superhuman citizens with advanced technology would be newsworthy. But these stories always turn out to be little or nothing to get excited about once the facts come out. However, this does not mean that the ruins of the Atlantis that Plato wrote about are not out there beneath the waves somewhere, awaiting discovery. No one doubts that the oceans are filled with spectacular archaeological sites awaiting discovery. I once interviewed Robert Ballard, the discoverer of the *Titanic*, and he is absolutely giddy over the archaeological treasures yet to be found. However, if there really was an Atlantis and if someone really does discover it one day, I am pretty sure that it will not prove anything other than a natural disaster caused an ancient city to slide into the sea. It might remind us about the need to have tsunami early-warning systems but it won't prove any of the supernatural claims made by the more colorful Atlantis believers. The confirmed existence of the true Atlantis would not be enough to prove that Poseidon is a real god. Okay, if an underwater archaeologist surfaces above the sunken city in possession of a glowing trident that regenerates amputated limbs, has the cure for cancer engraved on its shaft, and projects a hologram of Poseidon introducing himself to the twenty-first century, then, yes, it would be a good indication that it is time to start building new temples to the god of the sea. Short of that, however, clay pot shards, marble columns, and a few beads won't prove anything about gods—although some believers would surely say they do.

To be clear, I am not necessarily against biblical archaeology, Islamic archaeology, Hindu archaeology, Buddhist archaeology, Mormon archaeology, or anyone else's archaeology. So long as it is honest and follows the same scientific methods of mainstream archaeology, dig away, I say. The more trowels in the dirt, the better. We all benefit from more knowledge about the past. I don't care anything about the beliefs of a particular archaeologist if they can teach me something about our shared past. However, I do think that belief-motivated archaeological efforts are inherently risky because the goal of supporting a particular conclusion will always threaten objectivity. This bias could lead archaeologists to exaggerate some discoveries and ignore others. The best believers can do is read carefully and think skeptically when they see reports about discoveries that seem to support the existence of their god. Is the new find really evidence of a god, or is it just another artifact left behind by ancient believers?

CHAPTER 4 BIBLIOGRAPHY AND RECOMMENDED READING

McCrone, Walter C. *Judgment Day for the Shroud of Turin*. Amherst, NY: Prometheus Books, 1999. Everything that shroud-believers need to know is in this book.

Chapter 5

Only my god can make me feel significant.

Do you ever feel small and insignificant? There is not necessarily anything wrong with having those feelings occasionally. It can be a natural reaction to living on a big world in a very big universe. Being just one of billions of other people might also make it a challenge to feel special. The current global population is nearly seven billion. Over the last fifty thousand years or so, more than a hundred billion humans have lived. That's a lot of people. It's no surprise that some of us might feel lost in the crowd.

It gets worse. Consider the fact that you are not even "you," at least not as much as you probably think you are. Every human body, including yours, is actually a complex ecosystem made up of about ten trillion human cells (you) and also more than one hundred trillion microbes (not you). Weird as it seems, if you could conduct a census of the space your body occupies, you would find that what you think of as all you is actually mostly other lifeforms such as tiny arthropods, bacteria, viruses, and fungi. You are a minority in your own skin. But you are not only outnumbered, you are also tiny—*very tiny*.

How small are we? Most humans today weigh less than two hundred pounds and are less than six feet tall. Compare that to our planet's mass, which is estimated at an intimidating 6,000,000,000,000,000, 000,000,000 kilograms. The Milky Way galaxy, our immediate neigh-

45

borhood, is one hundred twenty thousand light years wide. (A light year is the distance it takes light to travel in one year, or about 5,879,000,000,000 miles.) Our galaxy contains more than a hundred billion stars. Our universe probably contains more than one hundred billion galaxies. It's anyone's guess as to how many planets there are.

So much is going on out there without us that it can seem as if we are invisible, even nonexistent. There are beautiful clouds of dust and gas called nebulae that are much larger than our entire solar system. Stars are born. Stars die. Sometimes an entire galaxy smashes into another galaxy. And this is just in the "observable universe." Some cosmologists think there may even be many more universes besides ours. Feeling tiny?

Size and numbers are not the only potential sources of human insecurity. By the measure of time we don't add up to much either. The universe is so old (fifteen billion years, give or take a few billion) that we might think of ourselves as mayflies, enjoying nothing more than a brief afternoon in the sun. A long life for an individual human today is about eighty years. That's a fairly small slice of time on a planet that is four and a half billion years old. It has been at least seven thousand years since we made the transition from the Stone Age to civilization. So many lives have come and gone in that period. Imagine all the dramatic events of those seven thousand years that we missed. Imagine all the interesting and beautiful people who died before our time.

Wouldn't it be nice if something or somebody, maybe a god, could make us feel important, relevant, and large? Maybe the god could even allow us to live forever. It sounds appealing. For some, the desire to feel important is sufficient motivation for them to seek out the comforting arms of a god, even if that god has never been shown to exist. But hope and desire should not be confused with certain knowledge about something. Many believers in many different societies say that believing in a god or gods makes them feel significant in a vast and intimidating universe. But this benefit from believing is not necessarily evidence for the existence of gods. It can easily be the believing alone, not a real god, that provides the reassurance.

Many belief systems make a big deal about this issue of the significance of the individual. Religious leaders are well aware that people often feel overwhelmed and lost in the herd of humanity so they are quick to offer a solution. Many Christian preachers, for example, talk about the "Book of Life" in which a god has written down the names of believers. Christians have told me that their god knew my name, even before I was born. Obviously this is a story that could make me feel special. But although having your name in a god's "Book of Life" may sound great, someone first should provide an explanation as to how we can know that such a book exists. Where is it? If it's up in a place called heaven that we cannot see, then how does anyone down here know about it? If the only source of information about this magical book is found in ancient writings by anonymous authors, then how can we believe with any confidence? Yes, the Book of Life, like the gods themselves, may help believers feel special but this does not mean they necessarily exist.

I can understand when believers say they feel good about a god who knows them and cares about them. I can imagine how such a belief might allow some to cope with life a little better. But there is another way. Everyone does not have to believe in Allah, Yahweh, Jesus, Ganesha, Vishnu, or other gods to feel significant. We can be happy, feel important, and lead meaningful lives without gods. Hundreds of millions of nonbelievers around the world manage to do it every day. One does not necessarily have to look any further than family, friends, and the joy from being productive or creative to find satisfaction and purpose in life. These real things can be so wonderful, in fact, that I wonder why anyone would ever want to take time away from them in order to worship a god who has not yet been proven to even exist. Believers might consider the possibility that every minute spent thinking about and talking to gods up in the sky is a minute wasted down here.

Believing in an unproven god may offer some level of comfort but it certainly is not the only way to feel a connection to something bigger than yourself. Besides, it is not really so hard to confront the intimidating reality of our place in the universe. It is possible to meet it head on by embracing the power and mystery of it all rather than shrinking from it. For example, when I was writing the opening paragraphs of this chapter, describing a universe that is billions of years old and billions of light years wide, I didn't feel overshadowed, overwhelmed, or intimidated. I felt excited and inspired. I love living in a universe that is outrageously big; anything less would feel claustrophobic. One does not have to be left feeling cold, hollow, or depressed by the realities of time and nature. Don't bow down and cower in the immense shadow of this universe. Stand up and claim your place in it. Be the opposite of those who glance up at the night sky and feel small. Look up and be a giant because you are a part of it all. Furthermore, you are special because, as a thinking and creative lifeform, you are one of the most fortunate collections of atoms in all the universe.

CHAPTER 5 BIBLIOGRAPHY AND RECOMMENDED READING

Sagan, Carl. *Cosmos*. New York: Random House, 2002.

Tyson, Neil deGrasse, and Donald Goldsmith. *Origins: Fourteen Billion Years of Cosmic Evolution*. New York: W. W. Norton & Company, 2004.

Chapter 6

Atheism is just another religion.

If atheism is a religion, then bald is a hair color.
—Mark Schnitzius

Some believers charge that atheism is just another religion. Atheism requires faith like any traditional religion, they say. "It takes more faith not to believe in a god than to believe," is a common quip these days. Some believers even claim that atheists worship humans and look to science as their religion.

These are strange but surprisingly common claims. I have heard them many times. Some believers apparently find it difficult to comprehend the existence of people who are not convinced that any gods are real. The weirdest thing about calling atheism a religion is that some religious people say it as if it's an insult. I know they don't mean it that way, but it sounds a lot like, "You atheists are as silly as we are." That aside, believers need to be aware that declaring atheism to be a religion does not help the case for the existence of a god. Whatever atheists may or may not be has no bearing on whether or not gods exist. Therefore, labeling atheism a religion is no justification for believing in a god. By the way, no atheist thinks Charles Darwin, Carl Sagan, or anybody else is a god. If they did, they wouldn't be atheists. They would be believers.

I suspect that many people who believe in a god are eager to call atheism a religion because thinking of it that way makes it more comfortable for them to deal with. Then it becomes just another rival belief system, easily dismissed as a mistake and ignored like all the rest. But atheism is more challenging when it is seen by the believer for what it really is: the absence of belief in gods. Atheism is not a religion, organization, club, philosophy, lifestyle, tribe, race, ethnicity, or team. Atheism is the absence of a belief in a god. That's it. It doesn't even necessarily mean that one is certain that no gods exist. It just means she or he does not believe in gods.

Some believers tell me that atheists think they are smarter and better people than believers. Unfortunately, some atheists probably do think that. But the assumption that nonbelievers are superior to believers is simply wrong. Yes, less religious societies tend to be more law-abiding and peaceful than more religious societies (Canada vs. United States; France vs. Pakistan; Sweden vs. Nigeria, for example). And yes, there are studies that show a decline in religious belief as educational levels go up. But any random individual atheist is not necessarily morally or intellectually superior to any random individual believer. I do understand, however, why some atheists might feel a twinge of superiority when they see images in the news of blood-soaked Shia Muslims flailing themselves with chains and cutting themselves with knives while chanting and parading; Hindus stabbing swordfish bills and other objects through their cheeks during a religious fesitival; and Christians allowing nails to be hammered into their bodies in gruesome crucifixion reenactments. But an atheist would be wrong to ever assume blanket superiority based only on the absence of belief. Intelligence and morality at the individual level can't be predicted based only on the presence or absence of belief. There is too much variation to generalize. Belief is just one ingredient in the complex recipe that makes up an individual's life.

When believers charge that atheism is "just another religion" I question them about what they think a religion is. In fairness, it's not an easy thing to define. Anthropologists are aware of so many beliefs and rituals in so many cultures that they know better than to make a narrow definition of religion because inevitably it would have too many exceptions. So they end up defining religion very loosely. Usually anthropologists say something like religions are behaviors and ideas that are an important part of a culture. With a weak definition like that maybe the believers are right. Maybe atheism really is just another religion. But the astronomy club and the chess team could be religions too, by that standard. Few nonanthropologists have any idea just how many varieties of religious belief there are today, much less in the past. It is staggering how productive we are when it comes to gods and religions. Humans have created millions of religions and confidently claimed that countless gods exist; so many that we can't even define religion very well because every definition threatens to leave somebody out.

So, is atheism a religion? No, it is not, at least not by the definition that people use outside of anthropology conferences. For most people religion includes belief in a god and atheism is, by definition, godless. Atheism is the absence of belief in gods. Most atheists don't seem eager to be united into an organization based on their absence of belief. I suspect that for many atheists, nonbelief is just not an overriding concern in their lives. Perhaps they have more important things to do than sit around discussing the unlikely existence of Thor and Odin. For example, I would probably list twenty or thirty personal attributes before I got down to atheism. I may care about how religious belief impacts the world and I may write about it, but I don't feel a need to dwell on being an atheist every day. It's just not that big of a deal. I'm far more interested in being a father, husband, friend, and writer than I am in being an atheist. There is a lot more to do in life than obsess over what you *don't* believe in.

Some believers suspect that atheists like science a little too much. A few have accused me of making science my religion. Not all but some nonbelievers may have a deep appreciation for science but it does not mean they worship it or necessarily believe in it as some ultimate source of wisdom and guidance. Science to me, for example, is simply the best method we have for figuring things out. That's as far as it goes. Science is not my surrogate god, as some believers charge. Science gave us napalm and the H-bomb so in my eyes it clearly is not a fountain of goodness that can do no wrong. I do not look to it to find personal meaning in life. It's not my mentor or guiding light. It is a tool. I think it is invaluable, irreplaceable, and inspirational but still just a tool.

Atheists do not worship humans as gods either, contrary to what many believers claim. This weird idea may have come from some believers' reaction to secular humanism. Secular humanism is a positive philosophy that promotes reason and ethics. It has no place for the supernatural, probably because nothing supernatural has ever been shown to be real in all of history. Some believers viciously oppose secular humanism, calling it a terrible evil that threatens the world. Christian TV preachers routinely attack it. Some believers even make the outrageous claim that Hitler and Stalin were humanists and mass murder is what you get when secular humanism runs its course. I find all of this fear and animosity toward humanism odd since the American Humanists Association defines it this way: "Humanism is a progressive lifestance that, without supernaturalism, affirms our ability and responsibility to lead ethical lives of personal fulfillment that aspire to the greater good of humanity."

How does this line of thinking threaten the good people of planet Earth? The following are some principles of the Council for Secular Humanism:

- We are committed to the application of reason and science to the understanding of the universe and to the solving of human problems.
- We deplore efforts to denigrate human intelligence, to seek to explain the world in supernatural terms, and to look outside nature for salvation.
- We believe that scientific discovery and technology can contribute to the betterment of human life.
- We believe in an open and pluralistic society and that democracy

is the best guarantee of protecting human rights from authoritarian elites and repressive majorities.

- We are concerned with securing justice and fairness in society and with eliminating discrimination and intolerance.
- We attempt to transcend divisive parochial loyalties based on race, religion, gender, nationality, creed, class, sexual orientation, or ethnicity, and strive to work together for the common good of humanity.
- We want to protect and enhance the earth, to preserve it for future generations, and to avoid inflicting needless suffering on other species.
- We believe in enjoying life here and now and in developing our creative talents to their fullest.
- We believe in the cultivation of moral excellence.
- We respect the right to privacy. Mature adults should be allowed to fulfill their aspirations, to express their sexual preferences, to exercise reproductive freedom, to have access to comprehensive and informed healthcare, and to die with dignity.
- We believe in the common moral decencies: altruism, integrity, honesty, truthfulness, and responsibility. Humanist ethics is amenable to critical, rational guidance. There are normative standards that we discover together. Moral principles are tested by their consequences.
- We are deeply concerned with the moral education of our children. We want to nourish reason and compassion.
- We are engaged by the arts no less than by the sciences.
- We are citizens of the universe and are excited by discoveries still to be made in the cosmos.
- We are skeptical of untested claims to knowledge, and we are open to novel ideas and seek new departures in our thinking.
- We believe in optimism rather than pessimism, hope rather than despair, learning in the place of dogma, truth instead of ignorance, joy rather than guilt or sin, tolerance in the place of fear, love instead of hatred, compassion over selfishness, beauty

instead of ugliness, and reason rather than blind faith or irrationality.

- We believe in the fullest realization of the best and noblest that we are capable of as human beings. (Council for Secular Humanism Web site)

Why would anyone have a problem with those principles? Who can honestly say that secular humanists are bad people based on what they stand for? I know the knock against all things supernatural troubles believers but I hope they can at least see that these are positive themes. Don't principles like these offer us a chance to improve our world, a much better chance than Sharia Law or the laws of the Old Testament, for example?

Whether one calls them members of a religion or not, isn't it obvious that people who are pushing "optimism rather than pessimism, hope rather than despair, learning in the place of dogma, truth instead of ignorance . . . and reason rather than blind faith or irrationality" are on the right side of human progress? While I am not a card-carrying member of any humanist organization, I am proud to say that I agree with their general attitude toward life and their goals for our world. They do not seem to be a group of people who would be likely to burn people alive for thinking differently or intentionally fly planes into buildings. They sound like the kind of people I wouldn't mind having as neighbors.

Having worked to make the case that atheism is not a religious belief, I will now confess that I have a secret belief about gods that I rarely talk about. It's sort of embarrassing because it is very similar to religious belief. I can't back it up with convincing evidence or overwhelming arguments but it's there, rattling around in my head nonetheless.

I believe there are no gods.

There, I said it. I'm a believer too, sort of. I can't prove that my belief is true and I freely admit that I may be wrong. I will change my belief if I'm shown to be wrong. However, based on what I know about the creativity of the human mind and the complete lack of evidence or strong arguments to support claims about gods, I can't help but "believe" that all gods were invented and do not exist. I don't know this and I can't prove it but I do believe it. I just have a hunch that if gods were real somebody would have come up with some evidence or at least a really good argument for them by now. After all, we have discovered three billion year–old fossils and identified galaxies far beyond our own. Surely we would have found some trace of gods by now if any were there. But we haven't so, reluctantly, I find myself believing in their nonexistence. This silly little belief is not my religion, however. I have none.

CHAPTER 6 BIBLIOGRAPHY AND RECOMMENDED READING

"The Affirmations of Humanism: A Statement of Principles." The Council for Secular Humanism. http://www.secularhumanism.org/index.php?section=main&page=affirmations.

Dawkins, Richard. *A Devil's Chaplain*. New York: Houghton Mifflin, 2003.

Robinson, B. A. "Definitions of the Word 'Religion.'" Ontario Consultants on Religious Tolerance, Religious Tolerance.org. http://www.religioustolerance.org/rel_defn.htm.

Smith, George H. *Atheism: The Case Against God*. Amherst, NY: Prometheus Books, 1989.

Wilson, Edward O. *Consilience: The Unity of Knowledge*. New York: Vintage Books, 1999.

Chapter 7

Evolution is bad.

I will destroy human wisdom and discard their most brilliant ideas.

—Corinthians 1:19

Reality is that which, when you stop believing in it, doesn't go away.

—Philip K. Dick

The good thing about the creationism vs. evolution debate is that it gets a lot of people talking about evolution. The bad thing, however, is that, despite all the talk, most people in the world today still don't know much about evolution. We are more than a hundred years beyond Charles Darwin's death and astonishingly inaccurate ideas about evolution continue to come out of the mouths of people who should know better. For example, President George W. Bush, a graduate of Yale University, said "the jury is still out" on evolution. During a 2007 Republican presidential debate, three candidates raised their hands to proudly declare that they did not believe in evolution. Somebody, whether it is the world's scientists, science teachers, or journalists, are failing to communicate to the public just how real evolution is. Someone is also failing to spark a sense of wonder and appreciation for evolution in young people. Many adults, under the mistaken belief that evolution is wrong, evil, or irrelevant steer clear of it and never learn what it really is. Even worse, many people walk around with ridiculous misinformation rattling around in their heads, thanks to the hard-working people who market creationism. For example, in the United States, the nation that put twelve humans on the moon, millions of citizens currently believe the earth is less than ten thousand years old and that the first human was created magically from dirt in modern form. How did this happen? Most American citizens spend at least several years in school. America has a very high literacy rate. Access to libraries and the Internet is very high compared to most other nations. So how can such a developed country end up with millions of citizens who have never heard of *Homo erectus*? And it's not just America. Most people in the world, based on my experiences, know little or nothing about human evolution. Australopithecus is a major character in the human story, for example, but I have found that very, very few people have ever heard the name. Perhaps a general failure of science education is partly responsible, but most of the blame for this points directly to belief in gods.

When someone goes down the path of belief they risk picking up a lot more than a god along the way. Sometimes ideas that contradict mountains of scientific evidence come with the territory. The widespread rejection of evolution in the United States is a sad example of how destructive belief in a god can be to human intellect. Not all, of course, but millions of believers trust preachers and creationism marketers over the world's top scientists to give them the facts on evolution. As a result, these people know virtually nothing about evolution. Today some religious leaders charge that evolution is an evil philosophy. This is particularly troublesome for those believers who are thoughtful and honest enough to want to know the real story of how life on Earth has changed over the last few billion years. But when a trusted preacher, rabbi, priest, or imam declares that the theory of evolution is immoral and could possibly destroy families, schools, and even civilization, many believers understandably shy away from the subject. This situation would be laughable if it was not so tragic. Here we have this fascinating—and true—story about ourselves and the rest of life on earth but it's feared, shunned, and ridiculed by hundreds of millions of people around the world. In many cases believers think that accepting evolution would anger their god. Many believers follow this strange line of reasoning faithfully, giving them one more justification to believe in a god. It goes like this: "Evolution is bad and false. Creationism is good and true. Therefore, my god is real." Flawed and twisted though it may be, this reason for belief is popular. Again, it is important to add that this does not necessarily have anything to do with intelligence. When a believer is bombarded with creationist claims and learns little about the science, it's probably not very difficult to come to the wrong conclusions no matter how smart the person may be.

The question of what claim is right is easily answered by any objective observer because creationism has no credible evidence to support its claims while evolution has strong evidence from numerous sources. The fossil and genetic evidence that supports the claim that life evolves is nothing less than overwhelming. It's not as if one little group of eccentric scientists is over in the corner pushing evolution all by themselves. This theory has been confirmed by decades of independent work by thousands of zoologists, biologists, botanists, microbiologists, and paleoanthropologists working in many different countries. And they say that nothing makes sense in their respective fields without evolution as the underlying theory. No matter what some American presidents may say, the jury delivered a verdict on evolution a long time ago. The debate continues today only because some believers refuse to face facts. Within the scientific community there is no debate. Evolution is real.

The unusual but resilient believers' claim that evolution is evil is more difficult to deal with. What does it mean, "evolution is evil," anyway? Okay, I agree that evolution is rough. It's part of a horrible and unfortunate way for life to have to exist because suffering, death, and extinction are the norm. But my personal distaste for predators, parasites, and extinction doesn't mean I can simply say, "I don't believe in it," and it will go away. Life on this planet will continue to compete, kill, die, and evolve whether we are all Baptists or evolutionary biologists. But believers are not hung up on the horrors of nature. When they make the charge that evolution is evil and threatens to degrade us all, they mean that it is a philosophy or way of life that rejects their gods. They think that accepting evolution is the godless road to ruin, a corrupt belief system that will turn us into monsters. Anti-evolution believers often point to eugenics atrocities committed by governments against "unfavorable" subgroups within their populations that they wanted to eliminate. Some cite examples of attempts to use evolution as a justification for racism. However, these attacks on evolution don't work. Obviously, people who may have tried to use the theory of evolution to justify murder, racism, or discrimination were wrong. But rejecting the theory of evolution because some bad people in the past attempted to use it to justify crimes is illogical. It would be like rejecting gravity because bad people on a rooftop once dropped rocks on somebody's head. It would be like condemning all religions because some of them were used to justify crimes. Nature works the way it works, no matter who claims to speak for it. If evolution was the rallying cry of every evil person in history, it still would not change the fact that plants, animals, and microbes evolve.

Some believers promote the extreme view that teaching evolution in schools is dangerous because it encourages children to think of themselves as "lowly" animals and gives them permission to steal, rape, and murder. Many people have expressed this concern to me. It is surprisingly popular. Believers seem to be sincerely worried that the theory of evolution can turn people into savages. There is, of course, nothing to base this on. Just consider the world's most fervent proponents of evolution—scientists. They certainly do not rape and murder at a noticeably higher rate than anti-evolution activists. I have no data to support it, but I would bet that the world's evolutionary scientists are, on average, more law-abiding than most other groups of people in the world.

This charge by believers that understanding and accepting evolution incites immorality, crime, or anarchy is nonsensical. Recognizing that an overwhelming amount of fossil and genetic evidence shows that life-forms have changed over millions of years does not give anyone the green light to hurt people. Believers who think that we cannot be moral without creationism are sadly misled by the idea that we need to have threatening gods standing over us with lightning bolts ready to strike us down if we misbehave. People are capable of moral behavior based on natural reasons alone. Scientists have observed apes demonstrating sympathy and sharing in the wild. That sounds like moral behavior to me. These "lowly animals" share and help one another because it is natural for them to do so, because they have learned to do so, and because it helps the group to survive. It is unlikely that chimpanzees exhibit what appears to be moral behavior because they believe in an ape god. If they can do it, we can do it. In fact, humans behave morally without gods every day all around the world. Remember, many millions of nonbelievers are alive and well today, leading quiet, peaceful, and positive lives.

The fear and loathing of evolution by so many believers is tragic because the story of human evolution and of all life is exciting, inspiring, and important. We can't ever really understand ourselves or the world around us without understanding evolution. It thrills me to think about the long line of life that led to me. I'm uplifted by it. I certainly don't feel degraded because I came from an Australopithecus instead of magic dirt. I am also confident that my acceptance of evolution will never lead me to kill a fellow human in order to get ahead in life.

I once spent a couple of weeks out in the east African bush. Not a day went by that I didn't think about the possibility that a *Homo erectus* or *Homo ergaster* may once have stood on the same spot I was on. I would squat down and scan the horizon, listen to the insects, and feel the wind—maybe exactly as my distant ancestors once did. I tried to imagine their rugged lives, their ingenious use of fire and stone tools. I was not ashamed, diminished, or immoral. I felt proud to be related to such fine people who did so much with so little. It is sad that so many people never think about such things because they know so little of the human story.

Evolution is not string theory or calculus. It is a relatively simple concept that anyone can grasp. Evolution simply describes how life changes over time. Contrary to creationist propaganda, evolution says nothing directly about how life began, only how life changes. These changes happen primarily due to (1) genetic mutation and (2) natural selection. Genetic mutation is just a fancy phrase for little surprises that turn up in genes. These mutations don't mean anything most of the time. Sometimes they are bad. Occasionally, however, they give the animal or plant a tiny advantage over others in the environment they currently inhabit. When this happens, natural selection can occur. Those who inherit this advantage from their parents are a little more likely to survive, prosper, and have more offspring than those who lack it. It might be a case where an animal is a little bit faster, a little bit taller, longer-legged, shorter-legged, smaller, bigger, whatever is significant in the given environment. Eventually, over many generations, individuals with this advantage could come to dominate the species. When this goes on for millions of years it is easy to see how gradual changes can add up to dramatic transformations.

Now, why would understanding this make anyone immoral? Who in their right mind would see this as justification for genocide or discrimination? Evolution is not bad. It may be nature's harsh, cruel, and indifferent way, but it's not the formula for human destruction that misguided or dishonest people claim it is. Teaching children how life on earth changes over time will not make them lose their minds and turn to crime any more than teaching them that the earth revolves around the sun did.

Evolution is a fascinating subject. It is sad that so many believers shut it out because they wrongly assume that it is too complex to understand or that it is a lie. They are missing out on something that likely would enhance their appreciation for their own life and life in general. Strangest of all, it is not even necessary to reject evolution for one to continue believing in gods. Many believers have it stuck in their heads that it must be one or the other. Although many religious leaders present it that way, it's not true. There are many millions of Christians,

Muslims, Hindus, Jews, and other believers all over the world who accept that evolution is real. They see the fossils in museums, hear the sensible explanations by scientists, and are able to accept it without letting go of their belief in a god. Scientist Francis Collins, leader of the Human Genome Project, believes that Jesus is a real god while simultaneously accepting that evolution is real. Of course he has no choice but to accept evolution because his work wouldn't make any sense otherwise. Collins was able to bend his belief around evolution so that it conformed to the obvious reality he saw before him. Other believers should at least go as far as Collins has. He and many others like him show that one can believe in a god without taking up the absurd position that life does not evolve. Believers should never allow themselves to be misled into thinking that they must choose between evolution and belief in a god. You can have both, as many people do.

CHAPTER 7 BIBLIOGRAPHY AND RECOMMENDED READING

Mayr, Ernst. *What Evolution Is*. New York: Basic Books, 2001. Outstanding book on evolution by a great scientist.

Zimmer, Carl. *Evolution: The Triumph of an Idea*. New York: HarperCollins, 2001. This is the companion book to the PBS series of the same name. This book is the perfect read for anyone who has doubts about evolution or just wants to understand it more. Includes the chapter "What about God?" which addresses the evolution-creationism controversy.

Chapter 8

Our world is too beautiful to be an accident.

During an interview with Apollo astronaut Gene Cernan, the last man to walk on the moon, I asked him if he had time for deep reflection in between the tasks on his busy schedule of exploration and setting up experiments. Cernan is one of the most eloquent of all the early astronauts and he didn't shy away from opening up about what he felt when he stood on the surface of the moon and looked up at his distant home.

"When you look back at the Earth, it is so overwhelming, so powerful and beautiful," Cernan said. "The world is too beautiful to have happened by accident. There must be something or somebody bigger than us who put it all together. When I stood on the Moon, I stood at a point in space and time where I witnessed science meeting its match. Science could no longer explain what I was witnessing at that point in time."

It is exciting to imagine how it might have felt to stand in Cernan's boots and see the tiny earth two hundred forty thousand miles away. Thanks to photographs taken by astronauts, we can feel at least a hint of that experience. Beginning with the classic "Earthrise" photograph taken from lunar orbit during the *Apollo 8* mission in 1968, photos of our planet have repeatedly shown it for what it is, a glowing oasis of life and hope in the cold blackness of space. During the *Apollo 17* mission, Cernan's final spaceflight, one of the crew, probably Jack Schmitt, took a brilliant photograph of the earth. Nicknamed "The Blue Marble," the shot may be the most widely used photograph in history—and for obvious reasons. Earth is stunningly beautiful in the photo, with its swirling white clouds and cool blue seas. So much life, so much potential, all contained on that little world. Observations of the earth from space can stimulate deep thoughts and even deeper reverence. But do awe and admiration provide a good reason to conclude that gods exist? Do the earth's complexity and beauty suggest that a god necessarily made it? Many believers claim that this abundant beauty reflects their god's handiwork, proof that he is real. But does this claim hold up if one takes a long hard look at our world from down here at ground level?

In answering claims about our world's "god-given" beauty, there is no better place to start than with ourselves. According to many believers, the human species is the crowning achievement of various creator gods. The gods who made the world and all its life, they say, warmed up with worms and birds but then made us, the pièce de résistance. Some religions even claim that we were made in a god's image.

Beautiful?

Us?

If we were designed and created by an all-powerful, all-knowing, and perfectly good god, as some religions claim, then how do we explain serial killers, slavery, and wars? Why would a good god who knows the future bother making a life-form that he knew would end up fighting, killing, raping, stealing, and generally running amok as many of us do? Many believers attempt to explain away the terrible behavior that is common to our species by claiming that their god gave us autonomy or "free will." But that misses the point. An all-knowing god would know in advance what choices we were going to make and how we would turn out. So why would he or she create us in this way? Why would any good god set the stage for so much misery and suffering? Why would a good god knowingly make tribal creatures who are so vulnerable to fear and hate? If he knew we would end up slaying our brothers and starving our sisters' children, why would he go forward with an obviously bad design?

Despite our many problems, I do agree with believers that life on Earth, including humankind, is profoundly beautiful, almost magically so. An Olympic runner in full flight and a child's smile are irresistibly gorgeous to human eyes. I am not so disappointed by our failures that I cannot see our achievements. However, we all should be honest enough to admit that the beauty of our species is at least matched by its ugliness.

If you suspect that I am being too hard on humankind, consider these statistics:

- There are an estimated twenty-seven million slaves in the world today. This is more than there were at the beginning of the nineteenth century when slavery was legal in Great Britain and the United States of America. (Leach 2004)
- About half the people on Earth struggle to survive on less than two dollars per day. (UN)
- More than 780 million adults cannot read or write. (CIA)
- More than a billion people do not have access to safe drinking water. (WHO)
- More than two billion people do not have access to basic sanitation. (WHO)
- The world spends more than a trillion dollars per year on waging war or preparing for war. (Global Security)
- About half of the world's children live in severe poverty. (UNICEF)
- More than nine million children die each year because of poverty. That's approximately twenty-five thousand each day. (UNICEF)

"Beautiful" may be one of our qualities but it certainly is not a complete description of our species. For every thing that is attractive about us, one can easily match it with something repulsive. We are smart enough to feed, house, and educate every child, but we choose not to do it. One man paints a landscape on canvas, another shreds it with cluster bombs.

As bad as we can be, however, it is the immeasurable suffering of nonhuman life that is even more of a problem for this claim that our world is the beautiful result of a god's creation. Yes, there is great beauty in nature. I know firsthand. On a black night I paddled a small boat up the Momon River in the Amazon rain forest, where a symphony of creatures serenaded me. Soaring silently in a hot-air balloon only a couple of hundred feet above Kenya's Masai Mara, I watched giraffes stir beneath me as the morning sun rose. Inside a tiny submersible, I enjoyed observing unforgettable deep-water wonders. Memorable as they may be, however, such encounters with beauty could never cause me to ignore or deny nature's ugly side.

It is a fact that the daily routine of life on Earth is a continual bloodbath of fear, suffering, and death. No Hollywood horror film could ever begin to approach the grisly reality of a single minute's activity in the animal kingdom. Every moment of every day, it is business as usual for animals to be eaten alive or even to have their internal organs devoured from within by parasites. For example, some bugs suffer that terrible fate when they are paralyzed by a particularly creepy species of wasp. This wasp injects an egg into the victim's body, converting it into an incubation chamber for their offspring. As the larva develops, it slowly eats its living host from the inside out. The larva is careful to save the most vital organs for last so the host stays fresh and alive for as long as possible. I have seen a video of this process. It's not pretty.

In Africa I saw two lion cubs gnawing on a zebra the older lions of the pride had taken down. Their victim was still alive, even as they worked to tear open its abdomen to devour the warm guts. It was difficult to watch an animal experience such misery. I will never forget the blood-soaked faces and ghoulish excitement in the lion cubs' eyes. But we cannot blame the parasitic wasp or the lion cub for such horrifying behavior. They are merely doing what nature demands of them.

Or, as believers might say, they are merely doing what the god who created them wanted them to do. The latter explanation is a bit more difficult to understand, in my opinion.

Failure and pain is the norm for life on this planet, predation and extinction the rule. Of all the species that have ever lived, scientists estimate that more than 98 percent have gone extinct. If the daily routines of the animal kingdom in this "beautiful world" are the work of a god, then I am confident almost any one of us could do far better if we possessed magical powers. It could not be that hard to come up with a system that is more humane—more beautiful—than the continual slaughter and constant failure that goes on day and night here on the "Blue Marble." To begin with, we could base life on photosynthesis and chemosynthesis in order to avoid this predator-prey madness that stains our world with so much blood. Had a human with a minimal sense of decency created this world, we might not have all these mosquitoes that spread misery and death in developing nations by delivering viruses into the bloodstream of millions of people— including children. Then again, one could just leave lethal viruses out of the creation recipe and not have to worry about mosquitoes, or that terrible influenza germ that killed millions of people in the twentieth century. Most species of bacteria do good work but there are a few we might be better off without. In a world created with compassion in mind, the populations of various species could be controlled by tinkering with fertility rates rather than disease and predation. Who knows what this world would look like if you or I had created it? I am confident, however, that it would be a lot more beautiful than the one we have now, the one believers say their god is responsible for.

CHAPTER 8 BIBLIOGRAPHY AND RECOMMENDED READING

"Causes of Poverty: Poverty Facts and Stats." Global Issues, 2007. http://www.globalissues.org/TradeRelated/Facts.asp.

Leach, Susan Llewelyn. "Slavery Is Not Dead, Just Less Recognizable."
    Christian Science Monitor, September 1, 2004.

"Military: World Wide Military Expenditures." Global Security.org, 2007.
    http://www.globalsecurity.org/military/world/spending.htm.

State of the World's Children 2008. UNICEF report, January 2008.
    http://www.unicef.org.

"Water Sanitation and Health: Health through Safe Drinking Water and Basic
    Sanitation." World Health Organization (WHO). http://www.who
    .int/water _sanitation_health/mdg1/en/index.html.

The World Factbook. Central Intelligence Agency (CIA). https://www.cia
    .gov/library/publications/the-world-factbook/index.html.

Zimmer, Carl. *Parasite Rex: Inside the Bizarre World of Nature's Most Dan-
    gerous Creatures*. New York: Free Press, 2000. Required reading for all
    those who think nature is nothing more than sweet-smelling flowers and
    pretty waterfalls.

Chapter 9

My god created the universe.

For me, it is far better to grasp the Universe as it really is than to persist in delusion, however satisfying and reassuring.

—Carl Sagan

Ignorance more frequently begets confidence than does knowledge. It is those who know little, and not those who know much, who so positively assert that this or that problem will never be solved by science.

—Charles Darwin

A classic justification for believing in a god is simply the existence of the universe and everything in it. How can anything other than a god, say believers, be responsible for trillions of planets and stars spread across billions of light years of space? It is inconceivable that all of this just happened by itself, they say. How could life have sprung up without a god, they ask.

This is a very appealing reason to believe for many people and it is easy to see why. Any thoughtful person who looks up at the stars, stares across the Grand Canyon, or simply watches a butterfly in flight cannot help but wonder how it all came to be. The explanation, "my god did it," is simple, convenient, and reassuring. The problem, of course, is that there is absolutely nothing to justify crediting a god for the existence of the universe. Yes, it seems incomprehensibly large and complex, and, yes, there are many questions that have stumped scientists so far. Some mysteries of the universe may never be solved. But this is ignorance, not evidence.

Unfortunately, the best scientific explanation we have today for the origin of the universe can be difficult to understand for many people and, for some, just too weird to believe. It's called the big bang theory and the mere mention of it causes some believers to laugh. They dismiss it as nonsense and refuse to consider the evidence for it. Other believers, however, embrace the big bang as "proof" of their god's creation. A sudden start like the big bang fits nicely with many religious creation stories. But is the big bang the handiwork of a god? Is there any reason, any hint that points to a divine being behind this big event?

First, we need to understand a little bit about the big bang. Charles Seife offers a fine account in his book *Alpha and Omega*:

> At first glance, the history of the universe, as told by scientists, will seem almost as farfetched as the stories told by Greek mystics or African storytellers. However, unlike the ancient myths, every part of the scientific narrative is backed up by hard scientific evidence. . . . And as strange as this tale may seem, scientists were forced to accept it to explain their observations of the heavens. Like many ancient myths, the beginning of the universe as seen by modern science, begins with nothing at all. There is no space; there is no time. There is not even a void. There is nothing.
>
> In an instant, the nothing becomes something. In an enormous flash of energy, the big bang creates space and time. Nobody knows where the energy came from—perhaps it was just a random event, or perhaps it was one of many similar big bangs. But within a tiny seed of matter and energy is all the stuff of our current universe. For a fraction of a second the universe expands at an incredible rate; it is inflated by an energy that scientists do not understand very well . . .
>
> Almost all the matter in the universe was born in the first few minutes of creation. (Seife 2003, 63–89)

Wow, so these scientists are trying to tell us that everything—and they mean everything—was compressed into a tiny space smaller than the period at the end of this sentence. They claim that, for unknown reasons, all this compressed stuff suddenly started flying apart and the result of that event was everything in the universe, eventually even us. That is a spectacular and admittedly difficult-to-believe story. It doesn't sound any more reasonable or likely than the numerous creation myths about a giant egg hatching the universe or gods simply wishing the universe into existence. But there is something very different about the big bang. This story, unlike all the others, comes from science and that means it must be supported by evidence. Unlike every other explanation that our species has come up with for the creation of the universe, this one has scientific observations and experiments that back it up. This explanation for how the universe started is not a belief and has no need for faith. However, it is not conclusive and remains open to correction or rejection, just like everything else in science. It's also important to understand that it doesn't even answer the question of why the universe started. The big bang theory currently does not explain what caused the sudden expansion of all that compressed matter. It only describes the process once it began.

The big bang was not easy to accept for some scientists when it was first proposed. It was more convenient when one simply could say that the universe was infinite, with no beginning and no end. But science is driven by evidence rather than convenience and the evidence points to the big bang. Interestingly, some believers claim that the big bang is the work of their god and go so far as to cite it as validation of their creation beliefs. (Note that it is always "their" god and never any other gods who might have been behind the big bang.) But at this time there is nothing to suggest that a god had anything to do with it. The big bang is a big theory with many components. Cosmologists are still working on it to see what holds up and what doesn't. As they make discoveries, wrong ideas will be discarded and the theory will be improved. If too much ends up being discarded, the entire theory would be tossed out. This is why the big bang is superior to all creation stories from religions at this time. It is not an inflexible conclusion based on inflexible belief. It is not a law written in stone that can never be changed—even if someone shows that it is wrong. The big bang is an excellent partial explanation for the beginning of our universe, but only for as long as the evidence supports it and not a second more.

Believers who see the big bang theory as science finally catching up to religion would do well to slow down and consider that science is still totally silent about the existence of any gods, much less a god being responsible for the big bang. Yes, some people try very hard to make that connection but they are way out of line with the evidence and do not represent the views of most cosmologists and astronomers. To date, all claims that a god has been discovered are hollow and misleading. Cosmology has not unveiled any gods, despite the statements sometimes printed on book covers and in magazine headlines. The most believers can do at this time is point to unanswered questions about the universe and attempt to plug in their god as the answer. But understand that what may seem like magic or a god today often becomes an elementary school science lesson tomorrow.

A final point about believers who see their god in the big bang is that attributing the event to a super intelligent being does not necessarily have to mean it was their god who lit the fuse. It just as easily could have been the god of a rival religion or even the god of a long-extinct religion. Or maybe it was the result of an experiment conducted by technologically advanced scientists from another galaxy or universe. There is no less evidence for this than there is for someone's favored god doing it. Maybe our religions have it all wrong and it really was aliens who gave our universe its start. Maybe they even seeded the earth with life. How could we know the difference between alien scientists and gods? I am not suggesting that we all start believing in super-intelligent aliens as our creators. There is no evidence or convincing arguments for that either. I bring up the alien idea only to show believers that one can fill in a mystery with pretty much anything. It's better to simply admit that we don't know everything at this time.

It is important for believers to understand that there are significant differences between "my god did it" and the big bang theory. The former tends to be an inflexible conclusion that is based on faith and has no evidence to support it; the latter is a scientific theory that is derived from the scientific method and open to correction. A common misconception that many believers have about the big bang is that atheists "believe" it in a religious sense. Some even call it a creation myth for atheists. This is not true. While I cannot speak for all nonbelievers, of course, I am confident that virtually no atheists "believe" in the big bang in the same way religious people believe in their creation stories. Most Christians, Muslims, and Jews, for example, would have a big problem letting go of the belief that their god created the universe. However, atheists who accept the big bang as a good explanation based on current evidence are unlikely to become enraged or feel emotionally devastated if overwhelming evidence turns up in support of a new "Little Burp theory" that overturns the big bang theory. It is safe to assume that atheists would not fill the streets weeping and gnashing their teeth. No atheists would threaten to behead the scientists who made the discovery or even burn them in effigy. It is doubtful that private atheist schools would pop up around the world to defiantly continue teaching the big bang theory to children in spite of the evidence. It is more likely that atheists would welcome the scientific advancement.

Wait, says the believer, the big bang had to have been caused by something. Nothing just happens. Science can't explain what caused the big bang but there had to be a cause and that cause was my god. This argument has been answered by atheists repeatedly for many years but it never goes away, so I will answer it too. The assumption that everything has to have been caused by something else might be incorrect. How does anyone know this? Maybe some things are infinite and uncaused. But, if believers are right and "everything" requires a cause, then that means something or someone must have "caused" their gods as well. They can't have it both ways. If, however, they say that there is an exception to the rule and their gods can exist without anything having caused them, then so can the universe.

The bottom line on how the universe began is that no one understands exactly how it happened. But our ignorance about the origins of the universe is not proof of the existence of gods. Atheists cannot claim that the big bang disproves the existence of gods. Believers cannot claim that unanswered questions about the big bang disprove a natural universe that is empty of gods. Those who side with the gods must find another way to justify their belief because cosmology offers them no help at this time.

CHAPTER 9 BIBLIOGRAPHY AND RECOMMENDED READING

Leeming, David, with Margaret Leeming. *A Dictionary of Creation Myths.* New York: Oxford University Press, 1994.

Seife, Charles. *Alpha and Omega: The Search for the Beginning and End of the Universe.* New York: Penguin Books, 2003.

Weinberg, Steven. *Facing Up: Science and Its Cultural Adversaries.* Cambridge: Harvard University Press, 2001.

Chapter 10

Believing in my god makes me happy.

I've got the joy, joy, joy, joy down in my heart.
Where? Down in my heart!
Where? Down in my heart!
I've got the joy, joy, joy, joy down in my heart.
　　　　　　—"I've Got the Joy" (Christian song)

Even when faced with good reasons to doubt, many people continue believing in their god because it feels good. If belief in a god makes them happy, why question it? This justification for belief may not carry much intellectual weight in the eyes of some but it deserves attention nonetheless. Simple as it seems, I find it honest and far more defensible than most of the extravagant arguments for gods that believers come up with. It feels good so they do it. It's tough to argue against this reason for belief. So I won't, at least not directly. After all, I want happy people and a happy world too. The last thing I want is to rain on anyone's parade. However, because I am convinced that people can be just as happy or even happier without gods, I won't duck this common reason for believing.

First of all, it is important to consider whether it is a real god that is making believers happy or merely something about the act of believing in a god that makes them happy. I certainly won't dispute religion's ability to make some people happy. I have seen religious joy up close. I saw it in the glowing eyes of a worshipping Hindu man in a temple in Nepal. I once found myself swept up in a whirlwind of smiles and singing inside a small-town church in Florida. I was enjoying it so much that I might have thought I was filled with the Holy Ghost if I didn't know better. I watched a Muslim man pray in Damascus, Syria. His expression was so intense and serious that I assumed he was in pain or deeply troubled by something. When he finished his prayers, however, he smiled at me in a show of pure joy. At that moment he might have been the happiest man in all the world. So how can anyone challenge all this happiness linked to religion? How can anyone deny that gods make people happy when the evidence is everywhere in the form of grinning believers? The answer, of course, is that none of this is evidence of anything other than the ability of belief itself and the activities that go along with it to inspire happiness. Happy worshippers prove nothing about the existence of gods. It could be that believing and worshipping are the sources of the pleasure. Believers may disagree but the most likely explanation for happy believers is that socializing with friends during worship gatherings, the relaxing process of prayer, singing and listening to music, and imagining that a god cares for you are responsible for the happiness. No real gods are necessary. Don't believe it? Then how do you explain Buddhists?

Orthodox Buddhists prove that religion can make people happy—even without a god. Contrary to what many Westerners think, traditional Buddhists do not worship Buddha as a god. Siddhartha Gautama, the Buddha, never claimed to be a god. Therefore, most Buddhists are atheists. However, they still may believe in other unproven supernatural claims such as reincarnation. Futhermore, Buddhism can be confusing because some versions of it have incorporated many gods and some Buddhists do revere and pray to Buddha in a way that strongly suggests they think of him as a god. This should not be surprising, however, as all religions branch out and change, creating many different versions over time.

So how do Jews, Hindus, Christians, and Muslims who credit their god for making them happy explain Buddhists who are just as happy if not happier? And do not doubt that Buddhists can be happy. I can personally vouch for it. I encountered many Buddhist monks in Nepal and Thailand who radiated remarkable happiness. They were exceptionally warm and content people. Just being around them made me feel happy. None of them asked me for money so I feel safe in assuming that they were sincere and every bit as happy as they appeared. But my random encounters around the world are not enough to make sweeping judgments, of course. Scientific studies are much better. One, in fact, indicates that Buddhists may be the happiest religious people in the entire world—despite not believing in a god. In 2003 researchers at the University of California San Francisco Medical Center reported that brain scans showed that Buddhist test subjects were likely to be happier and calmer than most other people. "The most reasonable hypothesis is that there is something about conscientious Buddhist practice that results in the kind of happiness we all seek," said Paul Ekman, one of the researchers. A second study by scientists at the University of Wisconsin found that Buddhist test subjects' brains showed unusually high activity in the area associated with positive emotions, self-control, and temperament (BBC 2003).

As a polite and positive person who happens to be a nonbeliever, I have no desire to see anyone unhappy or lose something they depend upon as a source of joy. But there is no reason for believers to avoid challenging their reasons for belief. The fact is, one can be a nonbeliever and still be very happy. I'm living proof of it. I smile far more often than I frown and I would describe my life to date as exceptionally happy overall. But I'm just one person. What about the entire world? Do gods really inject joy into the minds of their worshippers? If so, one would expect believers to be happier than atheists overall. Let's see if this is the case.

Although some studies have found that individuals who attend religious services tend to be happier than individuals who do not, the big picture is quite different. Adrian White, a University of Leicester psychologist, created the "World Map of Happiness" by analyzing more than a hundred studies that questioned eighty thousand people worldwide (*Science Daily* 2006). Although it was not the purpose of the study, his findings shed some light on the relationship between belief in gods and happiness. White's work clearly shows that high levels of belief do not guarantee high levels of happiness for societies. Based on the data, high levels of *nonbelief* seem more conducive to a society's overall happiness than belief. According to White's research, the top ten happiest nations on earth are:

1. Denmark
2. Switzerland
3. Austria
4. Iceland
5. The Bahamas
6. Finland
7. Sweden
8. Bhutan
9. Brunei
10. Canada

What immediately stands out about this ranking is that the happiest country in the world is also one of the least religious countries in the world. Denmark is first in happiness and third in the world for percentage of nonbelievers among its citizens. Between 43 to 80 percent of Danes do not believe in a personal god, according to research by sociologist Phil Zuckerman (2005). This must be surprising news to believers who think that belief in a god is the key to happiness.

Switzerland ranks second on the happiness list and is also one of the most secular nations in the world, ranking twenty-third for "organic atheism" out of more than one hundred seventy countries analyzed by Zuckerman. ("Organic atheism" is nonbelief by choice. Zuckerman's rankings exclude nonbelief among totalitarian societies where governments may attempt to impose it upon citizens and self-reporting of religion may be compromised due to persecution.)

Austria, third in happiness, is right behind Switzerland in nonbelief with 18 to 26 percent of its population describing themselves as atheist, agnostic, or nonbelievers. Cold but happy Iceland follows Austria and also ranks high in nonbelief (twenty-eighth with 16 to 23 percent nonbelievers). The Bahamas does not make the list of the top fifty nations of nonbelievers but sixth-place Finland does, at number seven with 28 to 60 percent of its population happily finding their way through life without gods. Sweden, seventh on the happy scale, has the highest percentage of organic atheism of any nation in the world at 46 to 85 percent. Bhutan's per capita income is less than a thousand dollars per year and most of its people are Buddhists with no belief in Yahweh, Jesus, or Allah. Nonetheless, the people of this small Himalayan nation rank in the top ten of the world when it comes to happiness.

Officially Islamic Brunei ranks ninth in happiness on White's scale, leaving Christians to ponder how they can be so happy without having Jesus in their lives. Maybe it is Allah, or maybe it's Brunei's oil-rich economy that makes them so happy, but it certainly is not Jesus or any of the Hindu gods. Number ten on the global happiness ranking is Canada, yet another nation with a relatively high percentage of nonbelievers. According to Zuckerman, cheery Canada ranks twentieth in the world for percentage of nonbelieving citizens, with 15 to 37 percent of its population unconvinced that gods are real.

What about the bottom of White's list? What are the least-happy nations on earth? Believers might be surprised to learn that the three countries occupying the bottom of White's happiness ranking are highly religious societies with virtually no atheists. They are: Democratic Republic of the Congo (ranked 176 in happiness), Zimbabwe (177), and Burundi (178). In the Democratic Republic of the Congo, nonbelievers are virtually nonexistent. The population is loyal to Christianity and traditional African beliefs. The people of Zimbabwe also are believers with very few exceptions. Most of them believe in both traditional African religions and Christianity. Burundi's citizens are mostly Christian but also include Muslims and those who follow indigenous African beliefs. All that belief, however, isn't enough to keep them from ranking last in global happiness.

I am not suggesting that atheism guarantees happiness. Of course it doesn't. But one can look around at the world today and see that belief in gods does not guarantee it either. There are many factors that determine happiness. Belief may indeed bring joy in many cases, but there is no reason to think that nonbelievers cannot find just as much happiness in their own way. For some, having a free mind that is unburdened by ancient beliefs is the best road to a happy and satisfying life. I suspect that security, health, food, shelter, family, romantic love, and friendships all weigh far more heavily than one's belief or nonbelief in influencing happiness. The important point here is that people can be happy without believing in gods and people can be sad even if they believe in gods.

Those who believe in a god and attempt to defend the reality of that god by claiming it is the source of their happiness are overreaching. Deriving joy from belief is not evidence that a god is real. It only means believing can bring joy for some people. Of course it can; no one disputes that. Those who go even further and claim that belief in a god is necessary for happiness need to consider the millions of Danes, Swedes, Swiss, Austrians, Icelanders, Finns, and Canadians who don't believe but are happier than most nonetheless.

Anyone who fears losing a bit of joy from life by daring to question his or her belief might consider that losing imaginary gods does not mean losing religion necessarily. There is no law that says one must believe Jesus is a god to enjoy singing "Silent Night" at Christmastime. One does not have to believe Allah exists to enjoy friendship and conversation at a Mosque. One does not have to believe that Kurma is real in order to enjoy participating in the beautiful rituals of Hinduism. Find your happiness where you can, but never cling to it at the expense of thinking freely and vigorously about everything—even gods.

CHAPTER 10 BIBLIOGRAPHY AND RECOMMENDED READING

"Buddhists 'Really Are Happier.'" BBC, May 21, 2003. http://news.bbc.co.uk/2/hi/health/3047291.stm.

Kurtz, Paul. *Living without Religion: Eupraxophy.* Amherst, NY: Prometheus Books, 1994. An excellent book capable of calming those who are worried about life with no gods.

"Psychologist Produces the First-Ever 'World Map of Happiness.'" *Science Daily*, November 14, 2006. http://www.sciencedaily.com/releases/2006/11/ 061113093726.htm.

Zuckerman, Phil. "Atheism: Contemporary Rates and Patterns." In *The Cambridge Companion to Atheism*, ed. Michael Martin, 47–65. Cambridge: Cambridge University Press, 2005.

Chapter 11

Better safe than sorry.

Fear was the first thing on Earth to make gods.
—Lucretius

Suppose we've chosen the wrong god. Every time we go to church we're just making him madder and madder.
—Homer Simpson

There is a snappy comeback that many believers are quick to use whenever someone suggests the possibility that their god may not be real. They declare that believing in and worshipping their god is the smart move, the safe option. Atheism, on the other hand, is both dumb and dangerous. Believing in their god, they say, is like placing a bet with your life and it's safer to gamble on the god being real than gamble on the god not being real. Better safe than sorry. After all, if believers are right the payoff will be spectacular. One might be rewarded with divine protection here on Earth and maybe even an eternity in heaven after death. If, however, their god turns out not to exist, that's okay too because they haven't lost anything. Atheists, however, take a terrible risk by not believing and worshipping because, if the god is real, they will be on the wrong side of judgment day and suffer severely for not believing. They might even end up in hell, the worst fate of all. So why not just play it safe and believe in a god? After all, hell sounds like a pretty scary place.

This suggestion to play it safe by believing in a god may seem reasonable at first glance, but give it a little thought and it quickly becomes clear that it makes no sense at all. First, there is no reason to feel threatened by any god's wrath because no one has ever been able to show that any gods are real. Why should we be concerned with judgmental gods and terrible places that most likely are not real? Before one fears hell and worships a god in order to avoid it, I think it is important to establish that hell is real. No one has managed to do that yet.

Whether they realize it or not, believers think about the threat of hell in much the same way as atheists do. For example, Christians do not fear the hell that Muslims say they will suffer in for rejecting the teachings of the Koran. Likewise, Muslims do not fear the hell that Christians claim they will burn in for rejecting Jesus. Each group of believers dismisses the threats of the other because they don't see any evidence or hear any compelling arguments to suggest that these alternate hells are real. They don't lose a wink of sleep over it because they know those claims are totally unsubstantiated. Meanwhile, atheists don't fear anybody's hell because none of them are backed up by any evidence. If believers want to use hell as a scare tactic or heaven as a lure to get people to believe, they first need to meet the challenge of showing that these places are real.

Another big problem with the "play it safe" idea is that believers are wrong about not losing anything if their gods are not real. People certainly do lose something if they spend a significant portion of their lives believing in and worshipping gods that do not exist. Consider the time and energy spent reading religious books, traveling back and forth to places of worship, praying, worrying, talking about, and fussing over a god who was never there. The total time wasted over a lifetime could be immense.

If we are lucky, we get about three billion heartbeats and then we are gone. Time is not something we should squander. Time spent carrying on one-way conversations with gods who may not exist is time that might be spent with family, writing letters to friends, exercising, and doing positive things for society. The fewer distractions we have in our lives the more we can get done. How many more sick people could Mother Teresa have helped if she had been less preoccupied with prayer and converting people to her religion? What else might Isaac Newton have achieved if he had devoted less time to magic and the Bible and more time to mathematics and physics?

The biggest problem of all with the "play it safe" idea, however, is that it is impossible to play it safe! Just how, for example, does one decide which god and which religion to line up behind? The majority of the world's believers cannot possibly be spending their worshipping time wisely because all religions can't be true. Most religions are far too contradictory in their claims for all of them to be valid. Some believers may promote the idea that all religions are paths to the same place and that all belief systems are expressing the same thing but this is nothing more than sweet-sounding double-talk. Islam, Scientology, and Jehovah's Witnesses are not on the same page, for example. They are mutually exclusive belief systems. Somebody is wrong. The fact is, a great number of the world's believers, possibly all of them, are wasting their time worshipping imaginary gods. Think about the hundreds of millions of people who are allowing belief in a god who is not there to consume valuable hours of their lives. Think about the hundreds of millions of people who base important real-life decisions on the imagined desires of a god who does not exist. It seems like an awfully inefficient way to run a species.

The difficulty with figuring out how to play it safe and worship the right god is that no god is more or less likely to be real than any other. There have been hundreds of thousands of gods that humans have claimed to be real, either in the past or today, and not one of them has a superior argument for his or her existence. So how in the world does anyone who wants to play it safe choose the right god to believe in? Simply going along with the religion of your parents and neighbors is too risky. It is also intellectually indefensible. That's an accident of birth, not rational decision making. Even if one is able to choose the right god, how does he or she decide which religion worships that god in the correct way? It seems like a believer faces a risky roll of the dice there as well. To really be safe, shouldn't believers spend several years studying at least a few hundred of the many thousands of religions and gods available so that they might have a better chance of making an intelligent decision? Like believers say, better safe than sorry. Surely it's too risky to just go with the first god one hears about in childhood.

Believers can never be sure if they made the right choice when it comes to a god. But even if they were fortunate enough to pick the correct god and correct religion in general, there still would be plenty to worry about. Can Christians, for example, simply repent their sins and accept Jesus and leave it at that? Or should they also try to follow the Bible's instructions and rule out shaving, lobsters, and a whole lot more? What about people who work on the Sabbath? Should Christians kill them, as the Bible commands? Should Christians hate their own family as Jesus demands in Luke 14:26 of the Bible? Should Christians accept the Book of Mormon as the word of their god, every bit as valid as the Bible? Why? Why not? Are communion and baptism necessary or not? Was David Koresh a modern-day prophet that all Christians should have listened to or was he a criminal who should have been ignored? Does Jesus want me to go to church on Sundays or Saturdays? Can I mow my lawn on Saturday? On Sunday? With more than thirty thousand versions of Christianity alone available today, choosing the right religion is anything but simple. What about Islam? Shouldn't we all be Muslims? Better safe than sorry. But shall it be Sufism, Sunni, or Shi'ite? Remember, you don't want to gamble foolishly with your life and your afterlife, so place your bet carefully.

In order to really play it safe, one could try worshipping all gods in all ways. Unfortunately, that would take about twenty-four hours per day, seven days per week—and a few hundred lifetimes! Just learning the names of the gods would take a lot of time and effort. Saying one brief daily prayer to even a small fraction of the gods would take all day and night. Work and family life would suffer. But since we're talking eternity here, it might be worth it. But then there is the problem of jealousy. Believe it or not, some gods are very jealous and they don't condone any worshipping of rival gods. The penalty for promiscuous worshipping is death in some belief systems. So we can't even spread our bets without risking trouble.

Face it, there is no safe bet when it comes to believing in a god. There are too many gods and too many religions to pretend that there can be a simple choice between belief and nonbelief. The choice is far more complicated than that. Perhaps the safest bet of all is to be an atheist and simply appreciate every second of life because it is probably all we get. One thing is certain, however, billions of believers around the world today are unable to agree on who the real gods are, how we are supposed to worship these gods, and what happens to us when we die. This uncertainty should give all of us reason to pause before gambling on belief with the precious hours and years of our lives.

CHAPTER 11 BIBLIOGRAPHY AND RECOMMENDED READING

Chaline, Eric. *The Book of Gods and Goddesses: A Visual Directory of Ancient and Modern Deities*. New York: Harper Entertainment, 2004.

Jordan, Michael. *Dictionary of Gods and Goddesses*. New York: Checkmark Books, 2004.

Chapter 12

A sacred book proves
my god is real.

This book is not to be doubted.

—Koran 2:2

*It ain't the parts of the Bible that I can't under-
stand that bother me,
it is the parts that I do understand.*

—Mark Twain

Many people depend heavily on a book to justify their belief in a particular god or gods. Where would Judaism be without the written Torah or Christianity without the Bible? The Bhagavad Gita is precious to Hindus. It is unlikely that Islam could have been so successful without the Koran. The Book of Mormon was the catalyst of a new religion in North America in the nineteenth century.

These books and others, various believers claim, are messages from their gods and, as such, they are invaluable resources for humankind. According to believers, sacred books may explain our origin, guide us through daily life, and even tell us what happens to us when we die. According to believers, their book offers conclusive proof that their particular god is real. It is important to note, however, that despite claims that these books are of divine origin not one of them has ever been able to convince a majority of the world's believers that it is anything more than a book written by people.

It never takes long for a devout believer to cite their sacred book as the ultimate authority for some point they are trying to make. In the minds of many believers, their book can withstand any challenge from doubters or even scientific discovery. Some believers claim that their book is perfect, completely free of errors or contradictions, so loaded with wisdom and correct predictions that it could only have come from a god. But are any of these books really perfect? More importantly, is there any book that contains any good evidence for the existence of a god?

No.

No holy book contains anything so special that it cannot be explained as the work of mere mortals. Believers have tried very hard for centuries but no one has ever found anything in any book that is clear evidence of a god. Furthermore, the impact of holy books seems to have a limited effect on people. No single collection of sacred words has ever managed to win over most people. This is odd. If one of these books really is a direct message from a god, then why has it failed so miserably to convince so many people? The Bible and Koran, for example, are by far the two most successful holy books ever, but neither one of them is impressive enough to silence the other or to convince even half of the world's people that it is the truth. Although both books have been remarkably successful at impressing believers, one of them is wrong. They make important claims that are contradictory and cannot be reconciled. For example, one says Jesus is a god; the other says Jesus is not a god. This means that, at the very least, more than a billion believers have been hoodwinked by a book that is not a message from a real god. The fact that one of these books must necessarily be false, yet still manages to convince so many people that it is true, shows how people can be entranced by a book that is *just a book*. And if that can be the case for one book, then it could be the case for all of them. It is possible that all holy books, no matter how old or popular, are the work of people and not gods.

It is fortunate that we have these holy books that supposedly justify belief because they can be analyzed by anyone to see if they really do present credible support for the existence of gods. If there is something supernatural contained within a sacred book, then believers would have a strong case for their god. If there is not, however, then believers may have one less reason to believe.

I have made the effort to read several books that serve as the foundations of popular religions. I was open-minded about finding any hint of magic within them. But they seemed to me like the words of ancient believers and nothing more. What I read was just about what one would expect from people who lived long ago in relatively unenlightened times. The Torah, Bible, and Koran, for example, suggest that slavery is okay, women are inferior to men, and critical thinking is a bad thing. After years of hearing about the peace and love that is supposed to be at the core of Judaism, Christianity, and Islam, I had not expected to find so much violence, cruelty, and hatred within the books that are the foundations of those religions. Overall the Torah, Bible, and Koran read like instruction manuals for achieving a divided, angry, and violent world. They do not appear to be a recipe for peace and love, as many believers claim. Yes, I found beauty in those books but not enough to forget the disturbing content. I cannot understand how honest and well-meaning people can pretend the negative and socially destructive content is not there. How can anyone claim that these books are good and perfect? Have they read them?

Many believers strongly deny that the Torah, Bible, or Koran, for example, contain any bad advice, errors, or immoral behavior by a god—until I show it to them. Even then, however, some refuse to believe it, preferring to think that there must be some explanation for it that is not easily understood. Most of the world's religious people, I suspect, do not actually read their holy books or, if they do, they avoid thinking critically about what they have read. Most Christians, for example, probably pick around the edges of the Bible, learn a few verses, but generally skip most of it. Considering what is in it, this may be for the best. If three billion Christians, Muslims, and Jews read every word of their books and tried to follow the instructions contained in them to the letter, our world would be even scarier than it is now. For example, millions of Christians today cite the Bible to justify their prejudice against gay men. Fortunately for gay men, however, most of these Christians missed the part in the Bible where their god says we are supposed go well beyond prejudice and actually kill gay men (see Leviticus 20:13). Obviously the vast majority of Christians wouldn't do this even if they read it and even if they considered themselves to be Bible literalists. Fortunately they have enough moral sense to resist murdering a gay person or even condoning it. But this is a problem for them because it seems to suggest that they think they know better than their god. Doesn't their refusal to kill gay men demonstrate that they have higher moral standards than the god they believe in? By refusing to pick up stones, aren't they admitting that their sacred book is wrong?

Some Christians claim that the bad stuff in the Bible is limited to the Old Testament and can be excused as historical content. But, according to Matthew 5:17, Jesus said that he did not come to abolish or change any of the old laws. One also can't forget that, according to the doctrine of the Holy Trinity, Jesus and God the Father are one— the same god who killed children by the thousands in the Old Testament. Even more troubling, how is the idea of Jesus sending everyone to hell who doesn't believe in him—the majority of humankind—anything but immoral? Does a child born in Agra, India, and raised by devout Hindu parents deserve to be punished in this way just because she trusted in what her family and society taught her?

As a nonbeliever I am not obligated or inclined to ignore the ugly parts of holy books. Some might suspect, however, that I only focus on the bad to use as ammunition against religion. Not so. For example, I admire Jesus's call for people to sell their belongings and give the money to the poor. Imagine how different our world would be if middle- and upper-class believers did that. There is a line in the Koran (5:32) that suggests that the taking of a single life is like killing everyone and saving one life is like saving all. How nice it would be if everyone embraced that attitude. Yes, there is wisdom and beauty in the world's holy books. But none so remarkable that it could not have come from human writers.

There is really only one way to respond when a believer claims that a sacred book such as the Bible is so special that it is proof of their god's existence. I encourage them to read it. If they have, and still think it is perfect, morally pure, and convincing evidence for their god, I encourage them to read it again. But this time I tell them to try to imagine themselves as one of the babies their god drowned in a flood or as one of the people who will be punished forever for the crime of having been born into the wrong religious family.

Believers may be negligent about reading their own holy books but they are even more so about reading the books that are important to other religions. Very few people investigate even the handful of more popular religions today. I have lived my life in societies that are dominated by Christians and I am repeatedly shocked by how many bright people I encounter who know little or nothing about Islam, Buddhism, Hinduism, Judaism, and animism. Those belief systems account for more than half the people on earth yet they are a virtual blank for most of the Christians I meet. To many, Hinduism has something to do with cows; Buddhism has something to with meditation; and Islam has something to with Osama bin Laden. It really is that bad. Believers should know that this lack of general knowledge about popular religions means they can't possibly make informed decisions about which belief system makes more sense or which one is morally superior. How can anyone be confident that they believe in the real god and worship that god in the correct way when they know so little about the many alternative gods and rituals that billions of other people are equally confident in?

Another problem with holy books is that they lure many believers into a bizarre loop of circular reasoning. Here is how it goes:

(1) How do I know my god is real?
(2) Because the Book of the Dead/Bhagavad Gita/Torah/ Bible/Koran/Book of Mormon, and so forth says my god is real.
(3) How do I know my holy book is true?
(4) Because its words were inspired by my god.

(5) How do I know my holy book contains the inspired word of
    my god?
(6) Because it says it does.

Obviously this proves nothing. If this line of thinking made any sense,
then Christians would have to believe that the Koran is the word of the
real god and Muslims would have to believe that the Bible is the word
of the real god because both groups rely on this circular reasoning to
support their claims. If it works for one holy book, then it would have
to work for all of them. But, of course, it never does. Typical believers
see right through this nonsense whenever a rival believer attempts to
use it on them. It seems that in most cases one has to first believe the
god is real before that god's holy book can make an impression.

Many believers claim that their holy book contains details of
future events and scientific facts that could not possibly have been
known by people when they were written. This, they say, is proof that
their book comes straight from a god. It's the Nostradamus approach
to proving a god is real. Although many of these claims are made,
none of them hold up under scrutiny. "The Bible code" or "Torah
code" is a good example of this. According to some believers, the
Bible is filled with hidden messages from their god that reveal star-
tling information about important events. Michael Drosnin's book,
The Bible Code, became a best seller in the 1990s and gave believers
one more thing to cite as proof for their god. Some nonbelievers may
be surprised by how popular the Bible code is. Although finding
"secret messages" in the Bible is nothing new, it warrants attention
because believers bring it up often and it doesn't seem to be going
away any time soon.

Bible code skeptics have demonstrated that one can find just about
anything in any large collection of letters simply by tweaking an
extraction formula. For example, code skeptics have "discovered" fascinating predictions within the novel *War and Peace* by Leo Tolstoy.
With a little work I am sure that they could find "Oswald killed
Kennedy" or "Giants win the Super Bowl" in this book.

Skeptic David E. Thomas writes:

Some believe that these "messages" in the Hebrew Bible are not just coincidence—they were put there deliberately by God. But if someone finds a hidden message in a book, a song played backwards, funny-looking Martian mesas, or some other object or thing, does that prove someone else put the message there intentionally? Or might the message exist only in the eyes of the beholder (and in those of his or her followers)? Does perception of meaning prove the message was deliberately created? (Thomas 1997)

To be consistent, Christians who insist on believing in the Bible code must consider the "Koran code." Yes, there is a Koran code. And some Muslims say it is the only true code that reveals messages from a god. There probably are others. What is important to know is that no holy code comes close to providing convincing evidence for the existence of a god. These are just cases of religion hijacking numerology's gig.

I once asked a Muslim why he is confident that the Koran is the word of a real god. He replied that it contains many facts that have only recently been discovered by science. This, he said, was proof that the Koran is the only book inspired by a god. I have learned over the years that it is not wise to allow a believer to swamp you with a long list of prophecies, "facts," and "revelations" found in their holy book. What happens is that they end up feeling that they have proven their case simply because they talked a lot, as if truth somehow correlates with the number of words spoken. The way around this that allows one to avoid being rude while wasting as little time as possible is to simply ask for the best evidence. Ask for the single most astonishing and detailed prediction that has come true or the most amazing fact that can be found in their book. My Muslim friend offered this: "The Koran describes a very young embryo as looking like a chewed up piece of gum. This is exactly what it really looks like but there is no way anyone could have known that when the Koran was written."

Do not think that his example was an aberration. Citing the embryo is a common "proof" many Muslims go to when challenged by a nonbeliever. Many thousands of non-Muslim biologists, medical doctors, and embryologists remain unconvinced, however. Christians usually answer the best-evidence challenge with Jesus or Israel. Jesus, they say, was predicted and then he came. But this doesn't work very well because the prediction and the fulfillment of the prediction both occur in the same book. That's just not good enough. They also like the prophecy that a new nation of Israel would be established. The big problem, of course, is that it was *people* who created the modern state of Israel. There is absolutely no indication that any magic, miracles, or gods were involved. It was the work of mere mortals that made Israel a nation in 1948. Harry Truman and David Ben-Gurion were not gods. Since people created every other nation on earth too, I hardly see how Israel qualifies as proof for a god's existence. What about the people who created the United States? That country is bigger than Israel. Does that mean John Adams, Thomas Jefferson, and the other founding fathers were more powerful than the Jewish god? The fact that so many believers cite the creation of Israel as the best proof of the Bible's validity says a lot.

Perhaps the most revealing shortcoming of popular holy books such as the Bible and the Koran is that they fail miserably at communicating a clear message to people, even to their respective followers. One Christian, for example, will read the Bible and immediately start giving time to help gay men with AIDS. Another Christian reads it and starts picketing the funerals of gay people and screaming, "God hates fags!" One Muslim reads the Koran and volunteers at a clinic to help sick people. Another Muslim reads it and joins al Qaeda to kill people. Why do some Jews reject evolution, based on their sacred writings, while other Jews embrace science, encouraged by their sacred writings? Why do some Mormons think their god wants men to have many wives while other Mormons think he forbids it? Forget squabbles between religions, just look *within* religions to see how ineffective these holy books are. Christianity has splintered into more than thirty thousand versions of itself primarily because Christians can't figure out exactly what it is their god wants of them based on the Bible. The reason for all this confusion is because these "inspired" books are not clear and often contradict themselves from page to page. Would real gods have done such a poor job of communicating vital information to believers?

CHAPTER 12 BIBLIOGRAPHY AND RECOMMENDED READING

Ehrman, Bart D. *Misquoting Jesus: The Story behind Who Changed the Bible and Why.* San Francisco: Harper, 2005.

Eliade, Mircea. *Essential Sacred Writings from Around the World.* San Francisco: Harper, 1967.

Green, Ruth Hurmence. *The Born Again Skeptic's Guide to the Bible.* Madison, WI: Freedom From Religion Foundation, 1999. If you don't have the stamina to read the Bible, then read this book to find out what sort of stuff is actually in it.

Helms, Randel McCraw. *Who Wrote the Gospels?* Altadena, CA: Millennium Press, 1997.

Thomas, David E. "Hidden Messages and 'The Bible Code.'" *Skeptical Inquirer* 21, no. 6 (November/December 1997). http://csicop.org/si/9711/bible-code.html.

Warraq, Ibn, ed., *What the Koran Really Says.* Amherst, NY: Prometheus Books, 2002.

Chapter 13

Divine justice proves my god is real.

I have always found that mercy bears richer fruits than strict justice.

—Abraham Lincoln

Many believers say they are grateful that their god watches over us and delivers justice to everyone sooner or later. Some believers say their god tracks every second of our lives taking note of everything we think, say, and do. As a result, we all prosper or struggle in this life according to a god's assessment of our behavior. Additionally we will all face some form of final judgment and be sent to a very good place or a very bad place forever. A world without all this divine oversight would be unbearably unfair, say believers.

The problem with these claims is that the world we see before us does not appear to be fair at all. What divine oversight? What justice? Good and innocent people suffer and die every minute of every day. Many people who have done horrible things live long lives in luxury and comfort and then die peacefully in their sleep. Ugandan Idi Amin was a terrible dictator, probably responsible for the deaths of more than three hundred thousand people. He had many thousands more people unjustly imprisoned and tortured. In an all too familiar story, however, Amin escaped justice and lived comfortably in Saudi Arabia with his four wives for the remainder of his life. He died of natural causes in 2003. His exact age at the time of his death is unknown but Amin was believed to have been about eighty years old. This is difficult to make sense of when you consider that many people with no blood on their hands suffer and die from diseases and natural disasters every year.

Cambodian leader Pol Pot enjoyed a much longer and far more comfortable life than the millions of babies in the developing world who die from dysentery each year. Pot's Khmer Rouge government was responsible for the deaths of an estimated two million people in the 1970s. Despite his crimes, he survived to the ripe old age of seventy-three.

Historians pin the deaths of more than a million people on Joseph Stalin, the brutal leader of the former Soviet Union. Some estimates are in the tens of millions. But Stalin's body count didn't get the attention of any gods and he made it all the way to the age of seventy-four. No lightning bolt ever cut down Chinese leader Mao Zedong either. His decisions were directly or indirectly responsible for the deaths of many millions of people but he lived to be eighty-four years old. Many believers are confident that their god deals out justice to the wicked, but where and when? According to many believers, Stalin and all other undeniably bad people get what's coming to them in the afterlife. Of course, we can't check on this and there is no evidence for it so we are left to just "believe it."

Those who say they could not live in a world without their god's perfect justice might consider the fact that they already are living in a world without perfect justice. If there is some kind of divine justice at work here on this planet, then it must be very different from the human concept of justice. Look around; life is not fair. What could be more obvious? Millions of malnourished and parasite-infested children in developing countries do not deserve their fate, at least not by any moral standards I understand, but they keep suffering and dying nonetheless. Wouldn't all these babies who die slow and painful deaths fare better if a god was watching over us? But more than nine million children under the age of five die of disease and hunger every year. And the suggestion that good times await these children in heaven after they die is not only impossible to prove, it's also heartless. Even if that extraordinary claim was true, these children still suffered tremendous pain and died far too soon while others—including murderous dictators—did not. If a god really is watching and judging us, then one can only conclude that the guiltiest people among us are little children in the developing world. After all, they are deprived of the most. They suffer the most. They die the youngest. One can only wonder what it is they are guilty of.

Another believers' explanation for such madness is that their god rewards and punishes here on earth in ways we may not detect. Perhaps the god torments the murderer, who only appears to have gotten away with it. Maybe he or she is haunted with painful guilt and terrible nightmares, for example. Maybe a god gives good people just a little more luck in life, spreading their reward over many years, making it less obvious but real nonetheless. To a nonbeliever, however, these explanations sound like desperate attempts to avoid facing reality in a world in which many bad people escape the consequences of their actions and many good people suffer and die for no reason.

The claim that everything gets sorted out after we die is very popular with believers. It can be expressed in different ways but the most common is the heaven and hell scenario. The good go up and the bad go down. Many versions of Christianity add a disturbing twist to this, claiming that a person can be truly terrible throughout their life but so long as they repent and "accept Jesus" in their last moment on earth, they will go to heaven. If true, it means Adolf Hitler, who was a devout Christian in childhood, might have jumped through the proper spiritual hoops a few minutes before he shot himself in that Berlin bunker. So Hitler could be in heaven right now while millions of people he sent to the gas chambers are not.

What kind of bizarre justice could place Hitler in heaven while someone like Anne Frank, as sweet and positive a child as has ever walked the earth, ends up in hell? Anne, a Jewish girl, wrote her famous diary while hiding in a house in Amsterdam during World War

II. Her words reveal a hope and optimism that reflects the best side of humankind. "I still believe, in spite of everything, that people are truly good at heart," she wrote. Eventually Anne was arrested and died in a camp at the age of fifteen. Sadly, she almost certainly is in hell right now according to a primary claim of the Christian religion. Anne was Jewish and therefore it is unlikely that she converted to Christianity before her death. Sadly for her, Christian dogma clearly states that Jesus is the "only way" to heaven.

A few years ago I interviewed Barbara Rodbell, a member of a Jewish underground resistance movement in Holland during World War II. She was also a friend of Anne's. Rodbell described Anne as a child who radiated goodness and hope. After all these years, there was still sadness in Rodbell's voice when she spoke about Anne. I challenge anyone who believes we all are beneficiaries of a god's justice to read *The Diary of Anne Frank* and then come up with a sensible explanation for why that girl should have died at the age of fifteen and currently be suffering in a Christian, Islamic, or any other hell.

A fair question that believers might ponder is why their gods kill so many people every year with natural disasters? For what reason do they shake the earth, stir the seas, and blow the winds with such violence? Why do they keep killing so many babies with viruses and bacteria? Wars and poverty can be blamed on us but we don't cause earthquakes and typhoons. We didn't invent the malaria virus or create dysentery. Where is the justice?

Believers have an answer for all this, of course. I've heard it many times but still find it shocking that sensible people think it makes sense. They attempt to explain the horror of children drowned by tsunamis or babies crushed by earthquakes as the result of "free will." Don't blame my god, they say, we corrupted the once-perfect world and now we get what we deserve. Okay, but how does free will excuse a god for killing babies who are not yet capable of making their own choices? If I could save all the children killed by natural disasters and disease each year, I would do it without hesitation. Wouldn't you? Why won't a god who is concerned with justice do the same? Some believers in the Jewish-Christian god say that when Adam blew it by biting the forbidden apple, we all would have to pay the price. The entire world and everyone in it "fell from grace," thanks to him. Think about that, long ago, long before you were even born, the actions of a prehistoric relative condemned you to a lifetime of being vulnerable to viruses, bacteria, predators, earthquakes, fires, floods, hurricanes, tornados, and tsunamis. Is this fair? Why would a god who is concerned with justice feel the need to punish people or allow them to suffer through inaction because of something their ancient ancestors did thousands of years ago? There is a good reason why court systems in developed societies do not punish innocent people for crimes their great-great grandparents may have committed. They don't do it because it would be unjust and barbaric. Shouldn't believers expect at least the same level of justice from their gods? However, rather than spend their time trying to think up reasons for why their god might need to kill babies with earthquakes, floods, hurricanes, tsunamis, and microbes I think believers would do better to simply consider another possibility. Can't all of this be explained more easily by the possibility that gods do not exist? Isn't it more likely that natural disasters kill thousands of people each year—regardless of their religion or behavior—because nature is an unintelligent and indifferent process?

Let's not forget women. They certainly must be included in any discussion about justice and the gods. Probably most of the belief systems that humankind has ever come up with have included outrageous injustice to women. Many religions have this injustice boldly written into their sacred texts for all to see. They don't just condone it, they demand it! Many people today continue to mistreat girls and women based on religious beliefs. Numerous belief systems still promote the idea that one-half of our species is the property of the other half. How can sensible believers who care about fairness and justice explain this? Those who say their belief in a god is confirmed by living in a world that benefits from divine justice must explain why women so often suffer in the name of gods.

Most people, upon reflection, probably will see that there is no warm and cozy blanket of justice covering our world. The next step would be to reject the claim that divine justice is a good reason to believe in a god. A protective god who guarantees justice for all is not readily apparent and never has been. It seems clear to me that the only justice we have is that which we make for ourselves.

Chapter 14

My god answers prayers.

Prayers and sacrifices are of no avail.

—Aristotle

If I thought there was any chance that it might work, I would pray that every member of al Qaeda reads this book, realizes that his religious beliefs might be in error, and vows never to kill in the name of a god ever again. I would also pray that those millionaire televangelists stop taking money from hard-working low-income people because a god "needs it." Unfortunately there is no convincing evidence that praying works, so I won't bother.

Requesting something by prayer is such a common practice that few believers ever stop to think about just how incredible a claim it is. People who say prayer works are claiming that we can ask a god for something—just about anything from good health to winning a war—and the god will consider our request and possibly grant our wish. Some even say the god is obligated to grant our wish, based on their interpretation of ancient writings. Despite the extraordinary nature of this claim, millions of people seem to go along with it without much thought. And, despite results that could more easily be explained as chance or as caused by the actions of people, they think it really works.

One would think that prayer could be analyzed or measured in a way that made it clear even to nonbelievers that it's a real phenomenon. Prayer is important to the big question of whether or not a god

107

or gods exist because many believers cite it as a primary reason for thinking that their god is real. It really could be the elusive proof for a god that atheists are always asking for. Imagine if the followers of one religion consistently had their prayers answered at a very high rate, high enough to discount chance, misinterpretation, or fraud. It would be powerful evidence that their god is real. But, of course, we do not see this. What we see are Hindus, Jews, Christians, Muslims, animists, and other believers praying to their respective gods in their specific ways and then claiming that their prayers work. The fact that followers of so many contradictory belief systems claim that their prayers achieve positive results is a bad sign for prayer proponents. For example, members of preindustrial tribes pray to a variety of gods for things like successful hunts and good weather all the time—and often they get what they asked for. But that's not proof that their gods are real. Nor is it proof that Yahweh, Jesus, Allah, or Vishnu are real when their respective believers get the results they prayed for.

Selective memory probably is the reason so many believers in many different religions think that their prayers work. For example, imagine a devout Christian who prays to Jesus for more money and then, after ten years of working hard and showing up at the office on time every day, she gets a raise. She might feel that this event in her life is confirmation that her god is real. After all, she prayed to Jesus for more money and she got more money. Case closed, at least in her mind. But would a typical Muslim accept this? Will he reject the Koran and begin believing that Jesus is a god based on this claim of a prayer answered by Jesus? It's doubtful, especially if the Muslim has experienced his own prayer successes that confirmed to him that Allah is the only true god. What about Jews who pray in their particular way to their god? They say their prayers get answered too. Millions of Hindus claim positive results from their prayers. Does it prove the existence of their gods? Mormon prayers get answered all the time, at least according to Mormons. Does that prove that Jesus was in North America like the Book of Mormon claims? If Tom Cruise prays for a box office hit next summer, and gets it, would that mean the claims of

Scientology are true? People in ancient Rome prayed and surely some of them believed that the gods answered their prayers on some occasions. If a Christian prayer can be called proof of Jesus, then a Roman prayer must be proof of Jupiter.

What is it that convinces believers that prayer works? If it did, if one really could get a god to grant wishes, wouldn't it be a lot more obvious that it worked and wouldn't we know which god was more likely to answer prayers by now? After several thousand years of praying, wouldn't trial and error have us all praying to the same god in the same way by now if there was something to this?

Isn't it possible that believing in prayer is a big mistake? Couldn't it be that believers simply are making the honest and common error of selective accounting when they review their personal prayer histories? Mistakes of this kind are easy to make and we all should be on guard against it. It seems to be human nature to focus on the few hits and forget all about the many misses when it comes to something we want to be true. Psychologists call it "confirmation bias" and psychics know all about it. When psychics claim to talk to dead people or predict a customer's future, they know that they only have to be right a few times because most people will forget the incorrect statements. Confirmation bias explains why many people believe in psychics even after they stumble through numerous incorrect statements. So when believers get excited about "answered" prayers it may have something to do with them forgetting all the prayers that resulted in nothing. People who do this are nothing more than the victims of a normal psychological phenomenon. Their only fault is thinking like a typical human. It has nothing to do with intelligence and it can happen to anyone.

Believers might also keep in mind that some "answered" prayers are not good evidence that a god is really at work for the simple fact that some requests are bound to turn out positively no matter what. For example, imagine if I was to list ten reasonable hopes for the coming year such as, "I hope I sell my car for a great price," and "I hope a hurricane doesn't rip off of the roof of my house." Then I record what happens over the next year. I am sure that some of my hopes would be fulfilled and some would not be fullfilled. Would the fact that some of my wishes came true mean that I have magical wishing powers? Of course not, this is just the way the real world functions. Some things work out like we hope they will and some things do not.

Comedian George Carlin has a lot say about religion, most of it too rude to include in a book that is meant to be respectful of believers. However, his commentary on prayer is not too harsh and it makes the point very well. Carlin says he gave up on praying to a god because the answer rate was unsatisfactory. So he started praying to Academy Award–winning actor Joe Pesci instead.

> So I've been praying to Joe for about a year now and I noticed something. I noticed that all the prayers I used to offer to God, and all the prayers I now offer to Joe Pesci, are being answered at about the same 50 percent rate. Half the time I get what I want, half the time I don't. Same as God, 50-50. Same as the four-leaf clover and the horseshoe, the wishing well and the rabbit's foot, same as the Mojo Man, same as the Voodoo Lady who tells you your fortune by squeezing the goat's testicles, it's all the same: 50-50. So just pick your superstition, sit back, make a wish, and enjoy yourself. (Carlin 1999)

Carlin is funny and right. Ask for a hundred things in the name of anything or anyone and you are bound to luck out on some of them. Praying to Joe Pesci, ridiculous as it is, is likely to generate a success rate that is similar to praying to Jupiter, Jok, Jesus, or any other god.

Health is a big concern for everyone sooner or later and prayer is often used by believers as a way of trying to fend off sickness and death. There may or may not be ways to conclusively test whether or not prayer works for this. Several studies in recent years have tried but none have shown that prayer works *and held up to scrutiny*. This alone indicates strong reason for doubt. Something that is supposedly so powerful should not be difficult to detect if it was really making an impact on human health.

Let's consider a special type of prayer for health, one that should have a very good chance of getting a god's attention. If any prayer works, one would think it would be a mother's prayer for the health of her baby. Few prayers are more sincere or more passionately delivered, especially if the baby is seriously ill. Unfortunately, these prayers do not seem to work well at all. This is obvious because there are many highly religious nations with horrible infant mortality rates. Meanwhile, highly secular nations with large percentages of atheists in their populations have very low infant mortality rates. How can this be? Why are the babies of so many atheist mothers faring better than the babies of so many Christian, Muslim, and Hindu mothers? Obviously the higher the percentage of believers in a society, the more praying is going on. How can prayer advocates explain why so many more babies die in very religious countries such as Nigeria, Yemen, and Niger than die in the much less godly countries of Sweden, Denmark, and England?

According to the UNICEF report, *State of the World's Children 2007*, the ten countries with the highest death rates for children under the age of five are: Sierra Leone, Angola, Afghanistan, Niger, Liberia, Somalia, Mali, Chad, Democratic Republic of the Congo, and Equatorial Guinea. These countries have populations that are virtually all Christian, Muslim, or followers of traditional African religions. None of them have a significant number of atheists in their population. No one can doubt that the mothers in these countries pray often and pray hard. But all this effort fails to save a shockingly high number of their babies.

To reinforce this point, *State of the World's Mothers 2006*, a report issued by Save the Children, ranked the best and worst countries for mothers based on available healthcare, education, and opportunity as well as risk for maternal and infant mortality. The list reveals the same pattern of countries with significantly high levels of atheism (less praying mothers) doing well and countries with high levels of belief (more praying mothers) doing poorly (Save the Children 2006):

Best Countries to Be a Mother	*Worst Countries to Be a Mother*
Sweden	Niger
Denmark	Burkina Faso
Finland	Chad
Austria	Guinea-Bissau
Norway	Sierra Leone
Australia	Ethiopia
Netherlands	Yemen
	Central African Republic
	Liberia
	Democratic Republic of the Congo

Even believers may wonder if prayers work for anything at all when they can't even save millions of innocent babies who are desperately prayed for by religious mothers. Who on earth is more deserving of a god's help than a baby? Some believers might argue that this disparity is about economics, failed governments, and healthcare deficiencies. I agree, but that's a godless explanation. Why should money matter to a god? Certainly believers think their god is capable of saving a baby, whether it is in a state-of-the-art European hospital or a dimly lit and underfunded African clinic. If prayer works, then it should be able to work anywhere regardless of the local economy.

The claim that prayer works may not go away any time soon no matter how many prayers fail. It may be easy to argue against it but disproving prayer is far more difficult, perhaps impossible. Although I welcome scientific prayer studies, it may be beyond science's ability to deliver a definitive answer. After all, how can researchers accurately record and measure prayer? Prayers can be nothing more than silent thoughts within the mind of a believer. They can be directed at people, even strangers, thousands of miles away. Believers can pray for people who are not even born yet. How can a researcher ever know which god the believer is really praying to, if they are sincere about it, or if they are really praying at all? How can a researcher determine who was prayed for and who was not? Some people pray for everybody on earth to be healthy, for example, while others might pray for the early death of all rival believers. How can researchers know if the subjects are praying or being prayed for in the "correct" way?

Former faith healer Hector Avalos, now a professor of religious studies at Iowa State University and executive director of the Committee for the Scientific Examination of Religion, is well aware of the difficulties:

> Even if someone prayed to the Christian god for healing and that person was healed, it would not prove that the healing was done by the Christian god. All religions claim to have answered prayers. For example, according to the Bhagavad-Gita, part of the sacred scriptures of Hinduism, the god Krishna claims that it does not matter which god human beings worship; it is Krishna who answers their prayer. Thus, it would not be scientifically possible to show that it is the Christian god who answered a prayer even if such a prayer was answered. (Avalos 1997)

Please forgive this wild thought, but could it be that most believers don't really believe in prayer? That's not as crazy an idea as it sounds. I know that many people make a lot of noise about how prayers can heal AIDS, change the course of hurricanes, and get a family member off the booze, but sometimes I wonder if they *really* believe in it. After all, it doesn't work most of the time. Privately at least, many believers must know that praying is no better than hoping. How can they not when sincere believers in every religion fail in relationships, lose jobs, suffer illnesses, die, and so forth every day despite desperate prayers? Believers likely have doubts about prayer, whether they talk openly about it or not. Dan Barker, the Christian preacher who became an atheist, certainly did:

> Looking back, I have to admit that my greatest doubt was the efficacy of prayer. Prayer simply does not work. Period. I know that I prayed thousands and thousands of prayers that were a waste of

time. That is, I know *now* that they were wasted. But since prayer is such a powerful doctrine of Christianity, I imagined that there was some meaning behind it all. . . . Some say prayer is an important exercise because, regardless of the outcome, it puts us in touch with God. But this contradicts the direct teachings of Jesus: "And all things, whatsoever ye shall ask in prayer, believing, ye shall receive" (Matthew 21:22), and "If two of you shall agree on earth as touching any thing that they shall ask, it shall be done for them of my Father which is in heaven" (Matthew 18:19). The writer of I John 5:14–15 said, "And this is the confidence that we have in him, that, if we ask any thing according to his will, he heareth us: And if we know that he hear us, whatsoever we ask, we know that we have the petitions that we desired of him."

Honest Christians know that these verses are false. It does no good to claim that many prayers are unanswered because they are not "according to his will." Even prayers that are clearly in line with the expressed "will of god" are rarely successful. Even if this reasoning were valid, it makes prayer useless as a means of changing nature. (Barker 1992, 108)

If prayer worked as well as many believers claim it does, it should not be so difficult to confirm even for those who are not predisposed to believe in it. The fact that it seems to work at about the same rate for all believers, regardless of which gods they pray to, suggests that this is probably about the human tendency to misinterpret chance and coincidence as something special. The Christians and Muslims, for example, who see their "answered" prayers as proof that their god is real must face the fact that hundreds of millions of other people say a different god answers their prayers. Of course, all gods cannot be real and all religions cannot be true. Therefore, it is more likely that so many "answered" prayers from so many sources shows that we have many problems but also an abundance of hope in our hearts. This is not necessarily a bad thing, but there is nothing about prayer at this time that provides a good reason to believe that gods are real.

CHAPTER 14 BIBLIOGRAPHY AND RECOMMENDED READING

Avalos, Hector. "Can Science Prove that Prayer Works?" *Free Inquiry* 17, no. 3 (Summer 1997). http://www.secularhumanism.org/library/fi/avalos _17_3.html.

Barker, Dan. *Losing Faith in Faith: From Preacher to Atheist*. Madison, WI: Freedom From Religion Foundation, 1992.

Carlin, George. "You Are All Diseased." HBO TV special, February 6, 1999.

State of the World's Mothers 2006. Save the Children, 2006. http://www .savethechildren.org/publications/mothers/2006/SOWM_2006_final.pdf.

Chapter 15

I would rather worship my god than the devil.

A religion can no more afford to degrade its devil than to degrade its god.

—Havelock Ellis

More than once I have encountered believers who were certain that all atheists are loyal followers of the devil or at least sympathetic to his mission. Simply because a person is unconvinced that Nanabozho, Hermod, or any other gods are real, some believers jump to the bizarre conclusion that he or she must be one of Satan's soldiers. This is related to the strange notion held by some believers that it is impossible to be a real nonbeliever. These people literally deny the existence of nonbelievers. To them, nonbelievers are nothing more than believers who switched sides and now serve Satan. Apparently they cannot imagine how anyone in their right mind cannot believe in at least one god. In an attempt to explain atheists these believers will insist that nonbelievers are enemies of god. They are not denying a god's existence. They know the god is real and they are fighting against him. All talk about nonbelief is a smokescreen meant to obscure their real agenda.

Yes, for those who doubt it, there really are people who hold this view. I have met several of them. And people wonder why so many atheists keep quiet about their lack of belief. It is, to say the least, awkward and uncomfortable to be thought of as a Satan worshipper. How does one even begin to respond to such an accusation? Such careless thinking can't be excused, of course, but I do understand how believers might not want to carpool or live next door to an atheist when they start out with this assumption. It's sad, however, to think that many believers would keep a fellow human at arm's length for this reason. It's a problem that is more common than most people may imagine. I encourage any nonbeliever who doubts this to go to Syria and strike up a few conversations at the souk about how wonderfully liberating atheism can be. Travel the "Bible belt" in America and see how warmly your atheism is received. Visit rural Tanzania and give a few public speeches on the merits of secularism. Good luck.

The worst thing about devil paranoia is that many believers are unwilling to consider that their god or gods might be imaginary because of it. They see the slightest movement away from belief in their god as a step toward Satan. Questioning religious claims is seen as being disloyal to their god and a dangerous flirtation with ultimate evil. The result is that many believers never analyze or challenge their beliefs. They may go through their entire life clinging to baseless beliefs because of this irrational fear.

Believers can relax, of course. Atheists are not Satan worshippers and they are not working to fulfill some evil supernatural agenda. Atheists do not believe in evil supernatural beings with pitchforks any more than they believe in good supernatural beings with halos. The devil is just another god to atheists. He can be dismissed as most likely fiction like all the others because there is not one speck of evidence or a single convincing argument that supports claims for his existence. Believers, please take note: one can be skeptical of gods—even disbelieve in them entirely—and still manage to elude the grasp of Beelzebub.

Anyone who really does worship Satan has far more in common with Christians, Muslims, Hindus, Jews, and other believers than they do with atheists. Satanists are believers, so anyone who is worried about rubbing elbows with a Satanist should check out their spiritual peers first. There is an odd exception to this, however. The late Anton LaVey, founder of the "Church of Satan," promoted a version of Satanism that did not claim Satan or any gods were real. Apparently, LaVey was an atheist who ran an organization dedicated to Satan, even though he didn't seem to think Satan existed. Whatever he was thinking, LaVey was not a typical atheist. Virtually every atheist in the world would consider praying to Satan as pointless as praying to any of the popular gods.

Even if Satan was real, Satanism seems like the wrong team to join if you think about it. If one were convinced that Satan existed, then he or she would probably have to agree that the Bible is accurate because that is the primary source for this character's existence. But, according to the Bible, Satan loses in the end. So why would anyone want to join up with him? Whether it is real or fantasy, Satanism makes no sense.

It is important to add that, despite the preoccupation with the devil that some believers have, there has never been any evidence of a large modern movement of devil worshippers. Stories of Satanists and their human sacrifices are great fodder for campfire stories and sensationalist news reports but the truth is that the devil has never won the hearts and minds of believers the way other gods have. He is little more than a plot ingredient for scary movies and a reliable scare tactic for religious leaders who want to keep the flock on their toes.

I once had a weird and frustrating encounter with a believer who suspected I was in league with the devil. She said that if I wasn't on her god's side then I had to be on the devil's side. According to her, I was a participant in some great spiritual war that was being waged even as we spoke. I politely explained that I was not now nor had I ever been a member of the devil's party. I assured her that I don't wear a pentagram pendant, don't own a ram's head mask, and never even once plunged a dagger into the belly of a sacrificial virgin to appease the Lord of the Underworld. But she shut me up fast when she suggested that I could be an "unwitting" agent of Satan. This was difficult to respond to. In fact, I couldn't. How do you reassure someone that you are not unconsciously serving Satan? If you were, you wouldn't know it. Of course you will deny it because the devil is controlling you without your knowledge. Sometimes you just can't win.

Undoubtedly some believers will see this book as a tool of the devil, filled with his lies to fool believers. But my goal is not to trick people into abandoning their gods with clever arguments. I only want to encourage readers to think for themselves and reconsider their justifications for believing in gods. I am only promoting a little bit of doubt, not declaring some definitive truth. People have to walk away from belief in gods on their own. I can't do it for them nor would I want to. If some believers want assurance that this book is not designed to turn people away from their god and into Satan's arms, then let me state clearly that I want people to think just as skeptically about Satan too.

Why do so many people believe in the devil anyway? I suppose with many religions it is a package deal and he comes with the god. The case for the devil's existence, however, is as weak as any god's. Many believers will disagree, of course. To them the devil is very real. They see evidence for him everywhere. It is astonishing how some believers see the devil's hand in just about everything bad. Drug addiction, murder, bank robberies, illness, and so forth are all the work of Satan, they say. I know that this seems to make perfect sense to believers who have heard it all their lives, but I encourage them to consider an alternative view. Bad things happen all the time and there is no evidence that any of it is linked to a supernatural being named Satan. Yes, humans misbehave. But there are explanations available for these events that are far more likely to be true. Drug addiction is a problem for many people because of the way the brain reacts to some chemical substances and creates a powerful craving for more. Some people commit violent acts because aggression is a standard feature of the human mind. People rob banks because that's where the money is. Don't these explanations for bad behavior seem more likely to be true than the claim that we are being manipulated and tempted by the magic spells of an invisible being who lives in a fiery dungeon somewhere?

Why do so many believers worry about this Satan character anyway? The whole story about him trying to take over the world seems highly unlikely. Why would he still be chasing that ambitious dream anyway? If Satan is a "fallen angel" and knew the god of the Bible up close and in person while he was in heaven, then wouldn't he know how this story turns out? Why in the world would he still be playing the game? According to the Bible, he loses in the end. Can't Satan read?

Believers can be assured that embracing skepticism and reason does not mean one is siding with the devil. Skepticism and reason not only tend to make gods go away. They chase away the devil, too.

Chapter 16

My god heals sick people.

The man in the white suit softly sings, "Hallelujah . . . Hallelujah . . . Hallelujah . . . Hallelujah." His song floats on the breeze of a cool Caribbean night. The mood is changing. After an hour of preaching, everyone knows that something very special is coming to Grand Cayman. Each word he sings seems to penetrate every believer. Most are standing now. They have come to this open-air sports stadium to see faith healer Benny Hinn call down miracles from heaven. And now he is about to deliver.

The small man with the big stage presence is now in full stride. He keeps singing that same word, "hallelujah," over and over. This repetition, combined with dramatic organ music, feels hypnotic. Perhaps it is. Hinn's eyes are closed now. One of his hands slowly extends toward the audience. Occasional shrieks rise and fall from the crowd. Some of the believers begin to twitch. Some cry. Many of them reach up with outstretched fingers. Trembling hands flail wildly. It's as if the believers are clawing at heaven, hoping to find a way in. Up on the stage, just twenty feet in front of me, Hinn continues singing that entrancing one-word song. My eyes dart about frantically trying to take in as much of the emotionally charged scene as I can. I'm adrift in a swirling sea of belief and the tide is rising. The emotional power of the moment is so intense that even I, a nonbeliever, feel slightly disoriented. The crying and the screams are louder now. A woman near me falls to her knees and begins convulsing. She looks as though she is reacting to severe electrical shocks.

Hinn sings on, "Hallelujah . . . Hallelujah . . . Hallelujah." Although I am skeptical of his ability to facilitate supernatural cures I can't deny the emotional power of this presentation. His voice, the music, and the crowd he commands all combine to create a potent psychological cocktail.

Suddenly, Hinn stops pacing and his illuminated figure freezes against the black sky behind him. He announces that the Holy Spirit is now with us. It's healing time. New waves of moans and mumbled prayers sweep across the audience. Many believers begin "speaking in tongues," that incomprehensible "language" that some believers claim their god enables them to speak. Hinn continues to work the moment like the master he is. His words are slow and gentle. He is like a kind father talking to his child. Hinn's smile glows. The stylish gray hair never once moves, even as the night winds blow across the stage.

"God heals today!" declares Hinn. "I don't know why they fall under the power. It just happens."

Hinn's eyes shut tight as he again extends his hand toward the mass of people before him. "Some will feel electricity, some will feel heat all over their body, some will feel vibrations."

"Take your healing now. Take your broken body, your broken life and fix it. Just look up and say, 'Fix it!'"

Contrary to what most people who have seen Hinn on television probably assume, this is when the "healings" occur at his services. Believers are not "healed" during Hinn's flamboyant touching action on stage. Those who appear with him on stage have already experienced their "miracles" while back in their seats. Apparently, that is the only reason they are allowed to go onstage in the first place. The people who end up making contact with Hinn are a very select group who claim to have already been healed by their god. On stage, Hinn merely applies a sort of final touch to complete their experience. And what a dramatic touch it is.

In assembly-line fashion, the flamboyant Hinn goes to work. Assistants feed him believers alternately from both sides of the stage. At times the pace seems frantic as if there is a time limit or some deadline to meet, but this only adds to the excitement. Hinn touches the face of a woman who says she had been addicted to drugs for many years. She trembles violently and then collapses into the arms of a man behind her. Now she is "free" of the addiction demon, declares Hinn. The crowd cheers wildly.

The rapid-fire touching continues. A young boy is "cured" of chronic eczema, says Hinn. Arthritis, diabetes, a heart condition, and many more ailments are "healed" by a god and certified or finalized by Hinn this night. I notice that when believers react strongly by shaking uncontrollably and falling down with above-average flair, Hinn usually instructs his assistants to pick them up so he can knock them down again. Believers in the audience explode with approving applause in response to these double and triple doses of the "Holy Spirit."

Hinn repeatedly credits his god for the "healings." This is an important detail. Hinn wields this incredible power on stage but then humbly denies having any power at all. I suspect that it makes him even more appealing to believers who might otherwise suspect that he is a little too godlike for their tastes. "I have nothing to do with this," Hinn says. "I am even more amazed than you are."

After a couple of hours of watching Benny Hinn in action up close, I was pretty sure that he was not a middleman or conduit for a god. I saw nothing to convince me of that. Everything I observed could be explained as nothing more than an audience that was predisposed to play along with a carefully choreographed performance. Remember, Hinn had more than two thousand years of tradition backing him up that night. It is not difficult to imagine how easy it can be for a revered holy man, of any religion, to whip up the emotions of a crowd made up almost entirely of true believers. They came with expectations and Hinn catered perfectly to those expectations.

Call it one man's charisma, gullibility run amok, or maybe the touch of a god. Whatever one concludes about an evening spent with Benny Hinn, his power to stir emotions cannot be denied. Hinn tours the planet "healing" believers and promoting Christianity. He is supported by millions of fans and his ministry's annual income reportedly exceeds one hundred million dollars. One cannot address popular faith healers without also addressing the issue of money because there always seems to be lots of money changing hands whenever they come to town. The night I saw him, Hinn became defensive when it was time to "pass the plate," or in this case, pass the very large and deep plastic buckets.

"When you give, it doesn't go to me," he declared. "All of it goes to the ministry. Not me, my wife, or my children ever touch one cent."

Hinn explained that the most important reason he asks people to give him money is so that God will "bless" them for it. "If you have problems, if you want to get out of debt, then give tonight. God said 'give and it shall be given unto you.' God cannot bless you until you put something in His hand."

Hinn then informed the audience that his ministry accepts donations by checks and credit cards. Scores of assistants fanned out into the crowd with big buckets. "Don't just give," he added, "Sow, so that you can reap a mighty harvest!" This is an interesting point Hinn makes at his services because it seems to eliminate any element of altruism from the donation. According to Hinn's claim, giving to his ministry is more like an investment than anything else. The promised payoff from a god seems to be the primary motivation to give, considering the emphasis Hinn places on it.

Hinn encourages believers, even those who are struggling financially, to "give to god." But how exactly does one "give to god"? Is giving to Hinn really the same as giving to a god? I humbly suggest that believers think long and hard before giving money to any person who is enjoying an extravagant and luxurious lifestyle that is far above their own. Clearly Benny Hinn is not sacrificing much, considering that he lives in a mansion, flies in a private jet, drives luxury automobiles, and wears shoes that probably cost more than my monthly mortgage payment.

Enough about money. Is a god really doing any healing at a Benny Hinn event or anywhere else? Do gods really heal us if we ask them to? Many believers have no doubt that their god can and does heal.

There must be millions of stories, sincerely believed, about prayers working to cure the sick. But, of course, no one talks much about all the prayers that failed.

If stories of faith healings prove that a particular god is real, then it means many other gods must be real too because numerous gods have been credited with miraculous healings since the beginnings of civilization. Anecdotes simply aren't good enough because every religion has them. Scientific studies might be able to answer the question. But there has never been a single credible scientific study that conclusively shows that faith healing or prayer works. Some studies have been hyped up in the news in recent years but upon further analysis all of them have been found to be unconvincing. In fairness, this is a very difficult thing to test. I'm not sure if it can ever be tested to everyone's satisfaction. Everybody is different and no disease or injury is exactly like any other. People may not be aware of it but most illnesses and injuries heal on their own and doctors aren't sure why. When Christians, Muslims, Hindus, Sikhs, Jews, and other believers recover from illnesses and injuries there is not necessarily a good reason to credit their gods, even if medical science can't explain it. Sometimes the human body just comes through on its own. There is still much to be learned about the immune system, for example. Therefore defaulting to the explanation that some unusual recovery must be the result of divine magic is premature.

One indication that faith healing is not a real phenomenon is that it just hasn't caught on despite centuries of hype spread across numerous religions all over the world. Yes, millions of people believe in it. Yes, some refuse medical treatment in order to gamble their life on prayers. But many more millions of believers are not convinced that it works and their actions show it. With the exception of people living in extreme poverty who have no choice, most believers in developed nations head straight to the emergency room when they cut their foot open on a piece of broken glass, for example. They are not content to pray for the skin to come back together infection-free. They find the nearest doctor as fast as they can. Why? If their god can cure AIDS and cancer, as many claim, then why not a simple laceration? Why aren't hospitals staffed with shamans and preachers rather than doctors and nurses? If faith healing really worked wouldn't we all be relying on it by now? After centuries of claims and stories of healed people, we would know for sure by now if the claim is valid. There would be no skeptics left. Furthermore, if one group of believers had a god that was real and consistently cured their diseases, then everyone would have noticed it and joined their belief system long ago.

Clever skeptics point out that the gods never seem to be able to heal amputees. Why is that? Surely some unfortunate guy who lost his leg in a car accident and some little girl who stepped on a landmine deserve divine healings at least as much as that drug addict whom Benny Hinn and his god supposedly cured. I can't speak for every nonbeliever, but I think that would do it for me. I would believe in a god who could regenerate flesh and bone right before my eyes. (Visit the "Why Won't God Heal Amputees?" Web site to read more about the gods' inability or unwillingness to heal people who are missing limbs.)

My skepticism about faith healing's ability to work as advertised does not mean I do not recognize the potential for it to offer some kind of meaningful boost to a patient's emotional state and maybe even aid healing in some cases. Yes, faith healing probably does help sometimes but not necessarily in the way believers think it does. It is not difficult to imagine faith healing "working" via the placebo effect. The placebo effect is a widely known phenomenon but still not fully understood. It occurs when a person seems to benefit from a medical treatment that is not really a medical treatment. Taking a sugar pill in place of real medication is the classic example. It seems that simply going through the motions of treatment, and believing that it is a valid treatment, helps some people heal from some illnesses sometimes. Something apparently happens between the mind and body that aids healing. This is the power of suggestion and it might explain some cases where people have claimed that faith healing helped them. But the placebo effect makes it difficult or impossible to know for sure if a god or the power of suggestion was responsible for any benefit. And we can never forget the possibility of a natural recovery that might have occurred with or without faith healing and the placebo effect. Finally, I have noticed in personal encounters that many believers will credit their god for improved health even though they were being treated by a doctor and taking medication at the same time they were praying for a cure.

I should add that I am well aware that faith healing, whether it works or not, can be comforting to someone who is hurt, frightened, or desperate. I know firsthand because I was once "healed" while lying on my back semiconscious in the middle of a street. I had been riding my bicycle when a careless driver pulled out in front of me. I was going too fast to steer around him so I hit hard and was launched like a space chimp. I'm fairly athletic, however, and reacted well, successfully pulling off a move so cool it would have impressed an Olympic gymnast. I managed to plant one hand on the car's hood as I sailed by. This helped to stabilize my flight and gave me a better chance of flipping my body far enough around to land on my feet on the other side of the car. Unfortunately, my moment of supreme athletic grace was followed by what may be the dorkiest belly flop in human history. My feet rotated too far under me and I crash-landed hard in the street. I was out for a minute or so but when the fog began to lift I discovered that my wild ride was not quite over.

On my back and looking up at the night sky, I saw that I was surrounded by several very large Jamaican women wearing shiny dresses and fancy church hats. Apparently they had just finished a worship service at a nearby church and were eager to practice what they had just heard preached. Circling above me like angels, or maybe zeppelins, they shouted: "Lord, heal dis boy!" "Come Jesus and help 'im, now!" said another. "In Jesus's name we pray!"

I was dizzy, hurting, but also quite flattered. "How sweet," I thought to myself. "They don't even know me and yet they care enough to try and heal me right out here in the middle of the road." I was touched. Despite the pain, I felt good.

Believe it or not, those ladies helped me feel better, a lot better. In no time I was back on my feet, bruised and scraped, but okay. To this day, I am grateful to those kind church ladies for their concern. I am sure I would have been down and out much longer without their efforts. But does this mean that a god magically cleared my head and soothed my wounds? No, more likely I benefited from the psychological boost of feeling loved. I was also under a bit of pressure to please the ladies and bystanders by showing them that I was going to be okay. They prayed so hard for me, I didn't want to let them down. I was highly motivated to get up and smile so I did.

It's likely that something similar to this goes on many times at faith healing events. The sick people know how the script is supposed to go and nobody wants to be the jerk that a god doesn't like enough to heal. So, chances are, many people are going to say they feel better no matter what.

The bottom line on faith healing is that, although it could be a real phenomenon, no one has ever been able to show that it is. If the scientific method can show that penicillin works, for example, shouldn't it have shown by now that faith healing works for millions of people all around the world? But it hasn't. Given the huge payoff if faith healing actually did cure people, it is very likely that we would have recognized it by now and fully incorporated it into modern healthcare accordingly. There would be no resistance if it worked. The fact that faith healing is still on the fringes and often used only as a last resort by virtually all believers who can afford the services of medical science indicates that it almost certainly does not work as advertised. Therefore, at this time, faith healing cannot be considered a good reason to believe in a god.

CHAPTER 16 BIBLIOGRAPHY AND RECOMMENDED READING

Randi, James. *The Faith Healers*. Amherst, NY: Prometheus Books, 1989.
"Why Won't God Heal Amputees?" WWGHA Web site, 2006. http://www .whydoesgodhateamputees.com/god5.htm.

Chapter 17

Anything is better than being an atheist.

The fool says in his heart, "There is no God." They are corrupt, they do abominable deeds, there is none that does good.

—Psalms 14:1

I don't know that atheists should be considered as citizens, nor should they be considered patriots.
—President George H. W. Bush

One of the reasons people say they hold tight to their belief in a god or gods is that they think atheism is a fate to be avoided at all costs. Many believers won't even consider the possibility that their god does not exist because an atheist, in their view, is not much better than a serial killer or child molester.

It should be no surprise that many people think this way considering how nonbelief is so often mocked, discouraged, and forbidden by religious leaders as well as within holy books. Some belief systems declare that atheism is an offense worthy of execution. It sounds like somebody is a little insecure about their beliefs.

Why are believers so uptight about atheism? These feelings run so deep and so strong that many people trust nonbelievers less than people who believe in rival gods. This is odd to say the least. Why, for example, do so many Christians feel more comfortable with Muslims than atheists, given the bloody history and current tensions between those two belief systems? Why do many Muslims feel more at ease around a Hindu than an atheist? Why is belief in any gods preferable to belief in no gods? Perhaps this is because it is seen as being better to at least play the game even if it is for a different team. Atheists, however, refuse to play ball at all and therefore may be a little disorienting to believers. My suspicion is that believers tend to feel this way because the mere existence of an atheist casts doubt on their assumptions that signs of a god are all around us and that belief is somehow necessary to live a normal life.

The popular notion among believers that nonbelievers are bad people by definition is so out of line with the facts that it is comical. I try to be understanding about it even though it is terribly insulting. I have been in churches and heard Christian preachers talk about their god being the only possible source of morality and how turning your back on this god leads to crime, drug addiction, wife-beating, gambling, pornography, jaywalking, and so forth. Not believing in a god can even lead to genocide and world wars, according to many believers. They love to cite examples of evil atheists in an attempt to prove that nonbelief really does make moral behavior impossible.

Adolf Hitler is almost always the first name believers drop to demonstrate the inevitable horrors of atheism. We will see later in this chapter why Hitler is the wrong choice for atheism's poster boy. But first it is important to understand that linking atheism to despicable people does not prove anything. The fact that some bad people in the past didn't believe in gods does not prove that gods exist any more than history's many religious tyrants and pious mass murders prove that gods don't exist. Furthermore, believers should not try to play the guilt-by-association game because they will lose every time. Over the last few thousand years religion has directly motivated far more hatred and violence than atheism. Remember, atheism is the absence of belief, nothing more. Many have killed for gods throughout history but few have killed for nothing. Believers often cite the twentieth century's "godless communism" and the horrific death tolls of atheists

Stalin, Mao Zedung, and Pol Pot as a strike against nonbelief, but the fact is those dictators were primarily motivated by power and politics, not an agenda of critical thinking and skepticism. They didn't have millions of people killed in order to make the world safe for free thinkers. They killed to gain and maintain social, economic, military, and political power. By stressing Stalin's atheism, believers seem to suggest that he would have been a much nicer fellow if only he had believed in a god. My hunch is that this former church choir boy and seminary student might have been even worse if he believed a god was on his side while he ruled the Soviet Union. Religious belief could have provided Stalin with even more motivation to murder just as easily as it might have cooled him down. Given its record, religion certainly cannot be counted on to always bring out the best in people.

Since Adolf Hitler lives on as the most notorious atheist in the minds of so many believers today, it is important to point out that he was not an atheist. Yes, Hitler was a believer—at least he was according to his own written and spoken words. Hitler was raised a Christian and was active in his local church as a boy. As an adult he quoted the Bible and drew upon religion for inspiration. Consider these lines from his book *Mein Kampf*: "Hence today I believe that I am acting in accordance with the will of the Almighty Creator: by defending myself against the Jew, I am fighting for the work of the Lord" (Hitler 1999, 65). And, "For God's will gave men their form, their essence and their abilities. Anyone who destroys His work is declaring war on the Lord's creation, the divine will" (Hitler 1999, 562).

Even more significant, virtually every one of Hitler's enthusiastic supporters were believers too, from most of his generals right down to the Third Reich's street sweepers. Millions of German troops marched off to battle in World War II wearing belt buckles with "Gott Mit Uns" ("God is with us") engraved on them. Christian crosses were prominent features at many Nazi rallies. There are many photos of Hitler praying and attending ceremonial events with Christian leaders. Atheists were not the ones forcing Jews to board trains bound for death camps. Believers did that. Anyone who knows anything about Germany under

Hitler would never call it an atheistic society. Of course it is possible that Hitler, an astute politician, simply pretended to be a believer when it suited his purposes. Maybe he secretly was an atheist, but that is impossible to know. Anyone who claims that would have to also agree that Stalin could have been a devout Christian secretly and only pretended to be an atheist to serve his political purposes. We can never know for sure what anyone really believes because belief happens in the privacy of the mind. Words and actions are all we can go by and Hitler's words and actions indicate that he was a believer in a god.

It is reasonable to assume that most believers, like most atheists, just want to be good people and live a good life. The thought of taking on the atheist label is scary for many believers because it carries with it suggestions of immorality, general creepiness, and perhaps even the sinister hand of Satan at work. But it doesn't take too much effort to think through the false idea that atheists are bad people. For example, if nonbelief leads to a less moral life than belief, then wouldn't atheists be convicted of crimes at a disproportionately higher rate than believers? But this is not how it plays out in the real world. Jails and prisons are filled with many believers and very few atheists. And what about the many obviously immoral wars fought exclusively between believers? For example, there are very few atheists in sub-Saharan Africa yet that region is plagued with numerous wars decade after decade. Who can be blamed but believers? Anyone who reviews history and surveys the world today cannot honestly claim that atheists deserve to be thought of as untrustworthy or dangerous people.

Regardless of the facts, sadly, someone who lives their life without believing in a god is still too suspicious for many believers to embrace as a friend and equal. As a result, atheists face significant prejudice, even in modern times and even in some developed and democratic countries that should know better. In the United States, for example, despite all the talk about tolerance, diversity, and freedom, there is a shockingly high level of prejudice against atheists. A 2006 University of Minnesota study asked people to identify the group that "does not at all agree with my vision of American society." Atheists topped the list with 39.6 percent. Muslims were second at 26.3 percent and homosexuals third with 22.6 percent.

The study also revealed that American parents are more likely to disapprove of their children marrying atheists than any other minority group. It wasn't even close, as 47.6 percent said an atheist is the last person on earth they want to see their child with. Second was Muslims (33.5 percent), followed by African Americans (27.2 percent). It must really be tough for gay African American atheists these days.

The study's authors, Penny Edgell, Joseph Gerteis, and Douglas Hartmann, were surprised to find such strong prejudice directed against atheists.

> Atheists are at the top of the list of groups that Americans find problematic in both public and private life, and the gap between acceptance of atheists and acceptance of other racial and religious minorities is large and persistent. It is striking that the rejection of atheists is so much more common than rejection of other stigmatized groups. For example, while rejection of Muslims may have spiked in post-9/11 America, rejection of atheists was higher.
>
> The possibility of same-sex marriage has widely been seen as a threat to a biblical definition of marriage, as Massachusetts, Hawaii, and California have tested the idea, and the debate over the ordination of openly gay clergy has become a central point of controversy within many churches. In our survey, however, concerns about atheists were stronger than concerns about homosexuals. (Edgell 2006, 230)

Most atheists are well aware of this prejudice. They often keep their nonbelief a secret, sometimes even to family members and close friends, because they don't want to upset or disappoint people they care about. They don't want to have to endure ridicule or rejection. Nonbelievers even may fear becoming victims of violence or workplace discrimination. Who can blame them? When believers tie atheism to Hitler, Stalin, and Satan, it can be a risky topic to bring up at the family dinner table or around the water cooler at work.

Apart from the morality issue, there is another reason why many believers are more uneasy about nonbelievers than they are about people who follow rival belief systems. Remember the classic fairy tale, "The Emperor's New Clothes"? People can debate the king's magical clothes and disagree over details about the workmanship, so long as they all "see" some clothes. But if someone points out that the clothes are not even there, the parade is in trouble. It is more comfortable, apparently, to bicker over what the gods are named, how they want to be worshipped, who speaks for them on earth, and what their clothes look like than it is to hear that gods might not exist at all.

Believers who dislike, mistrust, and discriminate against atheists base their decision to think and behave this way on nothing but plain, old, shallow-minded prejudice. This is precisely the kind of blind ignorance that is stupid, immoral, and usually harmful to everyone in the end. Atheism is not a club and atheists are not necessarily united by anything other than their lack of belief in a god. Atheism simply means no belief and that nets a diverse group of people. Just as it is with believers, there are good and bad atheists. Just as it is with religious people, there are kind atheists and there are atheists who are jerks. Deciding to dislike all nonbelievers rather than judge them as individuals is indefensible.

By the way, not that name dropping proves anything, but this "immoral" atheism crowd that many believers love to hate includes many notable figures who seem like fairly respectable people. Here are just a few: Thomas Edison, Ernest Hemingway, Isaac Asimov, Noam Chomsky, Mark Twain, James D. Watson, Bill Gates, Warren Buffet, Steven Hawking, and Carl Sagan. Are these evil people? Are these people you wouldn't want to hire or have as neighbors? Are they fools who have never done good, as the Bible claims about all nonbelievers?

No matter how illogical and unfair it may be, atheists do not find easy or broad acceptance in strongly religious countries such as the United States, Saudi Arabia, and Afghanistan. But it is important to keep in mind that this has nothing to do with whether or not gods exist. Some believers make the mistake of assessing truth by measuring popularity. Yes, atheism is not fashionable and atheists sometimes have to watch their back. But this is about who is prejudiced, not who is on the right side of reality. This is about being different. This is like the high school in-crowd determining who is cool and who is not. It's the majority looking down their collective noses at yet another minority. Without a doubt, future generations will shake their heads and wonder how such an attitude could ever have existed.

Perhaps some of the prejudice can be explained by believers misreading how atheists view their gods. Contrary to what many believers think, atheists do not insult or fight against anyone's god. They don't reject anyone's god. Atheists can't do any of this because for them gods do not exist. Atheists are not believers who choose not to worship a god. They are not people who have decided to hate a god. Atheists are people who do not believe any gods exist. How can one insult something that does not exist? How can atheists fight against something they do not think is there? Yes, some atheists might insult believers or strongly oppose a religion, but these are significantly different things from directing rage or rudeness toward a real god. Atheists, by definition, can only take issue with the belief people have in gods. Nonbelievers do not see themselves as the enemies of gods. They can't be because atheists are waiting to be convinced that the gods are even there.

A humorous side of prejudice against atheists is that believers are atheists too! Yes, every person on earth—including every believer—is a nonbeliever to a degree. For example, the Christian is a nonbeliever, just like all those atheists they don't trust, when it comes to the Hindu gods. Christians are skeptical of the claims of Hinduism and conclude that all those gods were simply made up by people long ago. Christians are hardcore atheists on this matter, despite the fact that Hinduism is much older than Christianity, has a billion confident believers, can cite ancient writings in support of its claims, and has countless stories of miracles and life-changing events that Hindus credit their gods for.

Muslims are staunch nonbelievers when it comes to Jesus being a god. Muslims declare loud and clear that their god never had a son. They take note of the absence of evidence and conclude that the resurrection story is fiction. More than a billion Muslims are atheistic toward Jesus, despite the claims of miracles, ancient writings in support, and all the miracles and life-changing experiences that Christians credit Jesus for.

Believers might benefit from asking themselves why it is they do not accept the claims of other religions. Why are they so much more skeptical of beliefs other than their own? If they apply their critical thinking and skepticism equally, believers may discover an entirely new perspective on their religion. Remember, both the believer and the atheist are doubters. They reject many gods alike. The only difference is that the atheist went all the way and left no god unchallenged.

CHAPTER 17 BIBLIOGRAPHY AND RECOMMENDED READING

Edgell, Penny, Joseph Gerteis, and Douglas Hartmann. "Atheists as 'Other': Moral Boundaries and Cultural Membership in American Society." *American Sociological Review* 71, no. 2 (2006): 211–34.

Head, Tom, ed. *Conversations with Carl Sagan.* University of Mississippi, 2006. Great selection of interviews and speeches by Carl Sagan.

Hitler, Adolf. *Mein Kampf.* Boston/New York: Houghton Mifflin, 1999.

Martin, Michael, ed. *The Cambridge Companion To Atheism.* Cambridge: Cambridge University Press, 2007. An excellent collection of articles and essays on nonbelief.

Chapter 18

My god made the human body.

If this is the best God can do, I'm not impressed.
　　　　　　　　　　　　　　　　　—George Carlin

Nothing provokes deep thoughts on life and death like an exhibition of skinless corpses in creative poses. I caught up with the touring Body Worlds exhibit at the Chicago's Museum of Science and Industry. As I expected, it was both fascinating and educational. But I was surprised that it ignited a philosophical flashfire within my mind.

I had never seen the human body presented like this before and it took me for a wild ride. Thanks to Gunther von Hagens's patented plastination process, lifelike dead people stood within arm's reach, no display-case glass between us, no clothes, and no more guessing about what a human liver really looks like. These were not textbook-style, unnatural anatomy displays. These exhibits weren't designed to collect dust and put pre-med students to sleep. I was wandering among the most creative collection of corpses ever assembled. These were interesting people who just happened to be dead and missing their skin. Their poses seemed anything but posed. They ran, played chess, rode horses, kicked soccer balls. Some were split apart to allow for easy viewing of internal organs. Who knew dead people could be so lively? (Note: Body Worlds' creator, Gunther von Hagens, denies ever knowingly using the bodies of executed Chinese prisoners for his shows, something a rival company reportedly has done. Von Hagens's Web site claims there is a donor roster of 8,688 individuals hoping to have their bodies plastinated and displayed in a Body Worlds show after their death.)

I suspect that many believers who visit a Body Worlds exhibit see it as a confirmation of their claim that the human body is the magical creation of an artistic god. I can understand their feelings; I was close to being seduced by the body's "divine design" too. So many organs doing so many jobs. Bones and muscles work in harmony to stand, walk, run, and jump. The vast and complex network of blood vessels. The heart that never sleeps. The brain's ability to store data and its infinite power of imagination. How can all of this have "just happened" naturally with no help from a god? It's a fair question and no believer should ever be faulted for asking it. Looking at the bodies of Body Worlds helped to open my eyes to the view many believers hold about the connection between the human body and their gods. Without a basic understanding of evolution, something most people don't have, nothing but a god can explain these magnificent machines. Any scientist or science literate person who turns snobbish and dismissive of those who see a god's work in the human body might consider that they probably would hold the same view if they had not been fortunate enough to learn about evolution. Yes, the human body can be easily recognized as the product of millions of years of evolution—but only if one has a basic biology education first. Short of that, a god seems like the only sensible answer.

The controversy over teaching evolution in the United States, and the popularity of creationism in that nation, has been well reported in the media; but what about the entire continent of Africa? What percentage of children there get a competent education about the biological history of life on earth? What about the Middle East? South America? The Caribbean? Probably the overwhelming majority of children on earth in any given year never hear a single word about human evolution. No wonder millions of people can't imagine how nature could be responsible for the complexity of the human body. They have no idea of the age of the earth and its life. They know nothing of genetic mutations and natural selection. I certainly never heard anything about evolution throughout my education in American public schools during the 1970s. Never once was human evolution mentioned, much less taught, in my classes. Through twelve years of elementary, middle, and high school, not one teacher ever told me about the *Australopithecus*, *Homo erectus*, or *Neanderthal*. Nobody bothered to mention how my ancestors shaped stones into tools and tamed fire. No one ever told me the story of humankind's great walk out of Africa to populate the globe. Today, I look back and feel cheated. I should have been taught what science has learned about who I am and where I came from. Fortunately, I made up for lost time and learned about human evolution on my own and in university anthropology classes. But what about all my friends and classmates from elementary school through high school who never did learn what human evolution is all about? They probably still have never heard about Olduvia Gorge, the Leakey family, or Charles Darwin's voyage aboard the HMS *Beagle*. Most Americans today wouldn't know a *Homo ergaster* cranium from their own. So when they hear about their ancestors and the evolutionary trail that led to them, they reject it as absurd. It's preposterous because they don't understand it. And in most cases the reason they don't know anything about evolution is because no one ever bothered to teach it to them. It's not entirely their fault. Their teachers, schools, school boards, and government failed them. No one should be surprised that half of the American population rejects evolution because it is easy to dismiss something you don't know anything about.

Around the age of ten, I stumbled across a book called *Early Man* (Howell 1965). It was loaded with great photos and artwork. I was fascinated by this story of human origins. I was amazed to learn that my ancestors lived in Africa, that they made stone chopping tools more than a million years ago, and competed against other hominid species who lived alongside them. What made it even more exciting was that

142   50 Reasons People Give for Believing in a God

this story had actual evidence; fossils you could see for yourself. And the scientists even admitted that they didn't know all the answers. They were still learning the story. It all seemed so sensible and respectable. It was believable.

Inspired by that book, I made my own stone tools in the backyard. I studied photographs of chopper tools and tried to reproduce them perfectly. I remember feeling uncomfortably inferior to my *Homo erectus* forebears because my tools never turned out quite as impressively as theirs. I even conducted my own digs. I remember once excavating a bone from the woods near my home and comparing it to a photograph of *Australopithecus* fossils in the *Early Man* book. They matched up pretty well and I was convinced that I had made a major discovery. Australopithecenes in Florida! I was going to shake up the paleoanthropological world. I was going to be famous! For some reason, however, my mother was not convinced and refused to alert the media. She may not have known much about human evolution, but she did know a chicken bone when she saw one.

My own experience with evolution prevents me from being too aggressive or judgmental toward believers who say evolution is nonsense and that creationism/intelligent design is valid science. Their schools probably failed them just like all of mine did. For this reason, I have never been inclined to argue with creationists. They don't need debates; they need information. They don't need to be beat up with superior arguments; they need books. I always prefer to simply share some basic information about evolution and leave it at that. For example, if someone came to me and declared that the earth is flat, I don't think it would make much sense to get all huffy and worked up over it. I know that the earth is spherical. People who think the earth is flat do not need to be argued into submission. They just need to be handed a few photos of the earth from space so they can go home and look them over in private. Most people who think evolution is a lie just need to be shown a *Homo erectus* skull. For example, I have museum-quality full-sized replicas of *Australopithecus*, *Homo erectus*, and *Neanderthal* skulls at home on a bookshelf. If a guest ever tells me that human evolution is a big, fat lie, I'm ready. I don't need to argue. I'll just point to those skulls and ask "Then I wonder who those guys were?" Evolution versus creationism is not smart people versus stupid people. It's not even believers versus nonbelievers, though many describe it that way. This is almost entirely a clash between people who have been exposed to the theory of evolution versus those who have not. I can never pretend to feel that I am necessarily smarter than a creationist who says biologically modern humans were created ten thousand years ago, or an intelligent design believer who says unanswered questions about the human body prove that a god designed it. I can't because I know that I easily could have ended up in their shoes. I suspect that if I had not come across that one book on human evolution many years ago in childhood, I might believe things like that too. There but for the grace of a good science book go I.

Progressing through the Body Worlds exhibit, I begin to pay more attention to the people around me as they react to the displays. Some of them never seem to get over their initial shock and horror. Others are obviously thrilled by it all. And there are some who shake their heads, as if in awe of the magnificent organic machine before them. Awe, of course, often leads people to gods. As I stood in front of one of the bodies I was okay with the fact that there are many things I do not understand about the human body and life itself. We are still a mystery in so many ways. One could graduate from medical school, work a long career in medical science, and still have more questions than answers. But is this reason enough to give up and declare that a god must have placed the lungs above the stomach and hair atop the head? I don't think so.

The human body is not quite as impressive as some of us assume, anyway. It is certainly not a perfect creation. Anthropologist Scott Atran makes that case in his essay "Unintelligent Design":

> Creationists and proponents of ID often point to the human body as evidence of God's plan—of his intelligent design and benevolence toward his creatures. A closer look at our parts reveals that the Deity

may never have been wholly pleased with his preferred creations. Why did he invert the retina and give humans (but not the octopus) a blind spot? Why, in making us upright, did he render us so liable to back problems? Why did he give us just one head, heart, and liver, instead of two, like the lungs and kidneys? After all, having two lungs and kidneys is surely better than having one of each: If you have one and it fails, you die; if you have two and one fails, you live. (Atran 2006, 131)

Atran picks the anatomy involved in childbirth as the most imperfect design of all. He writes that it results from "evolution's having jammed the outlets of three major expulsive functions into a narrow basin [pelvis]: the expulsion of the large-headed human fetus though a narrow region at childbirth occurs at considerable cost. The 'design flaw' of human childbirth has had cascading effects: Human offspring profit from having big brains, but only at substantial cost-to-fitness of relatively high fatality rates for child and mother, long periods of postnatal care, reduction in fertility rates, decrease in resource procurement, and so forth." No sensible god ever would have designed it this way, Atran concludes.

I remember my first reaction upon entering the Body Worlds exhibit was to cringe a bit, as one naturally does in a room full of corpses. But the desire to learn pushed aside that reflex. I began working hard to see every detail and absorb as much of the experience as I could. Lungs, brains, livers, muscles, bones, teeth, blood vessels, hearts—it was all fascinating. How impressive, I thought. So many parts work so well together, allowing us to do so many things. This human machine of ours has climbed Mount Everest, swum the English Channel, walked on the moon, invented calculus, and run one hundred meters in less than 9.8 seconds. It really is wonderful. But during my over-the-top adulation of human flesh and bone I suddenly remembered that my "glorious" human body is no more special than that of a dog or a rat. We're all just mammals. Size and proportion varies and we have a much more complex brain, of course, but overall we are far more alike than different. My initial excitement over Body Worlds is fading and I notice a shift in my thinking. These bodies all around me are not perfect. They were not magical creations. They were not miracles. They were convenient arrangements of atoms, shaped by evolution and made beautiful only by the whims of personal taste. These bodies represent the current version of fortunate meat whose ancestors managed to survive a gauntlet of natural selection spanning a few billion years or more. All bodies, not just the dead ones on display, are evidence of human evolution. We all walk around every day with the evidence of evolution. We are the proof. We have been designed by nature over millions of years. Our many imperfections reveal the absence of intelligence in the process. Our more impressive features, the brain in particular, reveal the blind but immensely creative potential of evolution. This explanation for who we are and where we come from may lack the satisfying simplicity and glory of a typical god story but at least it is an explanation that is supported by the reality of what we see when we look in the mirror.

I walked away from the Body Worlds exhibit convinced that the human body is no more special than any other warm-blooded, furry Earth creature. This vehicle we ride around in is more like plumbing and Tinker Toys than magic from the sky. But there is one exception. Our brains truly are something special. We sing songs, write books, and dream of things that can never be. We also use these brains to seek answers. I see no justification to ever slow or shut down this wonderful organ. All believers who claim that the "miraculous" human body is evidence of magic might consider calling on that "miraculous" brain of theirs to learn more and think more before giving all credit to the gods.

CHAPTER 18 BIBLIOGRAPHY AND RECOMMENDED READING

Atran, Scott. "Unintelligent Design." In *Intelligent Thought*, edited by John Brockman, 126–41. New York: Vintage Books, 2006.

"Gunther von Hagen's Body Worlds: The Original Exposition of Real Human Bodies." Institute for Plastination, 2007. http://www.bodyworlds.com.

Howell, F. Clark. *Early Man*. Life Nature Library, New York: Time Life Books, 1965.

Johanson, Donald, and Blake Edgar. *From Lucy to Language*. New York: Simon & Schuster, 1996. This large-format book presents brilliant color photographs of many important hominid fossils.

Tattersall, Ian. *The Human Odyssey: Four Million Years of Human Evolution*. New York: Prentice Hall, 1993.

Chapter 19

My god sacrificed his only son for me.

One of the most popular stories of all time is the one about a god who sent his only child on a mission to save the world, but in doing so allowed him to be killed so that all the people of the earth might know peace and salvation. After his brutal death, the son magically rose up to heaven where he lives with his father today. We may all go to heaven and be with him after we die, but only if we believe in him and repent our sins. This, of course, is the core belief of Christianity. It must be very a good story because Christianity is currently the planet's most popular religion with more than two billion followers. Although that leaves some four billion people who don't believe the story, it's still the most numerically successful religion of all time. As such, I thought it deserved comment, even though this justification for belief is specific to just one religion.

The story of Jesus is appealing to many people who see it as the ultimate example of love, sacrifice, and God's overwhelming goodness. Many believers have told me how it touches them and how inspired they are by it. It is especially powerful when you consider a typical father's love for his child. God must really love me, some Christians say, if he would let his only son suffer and die for me. If one thinks a little bit deeper about this story, however, some problems emerge.

First, what is the great sacrifice that God made? Was it really a sacrifice in the way a human father giving up his son would be? I have a young son and I cannot imagine the pain I would feel if, for some extraordinary reason, I had to let him suffer and die. I think it would be more than I could bear. But God did not lose his son; at least not in the way I or any other human would lose a son. God made no sacrifice. God lost nothing.

The Christian doctrine known as the Holy Trinity claims that God exists in three forms: the Father (the God of Abraham), the Son (Jesus), and the Holy Spirit (or Holy Ghost). Despite the fact that many Christians speak and worship as if these three are separate gods, Christianity considers itself a monotheistic religion, meaning it has just one god. So if one accepts the Holy Trinity doctrine, then one has to admit that God (the father) did not really sacrifice his son (Jesus). If anything, he was sacrificing himself or part of himself—but not really. Even if it somehow were a distinct and separate son that died, it wouldn't make sense as a great sacrifice because God the Father knows the future. How, then, can it be claimed that he "gave up his only son for us" when he knew that Jesus would rise from the dead and join him in heaven soon after? What is the sacrifice?

I love my son as much or more than any father ever has. There is nothing superhuman or supernatural about me, but I believe I would do precisely what many believers say God the Father did two thousand years ago. I would agree to sacrifice my son if I was confronted with the bizarre proposition of allowing him to die in order to save billions of humans now and for generations to come from eternal torment in hell. Like God, I would know that my son would be fine and back with me a few days later anyway. I would be saving him from hell as well. So the correct decision is obvious. I would be highly upset about having to put him through the suffering part of it but I would have to agree to the deal. Looking at the big picture—billions of people saved, including my son, and I get him back healthy and happy—would make it a no-brainer. And I certainly would not feel that I deserved heroic or godlike status for making the decision.

Many Christians emphasize the suffering endured by Jesus prior to his death. According to the story, Jesus was tortured by Roman guards and then nailed to a cross. That's a bad day by any measure. The pain and terror he felt would have been unimaginable. No one who saw Mel Gibson's blood-spattered, bone-crunching film, *Passion of the Christ*, will ever take crucifixion lightly. The courageous suffering of Jesus adds a great deal to the story's power and appeal. He could have opted out, say believers. He could have been selfish, forgotten all about saving souls, and avoided the crucifixion, but he didn't. He took the pain for us, believers claim. However, it is fair to point out that many other people have suffered horrible deaths as bad or even worse than what Jesus is supposed to have endured. And their suffering did not even save billions of people across future generations to come.

More than one hundred firefighters die on the job during a typical year in the United States, according to the US Fire Administration. They die trying to save the lives and property of strangers. Usually firefighters are not responding to massive disasters such as the World Trade Center attacks or dramatic chemical plant explosions. More often they are rushing into small, smoke-filled homes, hoping to pull out one or two unconscious occupants. Sometimes the firefighters die. They do this without divine powers or knowledge of the future. These are people who are far less capable than gods, yet they are able to summon up the necessary courage and compassion to risk it all for people they don't even know.

Throughout history there have been warriors who were willing to sacrifice their lives for the lives of comrades. Of course, most soldiers are no different than anyone else: they want to live. They would rather be a hero and survive than be a hero and die. Most expect or hope that their heroic deeds on behalf of someone else will not get them killed. But surely there have been many cases over the last several centuries when warriors were in situations where they knew they would die but still acted out of a sense of loyalty to a friend or for the sake of their society. How do these people compare to Jesus? They did not give their lives for billions and they did not have the absolute assurance that they would rise from the dead and be fine afterward. They suffered and died for a handful of lives, or maybe just one. Yes, many of them may have believed they would go to heaven, but they could not have known it as confidently as a god would. So how are we to describe these brave self-sacrificing mortals? Compared to Jesus, they gave up so much for so little. Don't we have to admit that the sacrifice they made was far greater than a god's?

There is something even more troubling about this dramatic tale of love, death, and resurrection. If it really did happen, why did it have to happen that way? I first asked this question as a child many years ago and have yet to hear a good answer. Why would somebody, anybody, have to be nailed up on a cross in order for me to go heaven? Was that really the best arrangement God could come up with? It makes no sense because he is the one who is writing the rules. Didn't he know how his creation was going to turn out? If so, then why would he make this whole redemption thing so cruel and barbaric? Why would a God set up a system that requires someone to be tortured and killed? I certainly wouldn't want anyone to have to suffer and die for me. It is odd that not all but many Christians today view animal sacrifice as a terrible ritual that no one should have anything to do with. But when the human sacrifice story of Jesus is presented as evidence of God's moral greatness, two and a half billion people applaud it.

How is it that you and I were born sinners, anyway? Christians are forever telling me that I was a sinner at birth. No matter how good I might try to be I am bad, they say. It hardly seems fair that being born means you immediately need saving. What do we have to do with Adam's and Eve's crimes? I never ate any apples in the Garden of Eden so why is it on my rap sheet?

Do Christians ever wonder if there might have been another way for their god to give us a ticket to heaven, some way other than human sacrifice? Why can't we all just say we are sorry, or pay a fine, or work it off with community service? Why can't God just forgive us and leave it at that? I'm sure most of us could think up several ways to award salvation to humankind that don't require torture and crucifixion. I wonder how Christians would react to a similar story if it took place today?

Imagine if the king of a small country announced that he was going to have his son beaten, whipped, nailed to a tree, and then stabbed with a spear. During an interview on CNN, the king admits that he is sad that his son will suffer and die but it must be done because it is the only way he can forgive the citizens of his country for their moral lapses and allow them access to healthcare and social services the following year. The king loves the people of his nation and wants their crimes pardoned, so his son must die. What would you think of this king? Weird? Cruel? Evil? Insane? But why would you expect a higher moral standard from the human king of a tiny country than you would from the god of the universe?

Another challenge to the Jesus story is that it may not be as unique as most believers think it is. According to scholars, there are several ancient stories that sound remarkably familiar. Randel Helms, author of *Fiction Gospels*, describes one:

> In the first century of the Common Era, there appeared at the eastern end of the Mediterranean a remarkable religious leader who taught the worship of one true God and declared that religion meant not the sacrifice of beasts but the practice of charity and piety and the shunning of hatred and enmity. He was said to have worked miracles of goodness, casting out demons, healing the sick, raising the dead. His exemplary life led some of his followers to claim that he was a son of God, though he called himself the son of man. Accused of sedition against Rome, he was arrested. After his death, his disciples claimed he had risen from the dead, appeared to them alive, and then ascended to heaven. Who was this teacher and wonder-worker? His name was Apollonius of Tyana; he died about 98 A.D., and his story may be read in Flavius Philostratus's *Life of Apollonius*. (Helms 1988, 9)

Perhaps the biggest flaw with the Jesus story is that it hasn't worked very well. Christians claim that Jesus died for our sins so that we could all be saved. But the problem is that now, two thousand years later, most people still aren't being saved each generation. Christians are a minority worldwide. The majority of people simply don't believe the Jesus story is true. Today there are about 2.2 billion Christians and 4.5 billion non-Christians. That's an awful lot of lost souls every generation. So, if it really happened, not only was the sacrifice of Jesus strange and gruesome, it was also a mostly wasted effort that has failed to save the majority of people.

CHAPTER 19 BIBLIOGRAPHY AND RECOMMENDED READING

Harris, Sam. *Letter to a Christian Nation.* New York: Alfred A. Knopf, 2006.

Helms, Randel. *Fiction Gospels.* Amherst, NY: Prometheus Books, 1988.

Price, Robert M. *The Incredible Shrinking Son of Man: How Reliable Is the Gospel Tradition?* Amherst, NY: Prometheus Books, 2003.

Russell, Bertrand. *Why I Am Not a Christian.* New York: Simon & Schuster, 1957.

Chapter 20

Atheists are jerks who think they know everything.

Of what use is a philosopher who doesn't hurt anybody's feelings?

—Diogenes

Atheists have an image problem. Some believers think all atheists are on Satan's payroll. Others imagine that atheists are immoral frauds who know a god exists but won't admit it for fear of having to give up their vices. Still other believers see atheists as arrogant jerks who think they know everything. Too smart for their own good, they say. So stubborn that they won't see the god standing right before them. Some believers say they would never stop believing in their god if it meant becoming one of those pompous fools.

Believers may have a point here but they go too far with it. There are rude and condescending atheists, of course. But aren't some believers rude and condescending too? It is important to keep in mind that personalities and attitudes do not necessarily have anything to do with the existence of gods. Gods still might not exist even if every atheist in the world were an obnoxious jerk. One could not assume that gods exist even if every believer in the world were polite and humble.

Much of this negative view believers have toward nonbelievers comes out of the clash of ideas about the world and universe around us. For example, it can be a challenge for science-literate nonbelievers to keep a cool head when in the presence of a believer who insists that the world is flat and ten thousand years old, or that angels and demons are all around us, or that life does not evolve. But this is no reason to belittle or abuse someone. Some of the more aggressive nonbelievers might try having a little more compassion and humility. For example, I never assume intellectual superiority when talking with a believer. They easily could be "smarter" than I am, regardless of how absurd some of their beliefs may be. If I had been homeschooled by Taliban or Amish parents, I probably would see the world very differently today. Would it be my fault? Would it be right for a nonbeliever to view me as a moron who can't think? Of course not. For most people in this world it all comes down to what your parents believe and which school district you live in.

The only fault that may be inexcusable is refusing to learn. Some believers accuse atheists of being stubborn and dogmatic. If they really are, then I join the believers in criticizing them. All of us, believers and nonbelievers, should maintain an open mind and be willing to learn new things, even if it contradicts some things we thought we knew for sure. I, for example, am willing to believe in a god, dump the theory of evolution, or embrace the existence of the Loch Ness Monster if new facts demand it. I just want to be on the side of reality. Don't you?

Evolutionary biologist Richard Dawkins is one of the world's most prominent and outspoken atheists. He delivered a powerful case against belief in his excellent book *The God Delusion*. I am a long-time fan of his work and I think *The God Delusion* is a positive contribution to the world. His goal is to encourage more people to think and stop wasting their time and intellectual potential on religious beliefs. Clearly, this is a message the world needs to hear. However, there is a tone that emerges from some of the pages within *The God Delusion* that may suggest to some believers that Dawkins thinks they are all a bunch of idiots and that atheists are a higher form of life. Although I am on Dawkins's side and I don't think his book was an all-out and no-holds assault on religion, I do understand why some believers feel this way.

To be clear, Dawkins believes in freedom of thought. He is not the atheist version of the Inquisition. He hasn't called for religion to be made a crime. He doesn't want to see people jailed for praying. His hope is that people simply will realize that gods are not real so that they can get on with more positive and productive pursuits. But while his arguments are direct and powerful, I'm not sure they will hit home with as many believers as they might have. For example, Dawkins sometimes refers to believers as "faith heads." I'll go out on a limb and guess that believers don't like that. "Faith head" sounds a lot like an insult. Okay, maybe some believers' heads are filled with too much of that intellectual poison called faith, but why call them "faith heads"? It's counterproductive and, more importantly, it's wrong to suggest that believers in general are dim or incapable of reasoning. Many of today's atheists were once "faith heads." There is always the potential for skepticism and reason to sneak in. We can't just give up on people. Yes, many religious claims are undeniably ridiculous, but one must never forget that millions of people are herded into holding these ideas because of the overwhelming power of family and culture. Calling them names because they have these beliefs is like making fun of someone because in their society people wear "odd" hats or eat "strange" food. It's a form of intellectual ethnocentrism sometimes directed against believers that is unfair. Nonbelievers must never forget how complex people are. Just because someone has a few potholes in his or her thinking is not a good reason to declare their mind a dead end. Smart people can be dumb about a few things and still be smart people.

I don't think that atheists necessarily are superior to believers by any meaningful measure. Yes, they are not going to hate and kill you in the name of a god, but there are many other factors that influence what kind of person the atheist is. An atheist might hate and kill you based on what sports team you cheer for or which political party you support. Not believing in a god does not guarantee that a person will be morally superior any more than believing in a god means that a person will be an antiscience dolt. As with gender, race, and nationality, it is usually a mistake to generalize.

Dawkins is excellent at dismantling the arguments of believers who still think they can prove their gods are real. But the way in which he knocks down their house of cards sometimes warrants a bit of criticism. Although some believers may respond well to being intellectually thumped, I suspect that most who are courageous enough to invest the time to read *The God Delusion* come away offended and feeling as if they had been scolded and maybe even pushed around by a bully. Again, I completely understand and sympathize with how Dawkins feels. He obviously is frustrated and irritated by religion because it so often discourages thinking while encouraging people to do bad things. But I am not sure that tough talk is an effective way to encourage a fellow human being to embrace reason and reconsider the validity of her or his cherished religious beliefs. In my own experiences arguing over religion, I have won many battles but few wars. The only people I ever felt that I might have influenced in a meaningful and lasting way were those who I simply shared a friendly chat with. Battering a believer with logic and data is usually a waste of everyone's time. Having a sincere talk with someone you respect as a fellow human being can change everything.

I don't know; maybe believers are right. Maybe there really is a shortage of polite and humble atheists in the world today. Regardless of whether this is reality or perception, atheists need to reach out to believers and encourage them to rethink their gods in a way that believers will listen to. I think this matters a great deal because the world can't take too much more religion. We can't afford to have billions of people loving their gods more than each other for much longer. Nuclear weapons, chemical weapons, and biological weapons hang over our heads. We are devastating the natural environment that we all depend on. Half the population is still far too poor. Meanwhile, belief in gods inspires a constant assault on science and human rights. Religious belief fuels the worst form of terrorism. (Isn't killing and dying for a god worse than killing and dying for land, money, or a flag? At least we all agree that those things are real.) Belief turns us against one another in a time when we need to cooperate more than ever. Religion is too great a threat to the world for it not to be confronted and taken down a peg or two by those who respect reality and believe in the positive potential of humankind. But how?

If more atheists would stop trying to win arguments and concentrate instead on offering their fellow humans a hand up from irrational beliefs, we might actually achieve the progress we need to survive in the twenty-first century. I am not suggesting that religion must be eradicated like some disease. There are many good things about religion and it is too deeply intertwined with human culture to be unceremoniously jettisoned. However, I do believe that atheists can show believers that there is absolutely no reason to take religion so seriously that it devours common sense and basic respect for other humans. But to make any headway, atheists have to respect believers as equals rather than think of them as a hypnotized subspecies. A popular mantra among believers is "hate the sin; love the sinner." Atheists might consider adopting a version of that: hate the irrational belief but love the believer. Atheists who respect life and care about our world have an obligation to share their wonderful worldview with those who need it most. Otherwise humankind may never wake up from its ancient dreams.

Religious belief for most people is not a logical conclusion that they arrived at after researching the world's faiths and deciding on the most sensible one. For the individual, religious belief usually comes during childhood and is wrapped up with many values and loyalties developed at the same time. Belief in a god or gods became a part of who they are. This belief in a god is more like a close friend, sibling, or parent than it is some cold concept in one's head or a club membership. The connection to a god is deep and strong for many believers. It won't be shaken easily. Losing a heated debate to an atheist usually doesn't make a dent in faith. The believer who did not make a rational choice to believe is unlikely to make a rational choice to stop believing. There are other things at play here. There is feeling. There is love. There is intuition. There is loyalty. The best a compassionate atheist can do is to set the table of reason with all proper manners and etiquette and then invite the believer to dine.

Some atheists underestimate how serious the more passionate believers can be about their gods. This is no casual thing for many of them. Hard as it is to understand for an atheist, many believers are being honest when they say they love their god. Belief is the most important part of their life, some say. I tend to believe them because I have seen their trembling hands and twitching bodies when they cried and prayed to their gods. I have seen this love and fire up close. I stood close by while Christians, Muslims, Hindus, and Jews prayed in their temples around the world. I've seen the tears run down their cheeks. I've heard the whispered word "love" from many believers. Sometimes it was beautiful. Sometimes it was scary. But it was always sincere, in my opinion. Name calling, complicated sparring over fine points of logic, and quoting dead philosophers won't put out the fire I have seen burning in the hearts of these people. Reason has virtually no chance when atheists approach the believers as bullies rather than friends because they won't give an inch. It only makes them believe harder.

Many atheists are too quick to dismiss the deep emotional commitment to belief that many people have. To a devout believer, it just doesn't matter if a nonbeliever bluntly declares that there is no scientific evidence for their god and therefore it's unlikely that the god is real. It just doesn't register. They won't even listen to what is being said because it is seen as an attack, an attempt to blow the house down rather than as a knock on the door. Imagine if someone came along and told you that your favorite color was wrong, that there is no evidence that it is the superior color. How likely is it that this would make you denounce your favorite color? You probably picked your favorite color for unknown reasons in childhood and remained loyal to it all these years. My favorite color is blue. I would love for someone to try and tell me that blue is not the best color. Why, just look at it! It's such a calm and peaceful color. It's the color of the sea and the sky. It's the best color of all and I don't care what anyone says to the contrary. I have faith that blue is best! Case closed!

I have engaged in both forms of the atheist-believer clash over the existence of gods. I have had bitter battles with supremely confident believers. I have also had friendly discussions with believers during which tough questions and contradictions came up. Without a doubt the latter is more enjoyable, more productive, and far more likely to leave believers thinking in ways they may never have before. I am convinced that one cannot force a believer into a corner with scientific facts or scriptural errors and hope to achieve something. If, for example, someone came at me ranting about flaws in the theory of evolution, I would react to their aggression by listening less to their ideas and concentrating more on how to launch my own arsenal of arguments at them. If, however, someone came to me and said that they want to know the truth about our origins but evolution seems to fall short in their view, I would be willing to listen, at least for a while.

I don't go looking for it, but if I find myself in the presence of a true believer and we drift onto the topic of gods, I mostly ask questions. That's right, I just ask how they know their holy book is a collection of words from a god; how they know the universe was made by their god; how they know the apocalypse is almost upon us; and so on. I let them do most of the talking. After listening for a while, I ask more questions. Socrates figured it out a long time ago. Asking questions is a great way to teach. Asking believers questions about their gods is better for everyone. It also is far more interesting and educational for the atheist because it offers a chance to learn more about how believers think and what it is they actually believe. For the curious believer, I imagine that hearing politely delivered yet challenging questions can be an eye-opening experience. I wouldn't be surprised if many questions from such an exchange linger in some minds for many years. Posing questions rather than simply firing off facts also tends to keep things friendly and pleasant. There is a world of difference between, "There are no gods!" and "How do you know that your god is real and all the others aren't?" The former tends to end meaningful conversations while the latter starts them.

Perhaps the charge some believers make is true. Maybe too many atheists really do lack sufficient humility. After all, shouldn't we nonbelievers be the most humble people on earth? Remember, we are the ones who don't know much of anything when it comes to the big questions. We are the people who don't know why or exactly how the universe started. We don't know how life started on earth. We don't know with absolute certainty what happens to us after we die. Yes, compared to believers, we don't know much at all. Atheists definitely should be the most humble people of all.

CHAPTER 20 BIBLIOGRAPHY AND RECOMMENDED READING

Dawkins, Richard. *The God Delusion*. New York: Houghton Mifflin, 2006.

Hunsberger, Bruce E., and Bob Altemeyer. *Atheists: A Groundbreaking Study of America's Nonbelivers*. Amherst, NY: Prometheus Books, 2006.

Wilson, E. O. *The Creation: An Appeal to Save Life on Earth*. New York: W. W. Norton & Company, 2006. E. O. Wilson is a scientist, environmentalist, and atheist. He is about as far away as one can get from the negative stereotype of the bitter, angry atheist. This book is his respectful plea to believers to do more to stop environmental destruction.

Chapter 21

I don't lose anything by believing in my god.

I wish I could stand on a busy street corner, hat in hand, and beg people to throw me their wasted hours.

—Bernard Berenson

Men in expensive suits work the aisles with quiet, focused efficiency. Like robots, they move through the audience without saying a word. No need to. Everyone knows what they want. The believers fill the collectors' containers with their money. I see twenties, fifties, hundreds, and checks go into the containers. Some believers request credit card slips from the collectors. The pace of this massive money transfer is impressive. Hundreds of people who came to take away "God's word" are leaving behind a considerable fortune. The collectors pick up the pace. They empty pockets and purses like emotionless army ants efficiently dismembering a still-living grasshopper for transport back to the nest. Meanwhile, the preacher up on stage repeats over and over how important it is to give money to god. He warns the faithful that god knows exactly how much they can give and exactly how much they do give. Even more cash flies into the containers. God made a lot of money tonight. Or did he?

Some believers won't reconsider their conclusions about the reality of a god or gods because they don't recognize that they pay a price for believing. It's all gain and no loss, say many believers, so why rock the boat? Why question it? Why think? Just keep on believing. First of all, I would suggest that nothing should be off-limits to questioning, not even cherished religious beliefs. The safest policy is to leave everything in life open to skepticism and analysis. No matter how wonderful something may seem, shutting off one's mind is risky. Skepticism, by the way, is not the dirty word some believers seem to think it is. Skepticism simply means thinking once or twice before accepting anything as true. What can possibly be wrong with that? Skepticism is a positive attitude and being a skeptic is a smart way to navigate through life. It should never be confused with cynicism. A cynic may drip with negativity and scorn but a skeptic merely questions claims before believing. There's nothing negative about that.

Despite what believers say, religion seems to cost believers a lot from the atheist's perspective. This is not to say there are not real and significant benefits to believing. For example, a believer who attends worship services might be healthier because she has a network of friends who will encourage her to get regular medical checkups as well as check on her when she is ill. But this could be a benefit of Islam and not necessarily Allah. Anthropologists say we are a social species and psychologists say we depend heavily on relationships for our happiness. So when a man finds joy in praying with others it could be the people who make him happy and not necessarily the Hindu gods he worships. Benefits that often come from belonging to a belief system do not prove that any particular god is real. However, because so many believers claim that believing in a god is cost-free, a closer look is warranted to see if this is true.

It is safe to say that belief in gods can claim a heavy toll from believers. This cannot be denied because there are many examples of believers destroying family relationships, losing jobs, draining life savings, and even killing or being killed in the name of a god. However, it's too easy to criticize unpopular religions that make extreme demands on members. (Believers like to call them "cults" to make them seem significantly different from popular religions. They forget, however, that virtually all religions pass through a time in which they are labeled cults.) Most believers understand that it would be a mistake to sell their house and car just because someone told them that the end of the world is next week. Most believers understand that it's wrong to release poisonous gas into a subway station. But what many people may not recognize is that believing, no matter if it is within a popular and peaceful religion, is not free. A price is paid.

Money is not the only price of belief but it is a good place to start. Believers around the world spend many billions of dollars each year on their gods. So many religions that cannot see eye-to-eye on anything else are somehow able to agree on one thing: the gods need lots of money. A god may be able to create a galaxy for nothing, but to get anything done here on earth apparently requires cash. Those who claim to speak for the gods say that giving money to a god is the right thing to do. Some go so far as to warn of severe punishment from a god for those who do not give. Many believers are encouraged to give so that they can get an even bigger return from their god. Some religious leaders tell believers that their donation is like an investment that is guaranteed to pay off many times over. To the atheists this all sounds very suspicious. First of all, why do gods need so much money? If they can make a universe can't they make a hundred-dollar bill? What is it that they need to buy, anyway?

The weirdest thing of all about believers giving money to their god is that none of them ever give money to a god! Okay, the pharaohs of ancient Egypt, Alexander the Great, and other "human-gods" may have collected funds in person. Other than them, however, no purely supernatural god has ever made a confirmed appearance on earth to personally accept a believer's donations. What happens instead is that believers give their money to a middleman, usually one who is wearing very expensive clothes and living in a very big house. Why do believers do this? Wouldn't it make more sense to burn cash as an offering to their god in some sort of ritual? Interestingly, some Chinese people do something very similar to that. They burn paper money in hopes of sending it on to the afterlife for use there. Or maybe a believer could be creative and give their money to the most needy people on earth, people who any good god should be concerned about. How about giving "god's money" to a few of those nine or ten million children who die each year in the developing world for lack of food or a two-dollar vaccination? Giving the money to them might impress any real gods more than giving it to some holy man with a private jet.

Stating the obvious, that religion is big business, is not meant to be insulting or an attack on believers. Surely all believers see that religion is one of the oldest and most effective ways to make money. One can argue whether the money is doing the work of a god or not, but the fact that religion is a booming global industry is clear. Admittedly, just because so much money is flying around in the name of so many gods is not evidence of fraud. What it does mean, however, is that many people on this planet today are wasting a lot of their money. The undeniable truth is that most believers in the world today who regularly give money to a god are throwing their money away because the god is not real or the religion is invalid. How, for example, can the Christian who gives money to help fund the distribution of Bibles and the Muslim who gives money to fund the distribution of Korans both be right about the wise use of their money? Either one of them or both of them are wasting their cash pushing a book that is wrong. The Bible and Koran contain opposing claims that cannot be reconciled. Therefore, at least one of these believers is wasting their money.

Some believers may argue that giving money to their god (or their god's representative on earth) is a good decision no matter if the god is real or not because the money goes to build schools, help the poor, or fund hospitals. But if schools, poor people, and hospitals are your concern then why not give directly to those causes? When money is given to a religious organization some of that money may indeed do good things. Inevitably, however, some portion of the money goes directly toward that organization's goals of marketing its claims about a particular god or gods who may or may not be real. Most believers probably would agree that it is a mistake to donate money to a belief system that is based on a fictional god. They only think it is wise to give money to their religion because they think it is true and their god is real. Therefore most believers probably agree with me that, in most cases, giving money to some guy who says he works for a god is risky. The Catholic believer, for example, is very likely to agree with me that a Muslim, Hindu, Sikh, or Mormon should make a donation to UNICEF rather than to people employed within their respective belief systems. The typical Muslim is probably on my side as well. He agrees with me that giving money to a local Wiccan priestess is probably not the best financial move to make. Both Christian and Muslim would agree with me that the average Scientologist is probably better off keeping her money rather than giving it to Scientology officials. So, really, there is a lot of agreement between believers and nonbelievers that too many people are giving their money away to organizations that are highly questionable.

Most disturbing, regardless of whether gods are real or not, is the fact that many believers give away money that they or their families need. Not all, but some religious organizations and religious leaders beg or demand money from their followers in the most despicable, heartless manner imaginable. They bully, threaten, or make wild promises in order to squeeze every possible penny out of the faithful, no matter how poor they may be. How people who do this can sleep at night is beyond me. Again, I am not necessarily condemning all religious leaders who ask for money. However, those who live in multi-million-dollar mansions should not be asking elderly people with little money to dig deep in their pockets and "give to the Lord." I have known a few victims of this racket and it is upsetting to say the least. People who are struggling economically should not be giving their money to a religious leader who is wearing a suit that costs more than they earn in two months. If the gods really do need money can't we all just wait until they ask for it themselves?

Although a lot of cash is spent, donated, earned, and stolen in the world of religion, money is not everything. Some people can afford to waste money. Some believers may feel it's worth it, even if the money is not used properly. It's their money and if they feel good giving it away, fine. But what about time? Time may be more valuable than money. There are probably few believers who ever pause to consider just how much of their time they sacrifice for belief in a god. Suppose a believer spends three hours every weekend taking part in worship rituals with others and then puts in another two hours with some sort of religious study group in the middle of the week. It adds up to two hundred sixty hours per year. Over fifty years, that's thirteen thousand hours. And this doesn't include time spent at special religious events, praying, and reading religious books. Maybe atheists are wrong and one of the gods really will give some believers an eternity of happiness after they die. But if atheists are right and the gods aren't really there, then wasting so much time is a tragedy. Believers agree with atheists about this in most cases. The Muslim thinks the Hindus are wasting their time worshipping all those gods, just as the Jew thinks the Christians are wasting their time worshipping a false messiah. Any given believer thinks most believers in the world today are worshipping an imaginary god while the atheist thinks they all are wasting their time. We are all a lot closer to agreeing on this than most people realize.

Many believers are quick to point out the wonderful bonds and networks that their religion provides. Yes, religions can be very good at bringing people together, but only in a limited sense. Unfortunately, religions do an even better job of keeping people apart. Disunity is usually overlooked or denied but it is one of the significant costs people pay for believing in gods. Worst of all, everyone on earth pays for it, believers and nonbelievers alike, by having to live in a world constantly troubled by religion-inspired division, hatred, prejudice, and violence. It should come as no surprise to most believers that their religion promotes these things. Just read the Torah, New Testament, or Koran for example. They do not promote tolerance and acceptance. Although some debate interpretations, they seem to clearly demand either allegiance or annihilation.

Imagine the countless lives that have been diminished by the barriers of prejudice that stand guard around and within religions.

Imagine all the friendships that never were because men said gods were against it. Imagine all the people who never learned anything about others from different backgrounds because they were not allowed to date or have friends outside their belief system. For millions of people to be denied full access to the human family is sad and it's a significant price to pay for believing in gods. It also is nothing less than one of the most serious problems our world faces today. Why do Christians, Muslims, and Jews so often find it difficult to get along? Many would respond to that question with a lengthy list of historical crimes and modern grievances. But really the answer is that they don't get along because they think of themselves as living labels. They are Christians, Muslims, and Jews first rather than humans first.

Another big price that many people pay for their belief in the existence of a god is the loss of scientific curiosity. This does not apply to all believers, of course. There are many who respect and appreciate science. Many believers have not shut down their minds to obvious realities about life, our world, and our universe. Unfortunately, many millions have. In hopes of appeasing a god they turn their back on science and in some cases common sense.

Although some believers and even some nonbelievers deny it, there really is a conflict between religion and science. Science attempts to explain things as we find them. This is done by discovery, observations, and experimentation. Religion is very different. It attempts to explain things by simply calling them magic and citing unproven claims of divine revelation. These are two very different ways of trying to figure out the universe and they are not compatible. When one gets in the habit of accepting things based on the authority of an ancient book or the words of a religious leader, scientific curiosity suffers. There is no way around this. Faith is like Kryptonite to the scientific mind.

In 1994 I visited a rural school in northern India. The students ranged in age from about seven to twelve. They took turns reading from the Koran as they rocked back and forth. India is mostly Hindu but also has many millions of Muslims in its population. The teacher told me that the Koran was the only book they wanted or needed because it contained everything that people need to know. I have seen American workbooks, written by Christians for elementary school students, that claim dinosaurs such as the Tyrannosaurus rex were on Noah's Ark and are still alive in the wild somewhere today. There is a cost. Our world loses something when millions of children are taught things that are probably not true (religion) in place of things that are probably true (science).

Chapter 22

I didn't come from a monkey.

Facts do not cease to exist because they are ignored.
—Aldous Huxley

When a believer is discussing evolution with an informed nonbeliever, and things are not going well, the believer often blurts out a strange retort: "I did not come from a monkey!"

I have heard this so many times from so many believers that I am beginning to think that they view our furry little friends as the scourge of the earth. What is so bad about monkeys, anyway? They're pretty smart and cute too. Why is "coming from a monkey" so much worse than coming from mud, dirt, a clot of blood, dust, or maize dough as some religions claim?

The truly weird aspect of this senseless controversy is that believers are the only ones who bring up a this monkey origin. They have created a bogus claim in their head and then recoil in horror from it. The truth is, no credible evolutionary scientist, paleoanthropologist, geneticist, biologist, or primatologist would ever say that humans came from monkeys. It is simply not true based on current evidence, and anyone who knows anything about human evolution wouldn't say it is.

When a believer hits me with the "I didn't come from a monkey" line, I respond by saying: "You're right. I didn't come from the lowly monkey and neither did you. We both come from that glorious and noble ape known as *Australopithecus afarensis*." Believers usually react with blank stares and a trace of fear in their eyes.

The simple explanation that many believers never hear, sadly, is that we do not "come from" monkeys or even modern apes such as chimps, bonobos, or gorillas. The reality, according to an abundance of fossil and genetic evidence, is that we—monkeys, apes, and humans—all share a common ancestor that lived many millions of years ago. That common ancestor might have looked similar to a modern monkey but it was not a modern monkey. If this also upsets some believers, and I'm sure it does, then they should protest against the claim of a common ancestor and leave monkeys out of it. But when they shout their rejection of descent from monkeys, it's embarrassing because nobody with any sense has ever claimed that in the first place. An important detail to add is that most people do not know the difference between monkeys and apes. Working my way through college as a zoological educational assistant at a major United States zoo, I was surprised by how little most people know about modern primates. Most people, for example, are not aware that apes do not have tails and monkeys do. Most people incorrectly refer to chimps as monkeys. And very few people know anything about bonobos, easily the most fascinating apes of all, in my opinion. I suspect this widespread ignorance about our closest living relatives has a lot to do with the mass confusion about our evolutionary history.

The fact that so many believers are misinformed about human evolution is partly the fault of religion's continual attack on science education. In most countries in the world today, very few people are taught in schools about the ancestors that we all owe our existence to. The stories told by fossils resting in laboratories and museums around the world never reach millions of believers because their religious leaders reject science whenever it threatens to contradict their ancient stories. To make matters worse, many religious leaders eagerly fill in the void with misinformation and lies, which make it even easier for people to reject evolution.

Highly religious nations such as Saudi Arabia, Afghanistan, the United States, Nigeria, and Turkey, for example, have banned or avoided the teaching of human evolution in schools to the point where a significant percentage of their populations are firmly against it without even knowing what it is. This is why so many believers end up saying strange things like, "my god is real because I didn't come from a monkey." If only they knew what they are missing out on.

I gained a good understanding of human evolution in university classes, read numerous books on the topic, and continue to keep track of news about the latest ideas and discoveries. I have also interviewed two of the most prominent scientists in the field: Tim White, discoverer of the oldest biologically modern human fossils to date (one hundred sixty thousand years old), and Donald Johanson, discoverer of the famous *Australopithecus afarensis* nicknamed "Lucy." I find the subject thrilling and important. I connect with it because it is personal. It's about who I am. Learning about *Homo ergaster* and *Homo habilis* is like looking through an old family photo album or researching a great-great-great grandfather. It's irresistible to anyone with a curious mind. How anyone can fail to find human evolution fascinating is a mystery to me. So much of it is inspirational. There was a long and dangerous path that led to us. Understanding it illuminates our important connection to the rest of nature. It also can help one think more clearly about our collective future. My awareness and acceptance of human evolution certainly hasn't degraded or dehumanized me, like so many believers fear it can. For better or worse, this is our family history. I believe we are better for knowing it.

The problem many believers have with human evolution is not about monkeys specifically, of course. It's the connection to anything nonhuman. They feel the suggestion of such a link is insulting. It's not like these believers would embrace Australopithecines if they knew about them. Evolution-phobic believers don't like any cracks in their imagined wall between humans and the rest of nature. They resist being pulled down from their pedestal into the animal kingdom. We are better than animals, declare these believers. We are above nature, blessed with a divine spark from a god, they say. I'm not so sure. I know history and follow current news so I have my doubts about that.

Contrary to the fears of some believers, admitting who we are, where we come from, and who we are related to does not condemn us to savagery. We have the most powerful brains on earth. We can use them to think ourselves clear of the destructive instincts we may have within us. We do not have to foul our own nest as we currently do. We do not have to kill our neighbors as we currently do. We do not have to be ignorant of our origins as most of us currently are. Believers who are anxious to put as much distance as possible between humankind and the rest of the animal kingdom should encourage science education rather than resist it. After all, it is science and science education, more than anything that keep us out of the jungle.

The Top Ten Myths about Evolution (Smith and Sullivan 2007) is a fine book that tackles common misunderstandings people have about evolution. Copies of it should be air-dropped over every country with a population in denial about evolution. It even includes a chapter named "People come from monkeys." Authors Cameron Smith and Charles Sullivan write:

> We can dismiss some critics' lamentation that believing in evolution will drag us down into the world of primates: we're already in it. And stacks of data make it equally clear, to any thinking person, that people *don't come from monkeys*. Around thirty million years ago, the African primates diverged into two distinct groups, taking up different diets, habits and habitats, as their environments changed and opportunities arose. One group developed into apes, which included—much later—chimpanzees, gorillas and humans. The other group developed into monkeys, and DNA and other studies prove that we belong in the ape group instead of the monkey group. Do people come from monkeys? Not at all. We do share a common ancestor with chimpanzees, and before them, with the group that became monkeys. But to say we come from monkeys is simply wrong, and evolution has never claimed it. (Smith and Sullivan 2007, 99–100)

Monkeys aside, religious people who say that accepting human evolution is incompatible with religion don't know much about religion. Today there are hundreds of millions of people in a wide variety of religions who accept the obvious truth that humans evolved. For example, the late Pope John Paul II made it clear in 1996 that Catholics' belief in their god need not conflict with human evolution. The official Catholic position is that human evolution was their god's process of creation. Of course, there is no evidence that a god guides evolution but I suppose it is possible. There are Muslims, Hindus, Mormons, even Baptists who accept evolution. Clearly it is possible to believe in a god or gods without running away from human evolution. Many believers recognize that there simply is too much evidence to deny it so they make their belief conform accordingly. Some people call it "theistic evolution." I call it a good start.

CHAPTER 22 BIBLIOGRAPHY AND RECOMMENDED READING

Lynch, John, and Louise Barrett. *Walking with Cavemen.* New York: DK Publishing, 2003. This book contains an abundance of information but it is the outstanding photographs of actors in makeup portraying a variety of hominids that make it special. This is the companion book to the memorable BBC documentary of the same name.

McKie, Robin. *Dawn of Man: The Story of Human Evolution.* New York: DK Publishing, 2000.

Sloan, Christopher. *The Human Story: Our Evolution from Prehistoric Ancestors to Today.* Washington, DC: National Geographic, 2004.

Smith, Cameron M., and Charles Sullivan. *The Top Ten Myths about Evolution.* Amherst, NY: Prometheus Books, 2007.

Tattersall, Ian, and Jeffrey H. Schwartz. *Extinct Humans.* Boulder, CO: Westview Press, 2000. This is an excellent survey of the field. Includes many brilliant photographs of important fossils.

Wells, Spencer. *The Journey of Man: A Genetic Odyssey.* Princeton, NJ: Princeton University Press, 2002.

Chapter 23

I don't want to go to hell.

Death, the most dreaded of all evils, is therefore of no concern to us; for while we exist death is not present, and when death is present we no longer exist.

—Epicurus

Many people say that their fear of hell is one of the reasons they believe in a god. But why? A desire to avoid ending up in hell is not a good reason to believe in a god. It might be a good reason to worship a particular god and to follow his or her rules but it is not a reason to conclude that the god exists in the first place. Before one can fear hell one must first believe that the god who created hell is real. For example I don't believe in any gods, including those who might have created a hell for people like me to suffer in. Therefore, I don't worry about hell. I couldn't if I tried because it's just not real to me. Maybe it really does exist somewhere deep in the earth's mantle or maybe at the core itself. Maybe hell is in another dimension. It could be that I am in for a terrible surprise after I die. But I doubt it. I'm open-minded and willing to be convinced that hell is real, but until then I simply can't bring myself to fear something that no one in history has ever been able to show is real or even come up with any evidence for. It's just another story, no different than stories about trolls or haunted houses.

If I believed in a god and hell, I imagine that an atheist's fearless attitude toward hell would bother me. How could I explain the lack of concern? Assuming the atheist was sane and had a normal distaste for fire and pain, how could she or he not be worried about hell? Something must be wrong here. Why would a god set up this horrible place of punishment and then make its existence appear so vague and uncertain that hundreds of millions of thoughtful and well-meaning people don't believe that it even exists? Surely a god with any sense of justice would not want to trick people into hell. Whatever purpose hell is supposed to serve, shouldn't the god who sends people there make sure that the danger is obvious to everyone? Wouldn't that be the least a god could do for us? It all seems a bit devious and evil otherwise. It's as if hell is meant not only to scare and motivate true believers but also to work as a cruel trap to snare all those who made the mistake of being skeptical and thinking critically about religious claims.

If hell is real, isn't spending eternity there a bit much? Who in their right mind can possibly believe that punishing someone forever is reasonable? Have you ever thought about how long eternity is? Wait a trillion years and you will be no closer to the end than you are right now. But these gods who create hells, we are told, seem to have no problem tossing atheists and people who believe in the wrong god into the fire forever. And for what? Because they doubted? Because they thought? Because they were born and raised in the "wrong" belief system? People deserve *eternal* punishment for that? Are you serious?

Worst of all, in my opinion, is the claim by many believers that those who believe in the wrong gods will be condemned to hell. Okay, the atheists may have thought things over and decided to pass on belief, but many people were born into families and societies that strongly pushed a particular god or gods on them virtually from birth. They hardly had much of a chance to think for themselves and find the "real" god. If I had been born into a poor family in rural Pakistan, for example, I might have ended up with the same views on gods that I have now, but the odds would have been heavily against it. Chances are I would be a fundamentalist Muslim today and well on my way to spending eternity in the Christian hell. Had I been born in Utah to Mormon parents, however, chances are I would be a devout Mormon right now and well on my way to the Islamic hell. Believers who care about other people and about justice must ask themselves if it is really a crime to believe in the "wrong" god or in no gods. If so, are they crimes that deserve eternal punishment? By the way, I am aware that some people prefer to believe in a softer, cooler hell, one in which there is no torturing and no fire. Where they get these details from I have no idea, but they claim hell is nothing more than existing apart from a god's love. It sounds like the ultimate time out for bad behavior. Nobody spanks you but you can't see your friends or play in heaven. You just have to stand in the corner—forever. While it sounds better than roasting in a lake of fire forever, it is still a severe punishment. If heaven is real, being excluded from the best thing ever just because you trusted what your misguided parents or society told you about religion seems too harsh. By the way, will the one billion Hindus alive today eventually go to both the Christian and the Islamic hell simultaneously or will they somehow split time between both? How does that work?

During the buildup to the 2003 invasion of Iraq by US and Coalition forces, there was a flood of government press conferences, TV documentaries, and news reports that described the despicable behavior of Saddam Hussein and his sons. Their apparent fondness for having rivals and enemies tortured was condemned repeatedly by appalled politicians, generals, pundits, and scholars. I noticed a recurring theme that stressed how these acts by Iraq's ruling family were immoral and unjustified, no matter what the victims had been accused or convicted of. What struck me as odd was that many of those who were upset by Saddam's use of torture—President George W. Bush, for one—claimed to be followers of a belief system that is supposed to include eternal torture for billions of people. It seemed inconsistent, I thought, for people to get so worked up about one dictator who had a few hundred or a few thousand people tortured over a period of several years when they did not seem troubled at all by their god who, according to them, has been torturing billions of people for thousands of years and will continue to torture them forever. Why is it that so often our sense of morality and fairness seems to be of a higher standard than the gods'?

Hell is just one more unproven religious claim. But it is special as the most barbaric and immoral one of all. By the measure of common human decency, isn't it obviously wrong for an all-powerful god to brutalize people forever because they failed to believe, failed to worship in the correct way, failed to behave in the correct way, or simply made the honest mistake of worshipping the wrong god? If my baby jammed a peanut butter and jelly sandwich into my new DVD player, I would forgive him within minutes. I once interviewed a woman who was subjected to cruel medical experiments as a child by the infamous Dr. Mengele in Auschwitz, the Nazi death camp. While she never forgot, she did forgive. Why is forgiveness so much easier for us than it is for some gods? If my children were to turn their backs on me one day and deny me love and respect, I would not wish them pain for five seconds, much less eternity. There is nothing they could do that would make me want to punish them forever. People who believe in a hell might consider asking why their god is so mean and unforgiving. Better yet, they might ask why their god left no clear evidence of hell so that all of us would at least know to fear it and try to avoid ending up there.

Finally, I would encourage believers to consider how it is they can believe in the existence of both a good god and a bad hell. I know that it is very important for most believers to think of their god as not only good but very good. But how could such a god operate a torture chamber? Believers cannot have it both ways. Either your good god is not real or your hell is not real.

Chapter 24

I feel my god when I pray.

The invisible and the non-existent look very much alike.

—Delos B. McKown

Although the intelligent design argument may get more attention these days, a justification for belief that is more difficult to challenge is the claim by many believers that they "feel" the presence of their god or gods when they pray. Many believers in many religions have told me that they know god is real simply because they "feel him."

How does one dispute a believer's claim that they saw a god, heard a god, or in some way felt a god without insulting the believer? I have found that it is not easy to have a respectful well-meaning conversation about such claims. No matter how gently the challenge is delivered, believers tend to interpret it as an accusation that they are either lying, unintelligent, or mentally ill. It is a tough position for a nonbeliever to be in, particularly one who genuinely cares about the feelings of believers. For example, when a believer says "God spoke to me," My first instinct is to ask whether or not it was an actual audible voice that was heard or possibly just the believer's own thoughts that were incorrectly attributed to a god. But some believers have interpreted that as rude and insulting. The polite nonbeliever must navigate carefully through a minefield to get anywhere with this one.

One believer told me that he had heard the actual voice of his god. He said the words were audible and could have been captured by a voice recorder if one had been available at the time. I asked him how he was sure that the incident was not imagined or some sort of hallucination. I reminded him that many people see and experience things that are not real every day around the world. It does not mean that they all are mentally ill or lack intelligence. The human brain is not reliable 100 percent of the time. Brains make mistakes. We are all capable of misinterpreting events, misremembering events, and imagining things that are not there. I asked the believer who said he heard a god how he can be sure that he did not imagine it. It was at this point that I began to sense his rising irritation and decided not to push any further. So how does one question this amazing but common claim of personal contact with a god? I believe there is a way.

There is a crucial fact about the phenomenon of believers feeling or hearing a god that cripples it as an argument for the existence of gods. When they understand it, honest believers have little choice but to rethink their position. It turns out that there is nothing unusual about sensing the presence of things that do not really exist. To prove this we only have to look at the claims of believers themselves. It may surprise believers who do not know much about other religions but claims of personal contact with gods are common, close to universal in human culture. And it's nothing new. Believers have been claiming to hear gods and feel the presence of gods for thousands of years. People who make this claim today must recognize that countless millions of other believers have felt or heard different gods. This is key: different god, same experience. This is a strong indication that believers are reporting some kind of psychological event that is common to the human mind rather than evidence of actually making contact with gods. Suppose, for example, a man hears Allah or an angel tell him to convert to Islam. Is this proof that Allah is real and Islam is the only true religion? A typical Christian might be too skeptical to agree with that, especially if she recently heard the voice of Jesus calling her to Christianity. And what about the animist believer who hears the voice of a god speak to him when the wind blows at night? What about tribal people who say they were visited by animal spirits during a vision quest?

The Hindus, Christians, Muslims, Jews, animists, Rastafarians, ancient Greeks, and so forth who claimed to have made contact with their gods cannot all be right about what they experienced. The only explanation that works is that most, if not all, of the believers who claim to have heard, seen, or felt a god are honestly mistaken about what they experienced. This does not mean that people who make these claims are lying, dumb, or crazy. It simply means they are human.

There is a tremendous amount of psychological energy that comes into play when the fires of religion heat up the human mind. Many believers cry, convulse, speak unknown "languages," laugh uncontrollably, or scream during worship rituals. It is stunning to see adults, tears streaming down their cheeks, wave their hands at the sky and shout up to their god. Yes, some are probably just going along with the crowd, trying to fit in and follow the script. But I am willing to believe that many of them really are experiencing a powerful psychological event in their minds. Some of the behavior that I have observed was too intense to be explained as a conscious performance, in my judgment. I have seen, for example, believers' bodies vibrate and twitch with a speed and intensity that would be impossible for most people to fake. I was convinced that there was a genuine explosion of excitement and emotion going on in their minds while under the spell of religion. It is not farfetched to suspect that a belief capable of generating such mental fireworks can also occasionally generate hallucinations.

Consider alien abductions. There are people who claim to have been kidnapped by aliens. The most common theme involves victims being immobilized, taken away, studied, and then returned. Just as it is with believers of gods, however, no alien abduction victim has ever produced any evidence to back up their story. So, how do god-believers feel about alien abduction claims? Some accept them as true, undoubtedly, but many are skeptical enough to have doubts. They probably would suggest that the person is either making it up or had some kind of a dream that only seemed real to them. But why do these god-believers have a double standard? If one person hears or sees a god and that is considered proof that the particular god is real, then why can't we consider alien abduction stories to be proof that extra-terrestrial beings are here on earth snatching and probing people at will?

My advice to believers who are sure they felt a god or heard a god's voice is to be skeptical and remember that believers have been hearing those same whispers from many gods for many centuries.

Chapter 25

I need my god to protect me.

One of the benefits of believing in a god who cares about you is the reassurance that you are watched over and protected by the most powerful being in the universe. As a child, I often asked for protection from the god that I believed in (or at least tried very hard to believe in). I didn't hesitate to ask for help when I was desperate, whether it was to shield me from disaster on a tough math test or to react fast enough to line drives hit my way while playing shortstop in Little League. I can't remember how reassuring those silent prayers might have been but I assume they served some purpose or I probably would not have bothered. But as the years went by I learned that the god my immediate society told me about was only one of many gods. And the way I was taught to worship this god was just one of many ways to worship him. By the time I reached my early twenties it dawned on me that none of these gods seemed very real and worshipping them in any way didn't seem like a very wise use of time. So there I was, all alone in the world with no gods to protect me as I made my way through life. Was I scared? Was I terrified of facing adversity, failures, and misfortune all by myself? Not at all. I figured I had already been on my own all those years before, whether I had realized it or not. Nothing had changed except my perception. How could I miss what was never really there?

In the 1990s I completed a long solo journey around the world. For month after month I had no friends, family, or gods to keep me company or watch my back. It was just me and my *Lonely Planet* travel books. I don't want to make it more than it was but there were a few dangerous and difficult moments along the way. In Africa, for example, I was struck with a mysterious fever while on a poor man's safari in Kenya. I was terrified that I might have contracted malaria or something worse. I spent an entire day on my back trembling uncontrollably in a tiny tent far from any towns or hospitals. It was not the best of times for me. My brain was close to cooking and I wondered if this was going to be the end of me. That night, I left my tent to urinate in the bushes. I felt a little better and the cool night air was a welcome change from the stifling tent. I believed that I was going to be okay and foolishly wandered a few hundred yards from my campsite. At some point during the walk I blacked out and collapsed in the tall grass. I awoke some time later in the night to discover a Masai warrior standing over me. It was a scary situation. I couldn't tell if he was planning to kill me or ask if I knew the latest World Cup results. Looking up from my submissive position in the grass, the tall man looked extraordinarily fearsome. I still clearly remember how his metal spear tip sparkled in the moonlight. After a long and awkward period of staring at each other and exchanging a few mutually incomprehensible words, I decided that I needed to appear a bit more manly and less of a pushover in case this was going to turn ugly. So I rose to my feet, inflated my chest and tried to look as confident and capable as any sickly, dehydrated, and disoriented man can look. The Masai said something. I forced a smile and slowly backed away while still facing him. Fortunately, he let me go without any confrontation and I made it back to my campsite.

The next morning the Masai man came to the camp and spoke with my safari guide. It turns out that he had found me lying there in the bush, easily the most pathetic tourist in all of Africa that night. He said he guarded me for a couple of hours while I slept off my daze because a lion was prowling nearby and he believed I was in serious danger. I was happy to be able to thank him for his kindness. I did not think about it until much later, but throughout the ordeal of sickness and even when I awoke in the bush in the shadow of that scary spear tip, I never once prayed for a god to help me. Somehow, I found the strength to ride out both the fever and the fear all by myself.

One day in Nepal I was feeling exceptionally strong and ambitious so I made a spontaneous decision to climb a mountain—by myself. I was very fit and it was a tiny mountain by Himalayan standards so it didn't seem like a foolhardy thing to attempt. To my surprise, however, reaching the summit almost killed me. Not that it wasn't worth it. Atop my own personal Himalayan hill, I experienced the unusual joy of standing inside a cool cloud as it lingered in the sky. My natural high faded fast, however, when I discovered that some twenty leeches had infiltrated my pants. Fortunately they had made it no higher than my knees, so I suppose it could have been much worse. The little beasts were firmly attached to my legs and some were even inside my socks. One white sock had turned completely red, soaked through with my blood because I unknowingly had crushed a couple of bloated leeches while climbing. I was too tired to panic but it was a bad feeling to have so many creatures simultaneously feasting on my blood.

Apparently the stealthy little monsters had slithered up my pant legs during the climb through the thick bush at the base of the mountain. As I stared in disbelief at my leech-covered lower legs, I realized that I was out of drinking water and starting to feel very thirsty, a condition that probably was accelerated by the high altitude. I felt exhausted in a way I had never before experienced. Nepal is a beautiful country with a fascinating culture and lovely people but it never seemed to have quite enough oxygen to suit my taste. I suddenly realized that I had to get off this mountain before the sun set or I would have serious problems finding my way back to the village in the dark. So I peeled off the leeches as gently as I could and let them go. (No reason to kill creatures for doing what they have to do, I figured.) After enjoying my moment on the summit and breathing in a bit of that cloud, I raced down the mountain. My legs ached and my lungs struggled to keep up. I moved as fast as I could without being reckless.

Halfway down I was still terrified that I wouldn't beat the sunset. But all I could do was keep moving. Interestingly, never once did I feel the need to ask a god for help. I just kept putting one foot in front of the other until I arrived at where I needed to be.

I never would have imagined that one could be surrounded by millions of people and feel lonely. But I was. Worn down by weeks of travel, risky food, and the constant barrage of con men, the dusty backstreets of Asia almost broke me. There was one haunting night in a rundown hotel in New Delhi, India, that I won't soon forget. I didn't cry that night but I'm sure it was only because I was too tired to work up a tear. I had always believed that I could handle loneliness better than most. I love being alone. It's the best time for reading, writing, and thinking. Solitude had always been so good to me. I never imagined that I needed people around me all the time the way so many others seem to. That long night in India revealed how wrong I was. I was more lonely than I had ever been in my life. I was in pain. But I never asked a god to comfort me. I just laid back in the filthiest bed I had ever seen, stared up at the bug-infested ceiling, and began planning how I would make tomorrow a better day.

These lowlights from my travels are personal and a bit embarrassing but they are worth bringing up to demonstrate a point. When I was in danger or emotional distress, I never called out to a god. Believe me, I would have without hesitation if I thought there was any likelihood that a god would have heard my pleas and helped. I could have prayed to one or a hundred gods but in the end I knew that I would be on my own to meet the challenges before me.

I am pretty sure that praying to gods for help and protection serves no practical purpose. The gods are probably invisible and silent because they are not there. One of the reasons their existence seems so unlikely is because they don't protect their believers. Our world is a place where suffering and loss are constant and indiscriminate. Good people get hit by buses and lightning at about the same rate as bad people do. Nothing could be more obvious than the complete absence of a god's justice and protection in this world.

There certainly was no divine justice on the morning of December 26, 2004. The Indian Ocean seafloor convulsed for eight minutes to launch a tsunami that killed more than two hundred thousand people—many of them babies and children. Of course, among its victims were people who had prayed that morning and many times before. It didn't help them. The massive surge of ocean water killed Hindus, Muslims, Buddhists, Christians, and Jews. Drowning or being battered to death in debris-filled water is a horrible way to die. It's likely that most if not all of the believers who died that day screamed out for help from their god as the waters consumed them. But they still died.

It's a tough challenge for believers to explain why their god kills people who pray to live. But they do have answers. Some believers will argue that a god does hear the prayers and comforts the victims as they die. Or they might claim their god has to do what he has to do because of some master plan. This is the "can't-bake-a-cake-without-breaking-some-eggs" theory. One of the more disturbing explanations I have heard from believers is that we all "deserve" disasters like tsunamis because we are all "sinful." This is what belief in gods does to the minds of some people. It actually leads them to think that babies are bad and deserve to be drowned in seawater.

According to a study by the World Bank and the Indonesian government, 37 percent of the people killed by the 2004 tsunami were under the age of eighteen. Approximately 13 percent were infants. More than seven thousand children lost both of their parents. Some thirty-two thousand children lost one parent. It's hard for an atheist to understand how children and babies deserved that. There is, of course, another possibility that fits perfectly with these disturbing facts. Perhaps people die tragically, seemingly for no reason, because there are no gods watching over us. Couldn't natural disasters such as tsunamis, floods, earthquakes, hurricanes, droughts, and tornados be unintelligent and indifferent events that can strike down anyone anywhere, regardless of which gods they pray to? This seems to be the most likely explanation because it matches the reality we see in our world.

Many believers operate under the mistaken assumption that life is too difficult to go it alone without a god. They think that not believing in a god would be reckless, like going through life with a death wish. One must have a god to lean on during hard times, they say. One needs a god for security. But this is not necessarily true. I believe that we all possess a lot more inner strength than we give ourselves credit for. Believers who say they must rely on their faith in a god to make it through life may be selling themselves short. I see no reason to think that the world's atheists are all psychologically stronger and more confident than the world's believers. Believers *can* do it alone. Most likely, they have always been on their own anyway. They just have never realized it or admitted it.

Too many believers refuse to admit the obvious: their god does not protect them. Of the popular gods today, all of them appear to be either unable or unwilling to keep people safe. For example, Christians who claim that Jesus protects them might visit a nearby hospital and take note of the Christians—including children and teenagers—who are there suffering from painful diseases and injuries. Most of the people in Darfur who have been facing forced relocation, rape, and murder for years are Muslims or Christians. I am sure that they prayed to Jesus or Allah for protection. But for tens of thousands of them, neither Jesus nor Allah helped them when the Janjaweed attacked. Millions of believers around the world are hit with everything from AIDS to abusive spouses, from house fires to hurricanes. If a god is keeping any one group of believers safe from misfortune it is a mystery who these protected people are.

More than one believer has told me that I will know their god is real one day when something terrible happens to me. (They never consider the possibility that a bad event in my life might lead me to someone else's god.) They suggest that I need a tragedy to bring me to my knees and humble me so that I will turn to their god for help. Could a personal tragedy or crisis force me to cry out for Allah, Jesus, or Hanuman? Maybe. It might happen if I am at the end of my rope. But so what? When humans reach out for gods in troubling times it does not mean that gods are actually there. If people really do need gods to get through life, then that may say something about human psychology but it says nothing about the existence or nonexistence of gods. Needing a god is not proof that the god is real.

The world we see around us seems to run precisely as one imagines it would without any gods involved. Haven't the last several thousand years of human history been pretty much what one would expect from a species that has nothing to work with but its own talents and flaws? Christians may say that life is too difficult to live without Jesus, but more than a billion Muslims manage to do it somehow. Muslims may say that life is impossible without Allah's guidance and protection, but some four hundred million Buddhists pull it off quite nicely.

I once worked as a live-in supervisor at a residential facility for abused and neglected children. It was the worst job I ever had. It was also the best job I ever had. Every day was an emotional rollercoaster ride with very troubled kids who had been abandoned, beaten, or sexually abused. In most cases it was their parents or a close relative who had abused or neglected them. They were let down by the very people they trusted more than anyone else in the world. These kids, ranging in age from about nine to thirteen, would have frequent destructive or violent outbursts. Often I was the only thing standing between them and serious injury to themselves or someone else. I was trained to use a simple technique called "containing" in these situations. It was really nothing more than holding a child in a bear hug until she or he regained self-control. Although I had to do it many times, I never got used to it. Holding a deeply wounded child and riding out the storm with him or her was both physically and emotionally draining for me. I could feel the waves of hurt, rage, and confusion inside of them as they struggled against my grip. I walked away from those incidents with tears in my eyes many times.

Some believers may argue otherwise but I am fairly certain that no gods were watching over those children. It was just me and the kids in the room, and I could never do enough to help them. Those children had lived horror stories that were consistent with a world that has no protective gods. If there really are invisible guardians around us, like so many believers claim, then why do they not do a better job of helping children like the ones I had to stop from cutting themselves and punching brick walls? If no god helps these little ones, then how can believers be so sure that a god is there for them?

Chapter 26

I want eternal life.

The Singularity will allow us to transcend these limitations of our biological bodies and brains. We will gain power over our fates. Our mortality will be in our own hands. We will be able to live as long as we want.

—Ray Kurzweil

W e live in exciting times. We are the first generation of humans ever that can sensibly discuss the possibility of beating death without calling upon unproven supernatural claims or pure science fiction. We may have a realistic chance of living extraordinarily long lives and this time we don't have to count on gods and angels. This time it's nanotechnology, robotics, genetic engineering, and computer power that some people are looking to for salvation. For thousands of years immortality was the exclusive domain of religion. Not any more. Science and technology have now progressed to the point where serious, sober, and sane people are talking about the possibility that humans in the near future may live for many centuries, maybe forever.

This is not as crazy as it sounds. There is a good chance that in this century, science will change everything, and it all could happen virtually overnight. Cyborgs, cloned body parts, robots with artificial intelligence, and human minds networked with a global brain are no longer wild fantasy. Today such things are viewed by many people as not

only possible but inevitable. What makes it all credible is the astonishing pace of progress. Science and technology are not trudging along
in linear progression. The rate of progress is consistently accelerating.
For example, computer power is growing exponentially and where it
will allow us to go, no one is sure. Some people predict that this radical transformation, the Singularity, may come as soon as 2045. Live
long enough to catch that wave, they say, and you may be able to live
forever. Inventor Ray Kurzweil is a leading proponent of this view.
His fascinating book, *The Singularity Is Near*, details his case for the
rapid approach of this moment when computers and other technolo-
gies accelerate to a point where unpredictable changes may occur and
we are able to become something far beyond human. If the Singularity
does come, and if it delivers even a fraction of what Kurzweil imagines, life and death will never be the same.

Religious leaders have been selling the idea of an existence
beyond death for as long as there has been religion. It's a powerful lure
and serves as an effective way to pull people into a belief system and
keep them there. But it only works because very few people ever
bother to ask these religious leaders to prove their claims. The one
thing that all promises of heaven, hell, and reincarnation have in
common is that none of them have ever come up with compelling evidence or even a strong argument to support the claims. The best
believers can offer are stories in holy books or stories from people
who say they "died," experienced some kind of an "afterlife," and then
returned to tell about it. There are also stories of people who died and
then either returned in the body of someone else or returned as a ghost.
Unfortunately these are all stories, no more credible than Elvis sightings and alien abductions. Many near-death or life-after-death stories
probably can be explained as the hallucinations and sensations that are
naturally produced by a dying brain. Seeing a ghost is more likely to
be either a hallucination or the simple misinterpretation of something
real that one encountered. After all, ghost stories have been accumu-
lating for centuries and there still is no concrete evidence that a single
ghost has ever existed. Heaven, hell, reincarnation, or some other

supernatural after-death experience may be real but, despite many centuries of confident promises from believers, there has never been a sensible reason to think that any of it is true.

Cryonics is an interesting nonreligious attempt at achieving a life after death. This is the claim that dead humans can be safely stored in extremely cold conditions until medical science advances sufficiently to be able to revive and cure them of whatever killed them. Dismissed by most people as impossible, cryonics is an intriguing idea nonetheless. Cryonics proponents say a slim chance is better than no chance. Technically they are right about that. Cryonics really does offer a better chance for reanimation in the future than, say, cremation. But is it a good enough chance to be worth the money? And doesn't it sound a little too much like ancient Egyptian religious beliefs? Don't cryonics customers seem like modern-day pharaohs? After dying they are placed in canisters and servants watch over them. The only thing missing is the pyramid. While the idea of cryonics is intriguing, I am not convinced that we currently know how to preserve brains in a way that would allow even unimaginably advanced technicians of the future to salvage them with memories and personality intact. Something that no longer exists cannot be revived, no matter how capable the available technology might be. For the moment, waiting on the Singularity seems like the better option for those who need to dream of beating death.

People who believe in reincarnation or heaven have always had the dream of eternal life all to themselves. Nonbelievers in such supernatural claims had no choice but to keep their chin up and pretend to be brave in the face of inevitable and permanent death. It has been left to atheists to be the mature minority of humankind, the ones capable of facing the cruel end without retreating into fantasy or unproven concepts. Only atheists surrender to death with courage and reason, or at least that is what they say in public. In private, however, I suspect that many atheists are a little more bummed out over death than they let on. But it doesn't have to be that way anymore. Thanks to science and this tantalizing idea of the Singularity, atheists can now harbor their own crazy dreams of eternal life. Furthermore, people who believe in a god can no longer justify clinging to their belief in a god because it is the only hope they have of fending off permanent death. There is another hope on the table now. Like heaven and hell, it, too, is short on evidence and nowhere near proven. But it is another option and it doesn't require belief in a god. If death is so frightening to you that you can't face it without hope of an escape clause, then try out the Singularity.

I am highly skeptical about the Singularity creating a secular heaven for us in this century, but no one can deny that we are heading somewhere very unusual very fast. It took about a million years to progress from stone tools to the Wright brothers' airplane, for example. But then it took less than seventy years after that to land humans on the moon. Computers recently filled large rooms, now we carry more powerful ones in our pockets. The next few decades will be mind-boggling—guaranteed. Of course there is also the important question of whether or not the Singularity will bring on the wonderful warm and fuzzy future that Ray Kurzweil predicts, or something more like the "Terminator" scenario in which super-intelligent machines exterminate us. Artificial intelligence researcher Hugo de Garis warns of the latter possibility in his book *The Artilect War*. Not only is there the threat of intelligent machines wiping us out, there is also the chance that terrorists and evil governments will find plenty of uses for supercomputers, robotics, nanotechnology, and genetics too. So there is the possibility that the Singularity will indeed occur but then promptly result in our enslavement or extinction. It is interesting how closely all of this seems to parallel many traditional religions. Even the Singularity offers us both a heaven and a hell.

The Singularity presents an intriguing new kind of hope. No longer are we limited to mummification or begging for help from the sky when death stalks us. One day soon we may have fleets of microscopic nanobots swimming around inside of us, finding and fixing wayward cells. We might have cloned body parts tucked away safely in storage, waiting for the day when we need to replace a liver or heart.

If we develop the ability to upload our minds onto a computer hard drive, we might then enter the age of true immortality. Imagine keeping a spare copy of your mind, wirelessly updated at regular intervals to keep it current. Then, if you get run over by a truck (or flying car) someone simply has to download your backup mind into a new cloned body or robot body and you are back in the game. (At least I think it would be "you.") All of this might sound like horrifying heresy to believers and utter nonsense to skeptics, but humankind is heading in this direction faster than most people realize. Whether or not we ever get there is an open question. Although I am fascinated by the Singularity and admit that Kurzweil and others make a compelling case for it, something prevents me from getting too excited just yet. Perhaps I just don't want to set myself up for a big disappointment. With my luck I'll probably die five minutes before the Singularity arrives.

Those who feel that the promise of an afterlife is a powerful reason to keep believing in a god might consider that such hope is no longer limited to religion. Those of us who live long enough to see the Singularity (if it happens) may go on living for a long time, if not forever. After thousands of years of praying and wishing, humankind might finally achieve immortality through science, an activity that makes no use of gods, miracles, or magic. It sounds way too good to be true and maybe it is. But at least it gives nonbelievers a chance to hope too.

CHAPTER 26 BIBLIOGRAPHY AND RECOMMENDED READING

de Garis, Hugo. *The Artilect War: Cosmists vs. Terrans.* Palm Springs, CA: ETC Publications, 2005.

Garreau, Joel. *Radical Evolution: The Promise and Peril of Enhancing Our Minds, Our Bodies—and What It Means to Be Human.* New York: Doubleday, 2005. A great review of the good and bad of fast-changing technology.

Kaku, Michio. *Visions*. New York: Anchor Books, 1998.

Kurzweil, Ray. *The Singularity Is Near: When Humans Transcend Biology*. New York: Viking, 2005.

Naam, Ramez. *More Than Human: Embracing the Promise of Biological Enhancement*. New York: Broadway Books, 2005.

Chapter 27

Without my god we would have no sense of right and wrong.

> *To neglect the common ground with other primates, and to deny the evolutionary roots of human morality, would be like arriving at the top of a tower to declare that the rest of the building is irrelevant, that the precious concept of "tower" ought to be reserved for its summit.*
>
> —Frans de Waal

> *True character arises from a deeper well than religion.*
>
> —E. O. Wilson

If my god wasn't real, declare some believers, we would have no reason to be good. Even worse, they say, we would not have the innate sense of moral judgment to even be aware that we were doing wrong. We couldn't possibly understand the difference between good and evil without a god. Laws would be hollow, without foundation. All attempts to be a good person or create good societies would ultimately fail because it is only through my god that we are something more than mere animals.

This view, common among believers in many religions, makes no

197

sense, of course. Do these believers ever pause to think about what it is they really are saying? Do they truly believe that people with no belief in a god are incapable of leading good lives and behaving morally? I understand why so many believers think like this. It is because religious leaders repeatedly tell them that their god placed moral instincts in humans and only their god can keep a lid on our worst desires. But just because you hear it over and over does not excuse accepting this absurd claim. To see how ridiculous it is, believers only have to look out their front door and view the world today. They are not perfect, of course, but hundreds of millions of non-believers are not robbing or killing. They are living peaceful and pro-ductive lives, apparently without help from any gods. Meanwhile, not all, of course, but many millions of believers are raping, robbing, and killing as if there is no tomorrow. It seems that, for some reason, the gods failed to inject them with that inner moral sense believers speak of.

Despite centuries of name calling, prejudice, and persecution, no one has ever been able to demonstrate that nonbelievers are less moral or more prone to criminal behavior than believers. ("Moral" refers here to the most basic concept of positive behavior between humans— i.e., respecting the life, freedom, and property of others.) Every day the world's newspapers include stories about believers doing bad things. The world's prisons are filled with believers who got caught doing bad things. Why is it that so many people who believe in a god keep getting themselves into trouble? If belief in a god gives one the moral high ground, at least compared to atheists, then why aren't non-believers more visible as a leading criminal element in society today? There are, after all, millions of nonbelievers in the United States alone. If they are the most immoral people in America we should notice their reign of terror. Strangely, however, atheists are not raping and pil-laging and generally clogging America's court systems at a detectable rate. These people, supposedly immoral by definition, seem eerily quiet.

I sometimes wonder how so many believers are able to do things that they say contradict their god's wishes. How, for example, can a male preacher carry on a long-term sexual relationship with a man in between sermons about god's condemnation of homosexuality? How do so many priests molest little boys between communion services? How can any Christian read Jesus's Sermon on the Mount and then store up millions of dollars for themselves in offshore accounts? How can any believer anywhere ever fudge their taxes, drive over the speed limit, or cheat at golf? Isn't their god supposed to be watching them at all times? If they truly believed that, wouldn't it motivate them to achieve near-perfect behavior at all times? This has puzzled me to the point that I suspect many believers may not *really* believe their god is real and always present, at least not as confidently as they claim. This is just a hunch, of course. I can't know what goes on in someone else's head so I would never accuse anyone of misrepresenting their belief. Based on what I see, however, I can't help but wonder if most believers mean what they say. I know that if I *really* believed that an invisible god was next to me at all times I am absolutely sure that I would never again so much as jaywalk or make a face behind my wife's back when she nags me to take out the trash. This strange disconnect between belief and behavior leads me to wonder if perhaps the only true believers are the ones we call "fanatics," "zealots," "extremists," and "radicals." Maybe the people who truly believe a god is beside them are the ones who kill strangers for their god, castrate themselves, blow themselves up, or give their lives to religion in a peaceful way such as monks and nuns do. Could it be that the vast majority of "believers" are just posing and pretending? Are they able to pull this off without feeling like frauds because they make sure to never entertain doubts about their god's existence? This might explain why so many weak reasons continue to be cited as justification for belief year after year, generation after generation. To be clear, I am not accusing believers of lying. I am only asking if perhaps they are able to keep believing because they consciously avoid thinking long and hard about why they believe.

If the topic is religion and morals, it never takes long for someone to bring up Adolf Hitler, Joseph Stalin, Mao Zedong, and Pol Pot. "These atheists killed millions of people in the twentieth century, more than religion can ever be blamed for," says the well-worn believer's line. Somehow they think bad nonbelievers prove that atheism is wrong and religion is right. It may be a ludicrous idea but it sure is popular.

Adolf Hitler is always the biggest and baddest name on the believers' monster atheists list. The problem, however, is that Hitler does not appear to have been an atheist. He spoke and wrote of God to support his views. Furthermore, the overwhelming majority of Germans who carried out his orders were Christians. (See chapter 17 about Hitler and Nazi Germany.) Late in his life Hitler seemed to have had some clear disagreements with Christianity but he is not known to have ever become a nonbeliever. It is a safe bet that if there was any good evidence that Hitler was an atheist, believers would have found it by now.

As a child, Pol Pot probably looked like just another cute kid sitting in class at the Christian school he attended. Unfortunately, he grew up to become one of history's most notorious mass murderers. As leader of the Khmer Rouge, Pol Pot took control of Cambodia (Democratic Kampuchea) and committed horrific crimes upon the population. Simply being an intellectual or being educated was reason enough to be murdered as the Khmer Rouge tightened its grip on the country. As many as two million people may have been shot or starved to death in labor camps. This estimate is even more shocking when you consider that the country's population at the time was only about eight million. Pol Pot's behavior was bad by any decent person's standards but what did it have to do with belief or nonbelief? I am an atheist and he was, too, but that does not mean that we share the same worldview or opinions on morality. I respect human life. He did not. I think people should be allowed to think freely. He did not. I respect intellectuals and highly educated people. He did not. I think that it's wrong to murder millions of people or even one person to achieve political goals. He believed it was acceptable. Yes, Pol Pot may have

been an atheist but no believer has ever explained how his behavior is
a strike against atheism. There is nothing to suggest that his crimes
were caused by or motivated by the absence of belief in a god. If
believers think that Pol Pot, Stalin, or any other atheists who committed great atrocities are proof that nonbelief leads to immoral
behavior, then what about the many more believers who have committed extraordinary crimes? What do they prove about belief in gods?

Francisco Pizarro, Saddam Hussein, Ted Bundy, Omar al-Bashir
(Sudan's dictator responsible for genocide in Darfur), Hernando
Cortez, Pope Urban II (launched the Crusades), and Jeffrey Dahmer
were all believers. Do they prove that belief in a god motivates or
causes immoral behavior? Virtually all guards and officers who ran the
Nazi death camps in World War II were Christians. Does this mean
that Christianity inevitably leads all Christians to commit evil acts?
Osama bin Laden thinks that it is acceptable to murder accountants
and receptionists to further his political and religious agenda. Do evil
believers prove that gods are not real? Of course not. And evil atheists
do not prove that gods exist.

A minor technical point to add is that believers are wrong when
they attempt to cite the body counts of atheist dictators in the twentieth
century to show that they were more evil than religious leaders who
went astray. This claim fails to consider available technology. Imagine
if Europe's Christian crusaders had invaded the Middle East with
machine guns, tanks, and four-engine heavy bombers instead of chain
mail, horses, and swords. Imagine if Cortez and Pizarro had mortars
and napalm to help them conquer the Aztecs and Inca. What would
their body counts have been?

End of Faith author Sam Harris offers this stinging rebuttal to the
believers' claim that bad dictators prove something negative about
atheism and something positive about gods:

> People of faith often claim that the crimes of Hitler, Stalin, Mao and
> Pol Pot were the inevitable product of unbelief. The problem with
> fascism and communism, however, is not that they are too critical of

religion; the problem is that they are too much like religions. Such regimes are dogmatic to the core and generally give rise to personality cults that are indistinguishable from cults of religious hero worship. Auschwitz, the gulag and the killing fields were not examples of what happens when human beings reject religious dogma; they are examples of political, racial and nationalistic dogma run amok. There is no society in human history that ever suffered because its people became too reasonable. (Harris 2006)

Harris is exactly right. None of these horrible atheist dictators oppressed, imprisoned, murdered, or started wars to impose a philosophy of free thought, skepticism, and respect for truth upon their nation and the world. I know of no mass murderer who ever had that as his goal. However, I do know of many men who oppressed, imprisoned, murdered, or started wars to impose their religion on others.

It is important to stress that all the talk about bad atheists and good believers does not directly have anything to do with the key question of whether or not gods are real. It has never been shown to be true, but even if believers really were better people than nonbelievers it wouldn't necessarily tell us anything about the existence of gods. It could be that religious belief simply helps to keep people in line through fear and hope. Maybe bad people like Stalin and Pol Pot were bad for reasons that had nothing to with gods. It could even be possible that atheism promotes bad behavior while belief promotes good behavior and yet gods still do not exist. So when believers push this "evil atheist" idea they are wasting their time because it proves nothing about the existence of their gods.

Another problem with the "god gives us morals" claim is that it doesn't make sense in light of what we know about morality. First of all, it is hardly a stretch to imagine that we came up with positive rules to live by on our own. I am pretty sure that humans, the most intelligent life-form that has ever existed on Earth, could have figured out that bashing a neighbor's head in with a rock is disruptive to the smooth running of a tribe, town, or nation. I don't think that rape is so ambiguous an act that a mere mortal could not think of making it illegal. And somewhere along the way some people might have realized all on their own that stealing leads to arguments and problems. Therefore, I can't believe that it was impossible for the species that was smart enough to tame fire, domesticate animals, and invent agriculture to also create a few rules that would help to limit self-destructive behavior.

What if some moral instincts are in our DNA as part of the package that comes with being human? Could natural selection over a million years or so have left us with an innate moral awareness? This is very likely true because we aren't the only primates who are moral. Apes in the wild have been observed doing things that I would interpret as moral behavior, or at least the beginnings of moral behavior. Chimpanzees, for example, are capable of quite nasty behavior but they also share, help one another, protect one another, and show sympathy for one another. Where does this come from? Did a god give them moral awareness too? More likely it was evolution, a process that can shape behavior as much as it shapes fins and eyeballs. Individuals who tend to share food more—and as a result have more food shared with them—might out-reproduce those individuals who only look out for themselves. The end result, after a sufficient number of generations, might be a species that is genetically programmed to share.

Primatologist Frans de Waal writes in his book *Primates and Philosophers*:

> Natural selection has the capacity of producing an incredible range of organisms, from the most asocial and competitive to the kindest and gentlest. The same process may not have specified our moral rules and values, but it has provided us with the psychological makeup, tendencies and abilities to develop a compass for life's choices that takes the interests of the entire community into account, which is the essence of human morality. (de Waal 2006, 58)

In this same book, de Waal cites a fascinating study that shows that what appears to be moral behavior is not exclusive to humans. Rhesus monkeys were trained to pull a chain in order to get their food and then an experiment was set up so that when they pulled the chain a monkey in a neighboring cage would get a severe electrical shock. This would happen within view of the monkey pulling the chain. After learning what pulling the chain would do to his neighbor, one of the monkeys refused to pull the chain for five days. Another monkey went twelve days without pulling! They chose to starve themselves rather than shock their neighbor. Although it was not as dramatic as the monkeys, the researchers even found that rats had this same reluctance to hurt a fellow member of their species. These animals were willing to suffer in order to prevent a stranger from feeling pain. Which is more likely, that a god blessed these monkeys and rats with the gift of moral awareness or that evolution shaped them into social creatures with a strong instinct to care about other members of their species?

De Waal writes in another book, *Our Inner Ape*:

Modern religions are only a few thousand years old. It's hard to imagine that human psychology was radically different before religions arose. It's not that religions and culture don't have a role to play, but the building blocks of morality clearly predate humanity. We recognize them in our primate relatives, with empathy being most conspicuous in the bonobo [an ape species] and reciprocity in the chimpanzee. Moral rules tell us when and how to apply these tendencies, but the tendencies themselves have been in the works since time immemorial. (de Waal 2005, 214)

Why must we view the inclination to do the good and right thing as something magical anyway? Why do we feel the need to credit gods for our sense of right and wrong? Isn't basic decency sort of, well, basic? What about just plain empathy? Why would a god have to give moral instincts to us, anyway? We are smart, we can think. We can imagine how others feel. If a clerk is rude to me at a store I don't go get a gun, come back, and kill him. I am pretty sure that I refrain from doing this not because a god embedded a rulebook into my subconscious mind. I don't even think that I have made it this far in life without killing anyone because I fear a long prison sentence. I don't kill people who upset me because I can imagine the terror they would feel if I pointed a gun at them. I can imagine the pain they would feel if a bullet ripped through their body and shredded one of their internal organs. I can imagine the tragedy of them dying younger than they otherwise would have. I can imagine their family and friends crying at the funeral. I am pretty sure that these are the primary reasons I haven't killed anyone to date. I don't hurt other people because it hurts them. No god had to tell me that and I didn't need to have it engraved on a stone tablet.

In 2006, one of the world's richest people, Warren Buffett, pledged to give thirty-seven billion dollars to another very rich person named Bill Gates. Buffett promised the donation to the Bill and Melinda Gates Foundation. Gates started that organization with his wife in 2000 to attack many of the most serious problems the world's poorest people face. It is nice to see that two of the wealthiest humans who have ever lived care about things other than yachts and mansions. Oh, by the way, Gates and Buffett are atheists. Apparently they were able to find the inspiration and the compassion to try and do some good in the world without a god prodding them.

This is not unusual, according to Marc Hauser, author of *Moral Minds: How Nature Designed Our Universal Sense of Right and Wrong*. "There are an awful lot of people who are atheists who do very, very wonderful things. As an objective question, do people who have religious backgrounds show different patterns of moral judgments than people who are atheists? So far, the answer is a resounding no" (Glausiusz, May 2007).

CHAPTER 27 BIBLIOGRAPHY AND RECOMMENDED READING

Ellerbe, Helen. *The Dark Side of Christian History*. San Rafael, CA: Morningstar Books, 1995.

Glausiusz, Josie. "The Discover Interview: Marc Hauser." *Discover*, May 2007. http://discovermagazine.com/2007/may/the-discover-interview -marc-hauser.

Harris, Sam. "10 Myths—and 10 Truths—About Atheism." *Los Angeles Times*, December 24, 2006. http://www.latimes.com/news/opinion/la-op -harris24dec24,0,3994298.story?track=tothtml.

———. *The End of Faith: Religion, Terror, and the Future of Reason*. New York: W. W. Norton & Company, 2004.

Hauser, Marc D. *Moral Minds: How Nature Designed Our Universal Sense of Right and Wrong*. New York: HarperCollins, 2006.

Joyce, Richard. *The Evolution of Morality*. Cambridge, MA: MIT Press, 2006.

de Waal, Frans. *Our Inner Ape: A Leading Primatologist Explains Why We Are Who We Are*. New York: Riverhead Books, 2005.

———. *Primates and Philosophers: How Morality Evolved*. Princeton, NJ: Princeton University Press, 2006.

Chapter 28

My god makes me feel like I am a part of something bigger than myself.

Many believers say they are energized and empowered by their religion. I don't doubt it. Belonging to a group made up of like-minded people with shared goals can be uplifting. Young people who feel unimportant and powerless, for example, might be able to find comfort by joining a criminal gang. Earning a place on a high school sports team can be a huge boost to a teenager's self-confidence. When an individual joins a group, especially a religious organization that has millions of members, many centuries of tradition behind it, and believes the creator of the universe is at the helm, there is a good chance that she or he will feel more powerful and perhaps even realize a new sense of purpose for her or his life. I don't know if it is a need or merely a desire, but we all seem to enjoy feeling that we are a part of something bigger than ourselves. An anthropologist or psychologist might just say we are social creatures and leave it at that. Some believers, however, cite this phenomenon as evidence of their god's existence. What else but a god could explain the sad individual who enters a church, mosque, or temple only to reemerge happy and vibrant? But maybe there is another explanation, a much simpler one.

I have had personal experiences that seem very similar to what believers say they feel when "connected" to their god. When I visit a good science, art, or history museum, I get a charge out of it that is difficult to put into words. Just being near giant dinosaur fossils, ancient Greek sculptures, and an *Apollo* command module that once orbited the moon excites me and stirs my emotions in ways that I cannot fully explain. Wandering among the trinkets and treasures of science and history can give me immense joy and, yes, it can even make me feel empowered and connected to something bigger than myself.

Whenever anyone asks me to name my favorite museum, I stammer and stumble because I can never do it. Chicago's Field Museum, the Smithsonian Air and Space Museum, the American Museum of Natural History, the British Museum, the British Museum of Natural History, the Louvre, the Smithsonian Natural History Museum, the Cairo Museum, the tiny but unforgettable Luxor Museum, the Metropolitan Museum of Art—how could I ever choose just one? Like my children, I love them all with equal, maximum intensity. I think my museum obsession helps me to understand a little about what believers feel when they are joyfully consumed by their religions. I know it's not exactly the same but it is similar. My heart rate literally rises when I walk up the steps to enter a great museum. Museums are my cathedrals. Artifacts in glass cases are my sacred relics. I truly believe I have felt something close to religious fervor inside some of these buildings. I even feel that I have experienced the occasional transcendent moment inside a museum.

My lifelong passion for science, anthropology, and history has rewarded me with a strong sense of belonging. It's a feeling that connects me to all humankind, to all life on earth, to all life that ever lived, and even to the whole cosmos. Believers may have their gods but I have an entire universe and that's not too bad. Thanks to a general understanding of how the universe works, I know that I am part of something bigger than myself. I am made out of atoms that were forged inside of stars billions of years ago. I am literally part of this vast universe. That's a big connection, certainly enough to prevent an inferiority complex. Clearly one does not have to look to the gods to feel a connection to something grand and spectacular.

I majored in history and anthropology in college and those subjects helped to enlighten me about my link to the entire human experience. Stories about the rise of humans in Africa, wars in Europe, and migrations of people into the Americas and Caribbean resonate with me because I know the characters involved were not aliens with no relevance or connection to here and now. What they did set the stage for the world I was born into. Their stories are my stories too. Their successes and their failures are mine. I claim them all and feel bigger for it.

Anthropology showed me that it's not optimistic fantasy to think of all humans as one big family (dysfunctional though we may be). What I learned in anthropology classes changed me. Later in my life I was able to walk the back alleys and country roads in faraway lands without ever once feeling like I was a visitor from another planet. I roamed around places like Papua New Guinea, East Africa, Fiji, and Ecuador without ever feeling like a stranger. I recognized many differences in cultures and peoples around the world, but ultimately I knew that I was nothing more than a guy wandering around in his own neighborhood visiting long-lost cousins.

The idea of race is one of humankind's all-time greatest mistakes. For centuries we thought it was sensible and morally acceptable to treat people well or poorly according to trivial traits such as skin color, nose dimensions, and hair texture. Now, thanks to anthropologists and geneticists, we know better. Or at least some of us do. Science has shown us that race is a lot more about cultural belief than biological reality. By exaggerating our trivial physical differences, we have divided ourselves unnecessarily, enslaved and murdered fellow humans. When I learned about the simple evolutionary reasons for the physical differences we see between populations, those differences no longer seemed very important. When I learned how closely related all humans are genetically, I didn't feel so distant from the Australian aborigine and the Mongolian nomad anymore. If you want or need to feel connected to a large group, try your entire species instead of some relatively small tribe or religion. There are more than six billion people alive today. I am grateful to the work of historians, anthropologists, and other scientists who have figured out so much about the world, the universe, and ourselves. By feeding off their work, I have been able to enjoy a connection to all humanity and even the entire universe—without having to suspend reason or ignore reality.

When believers say that their religion makes them a part of something bigger than themselves, they usually are not referring to simple membership in an organization with others who share their belief. They mean it is the god they believe in who gives them a special feeling. Believers talk about experiencing a connection to the master of the cosmos. This feeling, they say, could only be possible if the god is real. This is why believers often present the "something greater than me" claim as evidence of their god's existence. But again there is that reccurring problem of contradictory religions. Remember, all religions cannot be true and all gods cannot exist. So when a Hindu enjoys positive feelings of oneness with a god or gods, she is making the same claim that a Muslim makes when he prays and "feels the presence of Allah." But both cannot be correct because the many Hindu gods and the one Islamic god are not the same thing by any stretch of the imagination. Both believers may be sincere about what they are feeling but one, or maybe both, must be mistaken about the source of the feelings.

Considering how common it is for believers to feel connected and empowered through worship, regardless of what particular god is called on, it is clear that belief itself is capable of providing this feeling. A real god is not necessary to experience it. Therefore, no believer can be sure if her or his experience has a natural or supernatural origin. For example, Christians who feel the high of connecting to something "larger" might ask themselves if it is more likely that an invisible god named Jesus really made contact with them or they simply experienced the same psychological phenomenon that billions of other people experience when they worship their gods.

It is important for believers and especially nonbelievers to understand that feeling the presence of a god or sensing a connection to a god does not necessarily indicate mental illness or a lack of intelligence. I think believers sometimes mistakenly feel that they are backed into a corner when their claims are challenged. They see their choice as either stubbornly clinging to the claim that it really does come from a god or admitting that they are fools. But this is not a fair choice. Probably most humans have the potential to "experience gods," whether they exist or not. If anything, feeling a god's presence in the way that billions have done in virtually every culture throughout history is probably evidence of a normal and healthy human mind.

To show how this phenomenon may have more to do with the brain than the gods, neuropsychologist Michael Persinger has conducted experiments that appear to be able to summon a god with the flip of a switch. He has conducted experiments on more than a thousand people to see if there is a biological source for this feeling of connecting with a god. He believes that our brain's temporal lobes can be stimulated to produce what many people interpret as a religious experience.

Persinger wired a modified a motorcycle helmet with outputs that send gentle electromagnetic pulses into the brain of the person wearing it. According to a BBC report, 80 percent of Persinger's test subjects reported the presence of someone or something while they were wearing the helmet alone in a room. A fascinating and telling detail is that the subjects described their experience in ways that matched their cultural background. Muslims would report being in the presence of Muhammad, Islam's primary prophet, for example. Christians sensed the presence of Jesus or his mother, Mary (Hitt 1999).

Some people have raised questions about Persinger's work. They say that the power of suggestion may have led to the test subjects' experiences and not the helmet. Either way, whether it was electromagnetic waves or suggestion, there is plenty of justification to be skeptical about feeling the presence of a god as evidence that the god exists based on Persinger's work. If people can have such a variety of "religious experiences" in a lab, pretty much on demand, it suggests that biological and psychological forces are more likely to be at work than anything supernatural.

CHAPTER 28 BIBLIOGRAPHY AND RECOMMENDED READING

Hitt, Jack. "This Is Your Brain on God." *Wired* 7.11, November 1999. http://www.wired.com/wired/archive/7.11/persinger.html.

Joshi, S. T. *God's Defenders: What They Believe and Why They Are Wrong.* Amherst, NY: Prometheus Books, 2003.

Chapter 29

My religion makes more sense than all the others.

Since it is inconceivable that all religions can be right, the most reasonable conclusion is that they are all wrong.
—Christopher Hitchens

It is stunning how little the typical believer knows about the world's religions. Most Christians, for example, have never read their own Bible and know virtually nothing about Hinduism, Islam, animism, or Sikhism. Most Muslims probably know little or nothing about Mormonism, Scientology, Shintoism, or the difference between Catholics and Protestants. One result of this widespread religious ignorance is that few believers are aware of just how similar their justifications for religious belief are to the justifications cited by people who follow very different religions. They probably also do not know that almost all religions follow a nearly identical pattern. Most religions rely on authority figures, very old stories, early instruction to children, and faith in the absence of evidence. Discovering how similar religions are in the way they operate and survive can be surprising for many believers who have been misled to think that their justifications for belief are unique and superior.

It is nothing less than shocking, some might say scandalous, that so many believers know so little about their own religion. Christians may or may not be the worst offenders but they certainly are in the running. For example, many Christians love to mention that the Bible is the best-selling book of all time, filled with inspiring stories, moral guidance, and invaluable wisdom that can be applied to our daily lives. Despite their glowing endorsements for the Bible, however, few Christians ever bother to read it. It's difficult to understand how some Christians can be so forceful in defending and promoting their religion when they have never read the book that it is based on.

I read the Bible so I know why so few Christians read it from start to finish. It's long, confusing, much of it is boring, and some parts are painfully tedious to get through. The revered King James version is written in seventeenth-century English, which is pretty much a foreign language to most English-speaking people today. Even more troubling for would-be readers, the Bible contains numerous stories and laws that hopelessly contradict the popular image of Christianity as a religion that is about morality, peace, and love. I cannot count the number of times that I have mentioned bizarre or disturbing things that I found in the Bible and the response from a Christian was either a blank stare or absolute refusal to accept that I could possibly be telling the truth. But there really are many jaw-dropping items in the Bible. Most Christians probably know that God killed babies by the thousands, but how many know that mass rape was approved of, if not ordered, by God? In the Bible God doesn't condemn or forbid slavery. He offers tips and rules for how to do it well. God also orders executions for what most of us today would consider trivial offenses unworthy of even a small fine. In addition to the violence, there are also sexual stories in the Bible that would make most Christians blush—if they ever read them. I don't think I'm a prude, but some of the stories are so graphic that I don't think any child should ever be allowed near the book. Nevertheless some adult Christians call for the Bible to be used in public schools as a textbook. I challenge any of these Christians to read aloud Ezekiel 23:1–22 to a fifth-grade class in any school in the United States, for example. If it doesn't get them arrested it certainly will upset some parents.

Not only have most Christians neglected to read their own holy book, far fewer have read the Koran, the central document of the world's second-most popular religion. Probably no more than a handful of Christians have read books that are important to Hindus, Mormons, Sikhs, Buddhists, Scientologists, or other religious people. How, then, can these Christians know with confidence that their belief system is superior to all others? How can a Muslim or a Hindu say their belief system makes more sense than Christianity if they have not read the Bible? It's like a football team declaring themselves champions despite never having played against any another teams. Shouldn't a person know something about another belief system before declaring it invalid?

It is strange but true: religious people don't know much about religion. To be fair, however, no one could possibly be well versed in every religion even if they cared enough to try. There are simply too many. It would be an impossible amount of work, considering that there are probably more than a hundred thousand religions and more than a million gods. Still, if religion is half as important as believers keep saying it is, one would think that they would at least know a little something about today's most popular religions. But few do. Countless times I have heard believers refer to Buddha as a god. They are completely unaware that he never claimed to be a god according to Buddhist scriptures. I also know from personal experience that many if not most Christians are unaware that Allah, the god of Islam, is their god, too. They don't know that the Jewish god, Yahweh, Christianity's God the Father, and Islam's Allah are supposed to be same god. Of course, given how poorly these three groups get along, one can understand why people wouldn't think that Judaism, Christianity, and Islam have anything in common. Many Western believers think Hindus are "cow worshippers" and leave it at that. They know nothing about the diverse and colorful gods that make the Hindu religion so fascinating. Some believers think that all religions are equally valid and that all paths lead to heaven. This sounds wonderfully optimistic but it only makes sense to people who know nothing about the conflicting and irreconcilable claims of the world's religions.

Religious ignorance is of crucial importance to the question of whether or not gods exist because it seems to enable a sense of confidence and even superiority in the minds of believers. The less believers know about rival religions, the more confident they tend to be that they believe in the real god or gods. In the age of television and the Internet many more people than ever before have access to information about the world's various religions. Unfortunately, much of what they hear, see, and read only reinforces the worst stereotypes and therefore strengthens their feelings of superiority. Some Christians think all Muslims are crazy terrorists, for example. Considering the images and conversations that dominate the news media, it's no wonder. Some Muslims think all Christians are warmongers who want to conquer the world. Some Christians think Hindus are under the spell of Satan and worship demonic statues. Some Protestants think the same thing about Catholics. Some Christians and Muslims think all Jews are members of a secret club that controls the world. Some atheists think all believers are dim and deluded bigots. It is too easy to assume superiority for your group when you haven't taken the time to learn very much about other people. Arrogance comes when people are not educated about religions and cultures other than their own. Prejudice comes when we do not get out and mix with people who are in tribes other than our own. One of the biggest drawbacks of organized religions is that they provide more unnecessary and dangerous labels for humankind. Religions have always been very good at creating and maintaining groups. Religions too often give people yet another excuse to divide themselves up into teams so that they can fear and hate "outsiders." Sadly, ignorance within and between religions will continue for some time to be both a source of prejudice and a source of unjustified confidence in the existence of gods.

In case anyone suspects that I am biased against believers and judge them too harshly about their lack of religious knowledge, many surveys have confirmed that most religious people really are clueless about religion. Stephen Prothero, a professor of religious studies at Boston University, is the author of *Religious Literacy: What Every*

American Needs to Know—And Doesn't. His book offers a revealing look at just how ignorant many believers are about other religions and often even their own. He focuses on what American Christians don't know about Christianity and other major religions. The results are surprising for a country that takes its religion so seriously. "If religion is this important, we ought to know something about it, particularly in a democracy, in which political power is vested in voters," writes Prothero. "But the average voter knows embarrassingly little about Christianity and other religions" (Prothero 2007, 5–6).

He finds that Americans also stumble when asked about non-Christian belief systems. "When it comes to religions other than Christianity, Americans fare far worse. One might hope that US citizens would know that the most basic formulas of the world's religions: the five pillars of Islam, for example, or Buddhism's Four Noble Truths. But most Americans have difficulty even *naming* these religions" (Prothero 2007, 6).

Do not assume that Americans are unique. According to Prothero, most of the world's believers know very little about religions other than their own, too. My experiences in talking with various believers around the world confirm this. Prothero correctly points out that it is dangerous when billions of people passionately believe in things that they barely know anything about. It is also dangerous when two or more groups of believers are in conflict and neither side knows very much about the beliefs and motivations of the other. "Today religious illiteracy is at least as pervasive as cultural illiteracy and certainly more dangerous," Prothero writes. "Religious illiteracy is more dangerous because religion is the most volatile constituent of culture, because religion has been, in addition to one of the greatest forces for good in world history, one of the greatest forces for evil" (Prothero 2007, 4).

Prothero calls for schools to teach students more about religions to address this problem. Easier said than done, however. This would be a huge challenge as the line between education and indoctrination could easily blur in many schools. I agree that it would be good if students were taught about the history and the supernatural claims of at least ten or fifteen of the more popular religions. However, I am not sure that religious people would be happy with the likely results of such an effort because one of the fastest ways to turn a believer into a nonbeliever is religious education. Teach someone, especially a child, an honest and objective overview of Christianity, Islam, Hinduism, traditional Chinese beliefs, Buddhism, animism, Sikhism, Judaism, Jainism, Bahism, plus the basics of a few extinct religions, and there is a good chance that this enlightened person will have a hard time convincing themselves that one of these belief systems is valid and all the others are not. Religious ignorance is faith's ally. Religious education is faith's enemy.

I am convinced that one of the reasons, perhaps *the* reason, that I don't believe in any gods is because I took the time to learn a little bit about them. My academic background in history and anthropology left me thinking that it was less likely that gods created us and more likely that we created them. There are so many gods and yet not a single one of them has enough compelling evidence to jump ahead of the pack. This makes it difficult to justify believing in one above all others. The lack of religious knowledge that is common among believers also explains why virtually every believer on earth today believes in the god that his or her parents believed in and/or the god that is most popular in their culture. But how can anyone feel confident that they got it right if their choice of a god and religion was based less on information than on ignorance?

A common behavior that betrays how common religious ignorance and prejudice is in the West is that virtually every believer and nonbeliever consistently leaves out every god but one when they discuss belief. "Is there a God?" "Is God dead?" "Where was God on September 11?" It's always singular and with a "G" in uppercase. Why do most believers in North America, South America, and Europe act as if there is only one god worthy of talking about or debating? This makes no sense because believers say gods are unrestricted by time and geography. For example, an obscure long-forgotten Sumerian god could be the one real god and nobody even brings him up anymore. Isn't it an insult to polytheists when only one god is discussed as if that covers it all? After all, their claim that many gods exist is no more or less supported by evidence than the monotheists' claim that there is only one god. Perhaps if believers knew more about past and current religions, they would be more inclusive.

Competent religious education is a direct threat to belief because it is far easier to believe in a particular god when one operates under the false assumption that it is the only god belief on the table. When one discovers that there are many thousands of gods that humans have come up with throughout history, confidence may waver. "Wait a minute," thinks the newly educated believer. "If people have been making up gods by the thousands since the beginning of civilization and probably earlier, then how can I be sure that my god is not made up too? If other religions claim to have miracles, prophecies, and holy books, then what reason do I have to think my religion is true and theirs is not? If people who believe in other gods experience personal encounters with their god, then how do I know my personal encounter was real? How can I be sure my religion makes more sense than theirs when there are so many similarities between them?"

The believer who declares that his or her religion makes more sense than all others makes a hollow claim. There is no superior religion when it comes to claims about the existence of gods. Yes, some religions may have followers who are economically superior or may be rooted in societies with greater military power, but when it comes to the claims a religion makes about the existence of a god or gods there is no ascending scale of credibility. All gods are equal. They are equally without good evidence and equally without strong arguments. No one today considers it but the truth is, Hera is just as likely to be a real god as Jesus is. Jupiter has the same amount of evidence supporting his existence that Ganesha has. But believers who know nothing of other gods and other religions cannot know this. People who are confident that they belong to the one belief system that is superior to all others must ask themselves how it is that they know this. Most likely, it is a conviction that depends upon a lack of knowledge about other religions. Sensible believers who consider this are likely to realize that they must look elsewhere to justify their belief. A declaration of religious superiority is nothing more than evidence of ignorance.

CHAPTER 29 BIBLIOGRAPHY AND RECOMMENDED READING

Barna, George. *The Index of Leading Spiritual Indicators*. Dallas, TX: Word Publishing, 1996. Contains some surprising statistics about America's believers.

Bowker, John. *World Religions: The Great Faiths Explored and Explained*. New York: DK Publishing, 1997. Excellent artwork highlights this general reader on religion. Good for young readers.

Crapo, Richley H. *Anthropology of Religion: The Unity and Diversity of Religions*. Boston: McGraw-Hill, 2003. A good anthropological overview of religion.

Knott, Kim. *Hindusim: A Very Short Introduction*. New York: Oxford University Press, 1998. Excellent, easy-to-read introduction to one of the world's most popular but least understood religions.

Prothero, Steven. *Religious Literacy: What Every American Needs to Know—And Doesn't*. San Francisco: Harper, 2007.

Trainor, Keven, ed., *Buddhism: The Illustrated Guide*. New York: Oxford University Press, 2004. Beautifully illustrated sweeping survey of Buddhism. Great for casual browsing.

The Upanishads. Baltimore, MD: Penguin Books, 1965. Sacred writings of the Hindu religion.

Chapter 30

My god changes lives.

"**I** asked Jesus to come into my heart—and He set me free from homosexuality—forever. That day God changed my life, and I will be eternally grateful to Him for what He did. Within two days I was out of my partner's bed, and within two weeks I moved out of my partner's home and was on my way and walk with Jesus Christ. My life now is wonderful. I am truly free, and it is all because of Jesus Christ and His love for me."

These are the words of Stephen Bennett, a "former homosexual." His story is posted on a religious Web site called "Hope for Homosexuals" that seeks to convince gay people that Jesus can change them into heterosexuals.

Ted Haggard, a former White House adviser, antigay activist, and mega-church preacher, was exposed in 2007 for having a longtime sexual relationship with a male prostitute. After just three weeks of prayer and religious counseling, however, he was "cured" of homosexuality (Gorski 2007).

These are remarkable claims. Sexuality is a powerful thing and for it to be so dramatically reengineered is clear evidence that a god is real, say many believers. But the gods do not only change sexual orientation, it seems. According to believers, they also cure alcoholism, drug addiction, promiscuity, and many other problems. But is this good evidence for the existence of Jesus? No, it is not. It could be compelling evidence if it was only Christians who claimed their god changes lives. The reality is, however, that numerous people within virtually every religion make the exact same claims. Tom Cruise says Scientology cured or at least significantly improved his dyslexia (Morton 2008, 245). Does that mean Lord Xenu, a central character in Scientology doctrine, really exists? When Mormons say their religion changed their lives, are we all to conclude that the Book of Mormon must be true? There are countless stories of Jews, Hindus, Muslims, and animists who say a god changed their life. I have heard many of these stories firsthand. I have even seen a few of them happen right before my eyes. I can't say for sure that a god was responsible but that's what the believers claimed.

What is really going on here? How are so many lives being redirected in such dramatic fashion if there is not a god behind it? Christians, for example, have challenged me to explain how an imaginary god could possibly get a gay man to stop dating men. They are also curious as to how a make-believe messiah could ever get so many people to stop drinking, stop taking drugs, stop beating their wives, stop gambling, or stop smoking. The answer I offer is that Jesus must do it the same way that Allah does it, the same way Ganesha does it, the same way that Dionysus used to do it, and the same way thousands of spirits in the forest do it for animists.

People have been crediting a long list of gods for radically changing their lives for a long, long time. It is nothing new or unique to any one particular religion. Using these stories as justification for believing that a god exists reveals how little some people know about rival religions because they all make the same claims. "Scientology put me into the big time," says film star John Travolta (Morton 2008, 101–102). Allah changed the life of a petty criminal named Malcolm Little by turning him into Malcolm X, the famous black rights activist. This canceling-out effect of so many people in different religions making identical claims is only part of the problem for believers. Another weakness of this claim is that one cannot be certain that it was a real god who caused a person to change or merely the act of believing and participating in a belief system that did it. There are, after all, many other things that have the power to change lives without a god, including: training for a marathon, reading books, changing careers, moving to a new country, joining a gym, surviving combat, battling cancer, making a new friend, falling in love, getting married, having a baby, and so on. All of these are examples of activities and events that can radically change a person's life for the better and none of them require a god's help. Yes, deciding to begin making regular visits to a church, mosque, or Hindu temple may turn out to be the key to improving one's life but it would not be evidence for the existence of gods.

The most likely explanation for all these stories of gay men becoming heterosexuals and alcoholics putting down their bottles is one that omits the gods. These people probably experienced their life-altering shifts as a result of belief itself or from joining a network of people who supported them rather than from the direct manipulation of a real god. That would explain why Christians, Muslims, Hindus, Jews, animists, and other believers could all have their lives dramatically changed within the context of their respective belief systems. Across so many religions and so many cultures, belief, not real gods, is the one thing that they all have in common. What is most likely occurring with all these believers is that they were able to feed upon the inspiration and power of their belief system to change their lives. Perhaps making progress on the challenges before them had been hindered mostly by a confidence problem. Perhaps these individuals had the ability to change their lives all along but lacked sufficient belief in themselves to pull it off. Believing in a god, real or not, however, might have been enough to finally give them the boost needed to forge ahead with a new life. None of this suggests that believers who make dramatic life changes in the name of their god are mentally weak or lack courage. It is human nature to feel empowered when part of a team.

I was a member of my high school track and field team and I remember that running a leg on the 4 × 400-meter relay squad usually gave me the ability to dig a little deeper in the homestretch than I was able to do in my individual races. There was something about those other three teammates having a stake in my performance that inspired me to try harder. But they weren't on the track to help me when it was my turn to sprint that lap. I had to go it alone. They couldn't physically push or pull me any faster because they existed only in my mind during the difficult final one hundred meters. But it was enough to somehow squeeze a little more speed out of my tired legs. Perhaps it is this way for the believer too. Maybe their god is not really there but belief alone, a god in the mind, is enough for the believer to dig a little deeper and do what they feel they need to do.

It is clear that just being around supportive people and tapping into the emotional boost that all religions are capable of providing can have a positive influence toward achieving a goal or avoiding destructive behavior. This certainly is a sufficient explanation and it seems far more likely to be true than the extraordinary claim of an invisible superbeing magically injecting willpower into people. The problem with the idea of a god changing lives is that we cannot separate the god from the belief. What believers say is the power of a god might only be the power of belief influencing their actions. While no atheists can be absolutely certain that no god is behind dramatic changes in the lives of individuals, we all can see that many lives are changed dramatically all the time without any claim of a connection to gods. This makes the other transformations, the ones said to be the work of gods, less certain. Therefore it is fair to ask why, when there is a far more simple explanation available, should we accept the most extraordinary explanation of all?

CHAPTER 30 BIBLIOGRAPHY AND RECOMMENDED READING

Gorski, Eric. "Haggard Says He Is 'Completely Heterosexual.'" *Denver Post*, December 24, 2007. http://www.denverpost.com/ci_5164921.

Morton, Andrew. *Tom Cruise: An Unauthorized Biography*. New York: St. Martin's Press, 2008.

"Stephen Bennett: The Amazing Story of Stephen Bennett." Stephen Bennett Ministries, "Hope for Homosexuals." http://familypolicy.net/hope/?p=349.

Chapter 31

Intelligent design proves my god is real.

To surrender to ignorance and call it God has always been premature, and it remains premature today.

—Isaac Asimov

Even noble souls can become corrupted with wrong education.

—Plato

Science is a philosophy of discovery. Intelligent design is a philosophy of ignorance. You cannot build a program of discovery on the assumption that nobody is smart enough to figure out the answer to the problem.

—Neil deGrasse Tyson

If any positive evidence could be found of a super-natural guiding force, there would be a land rush of scientists into it. What scientist would not want to participate in what would be one of the greatest discoveries of all time? Scientists are simply saying—particularly in reference to intelligent design—that it's not science and it's garbage until some evidence or working theory is produced.

—E. O. Wilson

Look at a flower. Take note of the little pollen grains ready to hitch a ride on the next visiting insect. Try to remember your junior-high science class and marvel at how the plant uses the sun's energy to live.

Watch a bird in flight. Think about how all the bones, muscles, tendons, and ligaments in each wing must work in harmony to keep the bird aloft.

Think about the DNA molecule within a single cell of a dog or a horse. This microscopic stuff contains all the information needed to produce a complete animal.

How can life be anything other than the work of a god? After all, the design we see in all the plants and animals means there must have been a designer, right? How could blind chance ever produce the amazing variety of complex plants and animals we have on Earth? Estimates of the number of species alive today range from ten million to one hundred million. Individually or collectively, life is too complex to have just happened all by itself, believers declare. Cells don't just fall together to create giraffes and buffaloes. Only a god can explain life.

This is a very attractive reason to believe in gods. It must be appealing because it's been used to justify belief for a long, long time and it's still going strong. The complexity and apparent intelligent design of life may be the most common reason people give when asked why they believe a god or gods exist. It is a popular argument from virtually every religion. I can't begin to count the number of times a believer has said something like, "How can you doubt my god? Just look at a leaf or a butterfly." But do leaves and butterflies really tell us anything about the existence of gods?

Intelligent design is the idea that life's complexity is evidence of an intelligent designer, such as a god. It has made many headlines in the United States in recent years, primarily because of school-board battles over teaching it in science classes. However, it hasn't made many headlines in leading science journals because it is more about religion than science. Intelligent design is nothing new, however. It's just another name for traditional creationism. The best argument intelligent design can make is that life is too complex to be fully explained as the result of natural processes and therefore life must be the work of a super-intelligent being. That super-intelligent being could be anything. The vast majority of people who embrace intelligent design, however, do so to justify their belief in a god—more specifically, *their* god.

Although the intelligent design debate might seem overly complicated, there is really just one aspect of this issue that one needs to understand to recognize that intelligent design doesn't make sense and is not a good justification for belief in a god. Proponents of intelligent design say it in many ways but ultimately they only make one big claim: science cannot explain everything about life, therefore a god must have created life.

All this does is point out the obvious and then jump to an unjustified conclusion. Of course we haven't figured out all there is to know about life. No scientist denies that. But the world's scientists are nowhere near ready to declare that all remaining mysteries in biology can only be explained by gods and magic. They are too busy making new discoveries to even consider giving up. Yet, many intelligent-design believers make the outrageous suggestion that life is too complex for us to *ever* understand it fully. All intelligent-design believers are doing is giving up on science so they can declare the game over and say their god won. They want to end the hunt for answers prematurely because they imagine that they already have the answer—their god. They "know" intelligent design is real because they see design in life, the work of a super-intelligent being, which just happens to be their particular god. But this makes no sense. Several thousand years ago, people with this same attitude might have declared that the bizarre thumps heard within a human chest were obviously the rattlings of a magical soul and should never be investigated. But some people didn't give up the scientific quest for knowledge and today we know that the beating is not a soul knocking on the ribcage but a very important organ that pumps blood. Any "impossible-to-solve mystery" that intelligent-design believers cite today is very likely to end up as tomorrow's common knowledge. This is a trend that has held up for many centuries now.

Don't bet against science because you will probably lose eventually. Science has really only picked up speed in the last couple of centuries. A little patience might be in order here before we throw in the towel and grab at supernatural answers. In trying to understand our world we have come so far in such a short period of time. Due primarily to the rapid rise of computing power, it is likely that science will advance faster this century than ever before. So how can anyone suggest that science will never come up with a natural explanation for something, for anything? Shouldn't we work the problems a bit more before giving up? Shouldn't we have a little more faith in the power of science and of the human mind?

Intelligent design encourages us to stop looking for answers. It would have us steer in the opposite direction of scientific curiosity. So what if we don't know everything there is to know about cells, genetics, or the evolution of humans at this moment in time? We can't give up! Who cares if we do not yet know every detail about every species? Scientists are working on thousands of challenges right now and making progress. Some answers may elude us forever, but that's okay too. Not knowing is never a reason to give up, declare that a god did it, and go home. Ignorance should not be feared and it's never a good reason to fill in the blanks with gods. Admitting ignorance and being mature enough to live with it is far more honest and respectable than making up answers. Ignorance should inspire us to keep striving. Ignorance should drive science, not stop it cold. Imagine where we would be now if scientists a hundred years ago had decided that the questions before them were unanswerable and stopped trying. Where will we *not* be a hundred years from now if today's scientists actually embraced this intelligent design idea and began labeling the unknown as "explained as the work of God"?

An often-overlooked weakness of creationism or intelligent design is that, even if it is true, it does not offer an explanation of anything. It just says "god[s] did it." Okay, so *how* did your god do it? Evolution explains how life changes: genetic mutations, genetic drift, and natural selection. Proponents of intelligent design, however, just say "god" or "intelligent designer" and then act as if they have explained everything. Saying a god did it may be an attempt to explain "who" but it does not explain "how." What if Charles Darwin just wrote "nature did it" and left it at that? His book *On the Origin of Species* would have been very short and not very enlightening.

Since intelligent-design believers are always attacking evolution as the rival to their god's creation story, it is important to point out that evolution does not directly address the origin of life. Believers almost always frame the debate as creationism/intelligent design vs. evolution but this is misleading because creationism/intelligent design is primarily a claim about the beginning of life while the theory of evolution only claims to explain how life changes over time. The theory of evolution does not answer how life began on earth. Many believers may be surprised to learn that most scientists today freely admit that they don't know how life originated. There are some very interesting ideas under investigation but, given the time factor of at least four billion years ago, we may never know with confidence exactly how life got its start.

Another problem with intelligent design is that its own reasoning works against it. Intelligent design declares that complex things such as life must have been the work of an intelligent creator. If that is true, however, it means that the intelligent creator—obviously complex—must have been designed and created by some other intelligent being. So who is the creator of our creator? Shouldn't believers be more interested in worshipping this creator instead? After all, creating a god is far more impressive than creating barnacles, palm trees, and humans. Of course, believers usually respond to that by claiming that their god is infinite and did not need a creator. Well, if that is possible, then maybe life is infinite with no beginning too. Maybe life always existed and just arrived here on earth from somewhere else.

There are three primary problems with intelligent design that every believer should consider. First, it has no evidence to support it. Second, intelligent design doesn't say anything about *how* life was created. Third, intelligent design encourages us to give up on seeking answers. It suggests that some mysteries of life are too complex to have a natural explanation. That is the worst form of antiscience imaginable.

Intelligent-design believers are right about one thing. There really is design in nature. They are not hallucinating and they are not stupid for stating the obvious. When I look at an ant or a flower, I don't see a random and accidental collection of cells that were thrown together by blind chance. I recognize design the same as believers do. What I do not see, however, is evidence of an intelligent designer. What many believers may not be aware of is that the theory of evolution does not claim that life is the random, accidental result of blind chance. This may be what believers are repeatedly told by preachers and antiscience activists but it is a misrepresentation of the truth. There is a designer. But it's not intelligent and it certainly doesn't need to be worshipped. Its name is evolution.

CHAPTER 31 BIBLIOGRAPHY AND RECOMMENDED READING

Brockman, John, ed., *Intelligent Thought: Science versus the Intelligent Design Movement*. New York: Vintage Books, 2006. This is a powerful collection of essays that demolish the claim that intelligent design is science or even sensible.

Brown, Barrett, and Jon P. Alston. *Flock of Dodos: Behind Modern Creationism, Intelligent Design and the Easter Bunny*. New York: Cambridge House Press, 2007. I wouldn't recommend this book to more sensitive believers but many others would find it both educational and hilarious.

Dawkins, Richard. *The Blind Watchmaker*. New York: W. W. Norton & Company, 1996.

Forrest, Barbara, and Paul R. Gross. *Creationism's Trojan Horse: The Wedge of Intelligent Design*. New York: Oxford University Press, 2004. This is required reading for anyone who believes that intelligent design is science and not religious creationism.

Humes, Edward. *Monkey Girl: Evolution, Education, Religion, and the Battle for America's Soul*. New York: HarperCollins, 2007. A good story about what happens when science and religion collide.

Shermer, Michael. *Why Darwin Matters: The Case against Intelligent Design*. New York: Times Books, 2006. Shermer presents a readable concise case for evolution.

Chapter 32

Millions of people can't be wrong about my religion.

One man's theology is another man's belly laugh.
—Robert A. Heinlein

A popular though clearly misguided justification for belief in a god comes from the notion that there is strength and truth in numbers. It is understandable how believers fall into this faulty reasoning. The typical Hindu in India looks around and sees that he is surrounded by nearly a billion other Hindus—almost one-sixth of the world's entire population. Naturally he says, "My religion must be correct because all these people couldn't possibly be wrong." But the Muslim looks around her neighborhood, her country, her region, and sees millions of Muslims. Today more than a billion people worldwide are Muslims. Meanwhile, the Christian surveys the world and notes that he belongs to the most popular religion of all with more than two billion followers. They couldn't possibly all be wrong about Christianity, he thinks to himself. So who is right? Is anyone right when they make this claim? Can we really tally up the membership rolls and declare a winner? Or is it perhaps a bit more complicated than that?

One of the reasons that religions have thrived for so long is because most people are either nearsighted or virtually blind when it comes to other cultures. Sadly, most people are mostly unaware of what goes on in other places around the world. Even trying to keep track of international news is not enough to build an accurate picture of the world. News focuses on dramatic events and interesting people. It is by its nature a distortion of reality. People in the West may know there is an Africa and a Middle East, for example, but since they don't live there or visit, they are nothing more than names heard on television. They are no more real than characters in some TV drama. So when a typical child grows up in the United States or Mexico, for example, the religious isolation can be profound. Christianity will probably be imposed on the kid by family members. The broader culture probably will further reinforce the belief. During all of this, in the child's most formative years, there is little or no education or discussion about other religious beliefs or about nonbelief. The end result of this common process is usually an adult who knows very little about other religions, much less the option of atheism, and is totally ignorant of how the numbers of believers and nonbelievers stack up globally. For example, I have found that many Christians are surprised when I tell them that about 70 percent of the world's people do not believe that Jesus is a god. They are aware that other religions exist, of course, but know little about them. Why would they? Most Christians live with Christians, go to school with Christians, play with Christians, marry Christians, and work with Christians. They are told both directly and indirectly that Christianity is the true religion, the real religion. It is easy to see why many of them end up with greatly exaggerated views of their religion's global acceptance and credibility. The same thing happens to many Muslims. A typical child born in Saudi Arabia, for example, is immersed in Islam from birth. No one gives her an objective assessment of the varieties of religious belief available. There is even less likely to be an unbiased explanation of religious skepticism and atheism provided. From day one the child is told that Islam is right and by default all other belief systems are wrong. It is doubtful that anyone will ever tell the child the simple fact that 80 percent of the world's people do not believe the claims of Islam.

The top predictors of a person's religious belief are what their parents believed and where they spent their childhood. This impact of inheritance and geography upon belief is powerful and consistent. It also explains a lot about how the world's religions survive generation after generation. This pattern is exactly what one would expect to see in a world where gods are not real and the continuing belief in them is the result of childhood indoctrination. The geography of religion, the fact that we can speak of "Muslim countries" and "Christian societies," suggests that very little comparison shopping and even less deep thinking is going on when it comes to deciding which god is more likely to be real and which religion is more likely to be correct. Rarely is a god chosen based on the weight of evidence, or which sacred scripture makes the most sense, or which religion has the best human rights record. In virtually every case, the choice of a god is determined by family and culture.

There is no guarantee of truth to be found in the number of believers alone. It does not matter how many millions or billions believe in a particular god. Millions and even billions can be dead wrong. In fact we know that at the very least a few billion people are wrong because it is impossible for the Christians, Muslims, Hindus, and animists to all be correct. What matters when it comes to assessing the gods is the quality of the claims for their existence. Good evidence and powerful arguments can make a strong case, no matter if only one person believes. Conversely, if everyone on earth believed in Zeus that alone would not be enough to prove he was real.

CHAPTER 32 BIBLIOGRAPHY AND RECOMMENDED READING

Barker, Dan. *Losing Faith in Faith: From Preacher to Atheist.* Madison, WI: Freedom From Religion Foundation, 1992. This book reveals fascinating insights into the journey of a man who was a committed and sincere Christian preacher but dared to think freely and ended up an atheist.

Warraq, Ibn, ed. *Leaving Islam: Apostates Speak Out.* Amherst, NY: Prometheus Books, 2003.

Chapter 33

Miracles prove my god is real.

Psychologists have extensively studied the tendency for people's judgment to be dominated by a single, salient example when more accurate and representative statistical evidence is available.

—Keith E. Stanovich

My search for a miracle has led me to a small Florida church. I've heard about miracles all my life and today I want to see one with my own eyes. A traveling faith healer is here to work his magic so there is a good chance I will get my wish. But I have to wait. Standing with fifty or so believers, I pray and sing for about thirty minutes. I actually like the singing. The songs are beautiful. Yes, an atheist can enjoy religious music. I also enjoy Christmas Eve with my family even though I don't believe Santa Claus is really going to come down the chimney.

Suddenly, the singing stops and the preacher launches into a standard, but still scary, sermon. He warns everyone to get right with God before it's too late. Jesus can return any day, any moment, he says. If you haven't repented your sins and accepted him into your hearts before he comes, then you will end up in hell, he declares with a tone of utter certainty. The people around me seem impressed, maybe a little worried too. Many of them nod in agreement. I wonder if any of these believers know that many Christians in every generation over the last two thousand years have expected Jesus to return in their lifetime.

As miracle time approaches, I start to feel a bit nervous. Even though I prayed and sang just like the believers did, I'm not sure that I fit in. I doubt they would want me here if they knew I was just a tourist, just passing through to see the sights. I didn't lie to anyone, of course. Everyone just assumed that I believe in Jesus. I am, of course, harmless. I didn't come to mock these people, look down on them, or disrupt their event in any way. I don't think I'm smarter or better than them just because they believe in magic and I don't. The only reason I'm here is because I want to learn something new. I'm just curious. My subterfuge only goes as far as their assumptions, anyway. All it would take to expose me is one direct question. I wouldn't lie to them.

Another round of singing takes my mind off being outed, but not for long. A believer in the first row keeps glancing back at me during the song. Does he suspect? Did he glance in my car on his way into the church and see those telltale anthropology and philosophy books on my car seat? Did he notice that I don't know the words to most of these songs? Has he put two and two together? My heart pounds. I know from past experiences that some believers are so disturbed by being in the presence of a real live atheist that they will do anything to avoid all contact. It's not a nice feeling. It's like becoming an instant leper and nobody wants to heal you. Sometimes I think believers are under the impression that skepticism and critical thinking are contagious. Then again, maybe they are. Deep down, I really don't care for my own sake if they discover that I'm a fan of Charles Darwin and PBS documentaries. What concerns me is that I'm on their turf and I don't want to spoil the mood. Everyone is so happy and charged up. I wouldn't want to ruin the party.

Finally, it's miracle time. I made it. The visiting preacher takes over center stage. He has above-average charisma and a pretty good voice but I've seen better. If faith healing were pro baseball, this guy would be a minor league prospect hoping for a shot at the big leagues.

But today, here in this small church, he is a heavy hitter and the fans are on their feet and cheering.

After a short explanation about how God promised to heal the sick, he calls for the sick to come forward.

"Who's hurting? Who's ailin'? Who needs a miracle here today?"

A few hands go up and the preacher calls them up to the stage. All eyes follow the believers as they walk to the front of the church. The visiting preacher selects one and sits him down in a chair. He tells the audience that the man has back pain. There were no words exchanged so it seems as if we are meant to believe that the preacher read the man's mind or received the diagnosis directly from Jesus. Then he grabs the sitting man's feet and straightens them out. The preacher seems to line up the feet and then tells us that there is a problem. He invites anyone interested to come closer and see for his or her self. Without hesitation I move in fast for a good look. The preacher explains that one of the man's legs is shorter than the other and that this is the reason for his back pain. He's right, the feet don't line up. It appears that one of the believer's legs is at least two inches shorter than the other one. Or maybe it is just the way the preacher placed the legs together.

The faith healer begins to pray loudly. He asks Jesus for a miracle while violently shaking the man's legs. And then it happens. The miracle occurs. The preacher puts the man's feet back together and—"hallelujah!"—they are perfectly aligned. A miracle came, right on cue. Or maybe it is just the way the preacher placed the legs together. Audience members shriek and cry. They thank Jesus. Some speak in tongues. Then the "healed" believer shoots up out of the chair and, without any coaxing from the preacher, declares that his back pain is gone. He grins and dances around to show everyone how great he feels.

Sure it was dramatic and I have no reason to think the preacher or the man with back pain were faking. However, I'm not convinced I saw a miracle. Everyone else in the room seemed to accept it without question. But why aren't they considering other possible explanations? Did the preacher manipulate the man's legs by placing them at an angle or pulling one leg straighter than the other? Did the man know that it didn't work but decide to play along out of fear or politeness? Were the faith healer and the believer working together in order to trick us? Was the believer's back pain improved by the power of suggestion? I don't know what it was for sure, of course, but there was no way I could just accept this as a miracle, not when so many simpler explanations are available.

Religious people may not believe me but I would love to have seen an undeniable miracle that day. I'm not opposed to supernatural healings from a god. I think most of the world's nonbelievers would welcome such an experience. I certainly haven't closed my mind to the possibility of miracles. At this point, however, after so many centuries of unproven claims, it seems unlikely that any form of magic or miracle will ever be revealed. One has to ask why the gods seem to always direct their miracles toward people who lack skepticism and critical thinking skills. Don't hardened skeptics and by-the-book scientists have a right to enjoy the excitement and wonder of an occasional miracle as much as anyone else? In fact, one would think that they are the people who would benefit most from them. Who needs a miracle more than an atheist? Why do the gods seem to waste them on people who already believe?

Although I was let down by the faith healer who stretched a man's leg and called it a miracle, I am not suggesting that this one experience means all claims of miracles are invalid. It is, of course, possible that there have been real supernatural events caused by a god. But if miracles were anywhere near as common as believers have claimed for centuries, there should be at least one that the world's scientific community would be able to confirm as undeniably the work of a god. But there are none, not a single one.

Sometimes I wonder if people who say they believe in all these miracles really do. I have seen faith healer Benny Hinn call down miracles from heaven to "cure" cancer and AIDS. But why didn't this astonishing medical achievement lead the evening news that night?

Why wasn't Hinn on the front page of the *New York Times* the next day? Every branch of the United States government's leadership is dominated by Christians. Why hasn't the government recruited Hinn to empty hospital beds across America? The answer, of course, is that most believers know that miracles are not real. If a holy man or praying could cure AIDS and cancer, then we wouldn't see many deaths from those diseases anymore. The only people who would be in danger of them would be atheists. And there wouldn't be very many atheists for very long because they would eventually notice that believers never get sick and promptly get with the program.

Supernatural events caused by a god may or may not be real, but they certainly have not been scientifically confirmed. It is therefore a mistake for believers to cite miracles as good evidence for the existence of their gods. There is also the fact that miracles are not exclusive to one god or one belief system. Just about everybody has miracles so how believable can they be? For example, how can a Catholic claim that a "weeping" statue of the Virgin Mary is evidence of their god's existence when we also have milk-drinking statues of a Hindu god to consider?

It had happened before, but when new reports came out about a statue of Ganesha drinking milk in New Delhi, millions of Hindus immediately were electrified with joy and excitement over the "miracle." Ganesha is the popular elephant-head god and a temple statue of him reportedly was "drinking" milk from pans, bowls, and even cupped hands. "People observed that Ganesha is drinking milk around 8 pm," a New Delhi temple priest told the *Times of India*, "after which the word spread and thousands thronged the temple to try it out. Lord Ganesha drank milk from all and sundry."

"It was actually happening," said Meenakshi Kumar, an excited believer. "Ganesha drank milk from my hand!" (*Times of India* 2006).

It is important to note that miracles such as health cures, weeping statues, and thirsty gods are not enough to convince most people that a particular god is real. They tend to only reinforce belief in those who already believe in the god credited for the miracle. Those who are outside of a particular miracle's belief system tend to favor explanations such as fraud or mistaken interpretations of natural events. There seems to be a necessary predisposition for belief in the god associated with the reported miracle in order for most people to be impressed by it. This is why we do not see millions of Muslims converting to Catholicism because some Catholics have claimed to have been healed in Lourdes, France. This is why we do not see Catholics becoming Hindus when a statue of Ganesha is said to be drinking milk. The fact that people in virtually every religion claim that miracles exist would seem to suggest that there is something less godly and more human about miracles. It is doubtful, for example that Ganesha would make a statue of the Virgin Mary cry and it is also seems very unlikely that Jesus would drink milk through the statue of a Hindu god. A much more reasonable explanation is that miracles of all religions are probably hoaxes, hallucinations, or simply natural events we do not yet fully understand. This much is clear: claims of miracles are not a good reason to believe in a god.

CHAPTER 33 BIBLIOGRAPHY AND RECOMMENDED READING

"Ganesha Drinking Milk Again." *Times of India*, August 21, 2006. http://timesofindia.indiatimes.com/articleshow/1910537.cms.

Gardner, Martin. *New Age: Notes of a Fringe Watcher*. Amherst, NY: Prometheus Books, 1991. Great writing from a great skeptic.

Nickell, Joe. *Looking for a Miracle: Weeping Icons, Relics, Stigmata, Visions & Healing Cures*. Amherst, NY: Prometheus Books, 1998.

Sagan, Carl. *The Demon-Haunted World: Science as a Candle in the Dark*. New York: Random House, 1995. If you only read one book on science, skepticism, and critical thinking, make it this one. My highest recommendation.

Vyse, Stuart A. *Believing in Magic*. New York: Oxford University Press, 1997.

Chapter 34

Religion is beautiful.

Religious awe is the same organic thrill which we feel in a forest at twilight, or in a mountain gorge.

—William James

I am in a small room in a shopping plaza in the Cayman Islands. All around me are Jamaican immigrants who have crammed themselves into this makeshift church to worship their god. The glare of bright dresses and fancy hats fills my eyes while the song "Old Rugged Cross" fills the room. About thirty of us sit in metal folding chairs surrounded by bare walls and not much else. The room is smaller than the closets in most churches but it does have one thing going for it. There is an unpretentious outpouring of love all around me, enough to make an atheist wonder if these believers might be on to something.

These Jamaicans are among the hardest-working people in Cayman. They do the tough blue-collar jobs that Caymanians prefer to avoid. They are construction workers. They clean homes. They cook. They care for other people's babies. Probably all of them work at least six long hard days per week. I imagine that this time must be a precious escape from their burdens.

Some of them smile. Some cry while smiling. One old man's scarred and calloused hand tightly clutches his Bible. He opens it and I can see tattered pages soaked through with yellow highlighter ink.

Some sentences are underlined in red. A large woman in front of me suddenly begins to shake. Her hands shoot up as she appears to be suffering, or enjoying, involuntary spasms. "Let's welcome the Holy Ghost!" someone shouts as the singing continues.

It's difficult to resist the rising flood of emotion and excitement. Why fight it, I ask myself. The believers are swept away by the moment and, before I know it, so am I. No, I don't see any gods or feel that Holy Ghost they keep screaming for, but I am definitely feeling the power of the people. The sentimental lyrics, delivered with rare passion, seem to surge right through me. I notice that I have been swaying with the music without even realizing it. I feel like I belong here. As the song concludes, their joy, tears, and voices have touched me deeper than I ever would have imagined possible. I look around the room and know that I am surrounded by something beautiful. Yes, they are worshipping a god who probably isn't real, but that's okay. It doesn't diminish my respect for these people or for the beauty of a moment like this.

Immediately upon entering the Church of the Holy Sepulcher in Jerusalem I am drawn to the Stone of Unction. An excited believer tells me that it was on this actual slab of rock that the body of Jesus was cleaned and wrapped for entombment after he was taken down from the cross. The people around me obviously believe the story. They also seem to think that the stone possesses some sort of magical residue of Jesus. No one seems to be concerned about whether or not there is any evidence that a god was ever laid on this particular rock or that it has magical powers now.

Just a few feet away from me, an old woman is "bathing" in the Stone of Unction. With closed eyes, she gently wipes the surface of the rock with her hands and then rubs her face, neck, and arms. She moves slowly, with grace and purpose. It's as if she is performing an intricate ballet, yet nothing about her movements seem artificial or rehearsed. I interpret her actions as an attempt to capture and apply the stone's magic to her body. Yes, her behavior seems odd, maybe even ridiculous, but I am absolutely captivated by it. I can't look away. Much to my surprise, I can't help but smile as I watch her attempt to sop up the stone's powers. Something about the scene is beautiful.

I later researched the Stone of Unction and discovered that there is no chance at all that this stone could possibly be the actual stone that the body of Jesus once rested upon. The stone that is there today was placed in the Church of the Holy Sepulcher in the 1800s. If there ever was such a stone it's either under the rock that is visible today or it's not there at all. I wonder how that woman who bathed in the Stone of Unction would react if she knew that Jesus could not possibly have touched it two thousand years ago. Maybe she did know or at least suspected that it wasn't a magical stone, but still didn't care. Maybe for some, truth and reality do not matter when it comes to religion. This is not beautiful.

I am standing at the center of the courtyard in the Umayyad Mosque in Damascus, Syria. Ancient Romans once worshipped Jupiter in a temple that stood on this same site. But Jupiter's fame crashed long ago and he is left with few believers today. Not that anyone ever proved that he does not exist. Like thousands of other gods, Jupiter simply faded away. This leads me to wonder: can a god still exist even if no one believes in him or her? What if all the gods we know are fiction but the one real god has no believers? Wouldn't that be weird?

Today, Umayyad Mosque stands as one of the oldest active mosques in the world. Some believers in Damascus tell me it is the oldest in the world. Colorful tiles, white stone, and religious passions synchronize to create a remarkable atmosphere. Overall, the building is beautiful. The architecture is not overbearing but still powerful. I feel small here. I'm not a Muslim but I do sense the energy and presence of more than a billion people who are. Most of the believers I encounter in Syria are friendly and every believer I meet in the mosque is friendly. Their kindness and hospitality add to the beauty of the scene. I feel welcome. But not for long, as I cannot forget the unspoken ugliness that taints the beauty here.

Some Muslims think it is justifiable to kill nonbelievers if they refuse to convert to Islam. I read the Koran and understand why some more passionate believers would think that Allah wants this. There are statements in the Koran that seem to suggest that killing nonbelievers is not only acceptable but a duty as well. Fortunately, most Muslims disregard this or offer softer interpretations of the scarier passages and point to peaceful quotes within the Koran that would seem to counter calls for violence against nonbelievers. Still, some Muslims do believe that "kill the infidels" means kill the infidels. This is not beautiful.

Religions have been an inspiration and guiding force for human passions for thousands of years. Belief in gods has generated songs, architecture, paintings, sculptures, smiles, and laughter. It would be foolish to deny that there is great beauty to be found in religion. However, it would be equally foolish to celebrate and fixate on the beauty while ignoring the ugliness that is also there.

Religion is similar to nature in that many people think of the natural world as universally beautiful. But this ignores reality. For every gorgeous waterfall to photograph there is a deadly tornado to flee. For every bright flower bouncing in the summer breeze there are millions of microbes waiting to kill us in slow and agonizing ways. So it is with religion. Every time good people sing "Old Rugged Cross" beautifully and from the heart, there is a preacher out there somewhere who is delivering a poisonous sermon that encourages believers to hate others and to embrace a medieval ignorance of the world. Wars and evil deeds that were inspired by or sanctioned by religion provide a counterbalance to all the goodness that comes from religion. For every life improved by belief in a god, there are lives damaged by it. The belief-inspired mistreatment of countless millions of girls and women alone proves that. It is either a mistake or outright dishonesty to describe popular religions such as Christianity, Islam, Hinduism, and Judaism as completely peaceful and wholly good.

It should not be seen as a blanket condemnation of religion to speak the truth. Honest believers have an obligation to admit that their religions are less than beautiful. For example, how can a science-literate Christian refuse to call it anything but ugly when other Christians insist on teaching children that the world is ten thousand years old and life does not evolve? How can a sophisticated and worldly Jewish person not cringe at the segregationist behavior of some Jews? How can a peace-loving Hindu call all of Hinduism beautiful when it inspires some to hate and even kill those who follow a rival religion? And how can good Muslims see Islam as completely beautiful when its prayers are whispered by a suicide bomber the moment before he kills himself and others?

At best, we might call religion a complex part of human culture that includes the potential for both good and bad. It is beautiful *and* hideous. Those who insist on denying that religion is often repulsive are dishonest. Religion was not beautiful when an Aztec priest plunged a stone dagger into the chest of a living, breathing human being and then ripped out his still-beating heart. It wasn't beautiful when religion inspired the Crusades and the Holocaust. And religion is not pretty when it motivates terrorism, antiscience activists, and prejudice among people who might otherwise be cooperating to build a better future for everyone.

Religion has caused unimaginable suffering for so many people throughout history. For example, can any one of us sense how terrible it really must have been for the women who were burned alive after believers condemned them for being witches? Don't skim over this little historical item just because you have heard about it many times before. Try to imagine how astonishingly evil it is to tie a woman to a wooden pole, pile up branches around her feet, and then burn her alive. Imagine the terror and intense pain they suffered. And this kind of thing didn't just happen to a few people. Thousands of people in Europe and around the world have been killed for allegedly practicing witchcraft. Today, despite the fact that witchcraft is still as unproven as any other supernatural claim, the killing continues. Every few months or so, a news report is published that describes the murder of an accused witch somewhere in the world. For example, the BBC reported in 2006 that more than one hundred people in a rural village in India took part in the beheading of a man, whom they accused of practicing black magic. Just to be thorough, the mob also chopped off the heads of four of his children. "They said the killings would appease the gods," explained an investigating police officer. The BBC report added that police records reveal that approximately two hundred people have been killed for practicing witchcraft in that same area in the previous five years (*BBC News* 2006).

Religion can be ugly. Very ugly.

Defensive believers can rest assured that it is not a total condemnation of religion to point out obvious problems. Keep in mind that virtually everything in human culture is a mixed bag. Sports, politics, art, business, and education are all messy combinations of good and bad, beautiful and ugly. Sports has both champions and cheats. Politics has both servants and crooks. Science is wonderful until it sells out to irresponsible corporations and ignorant politicians, or is used to create weapons and technology capable of bringing about our extinction. Nothing we humans do is perfect or perfectly beautiful.

Believers might consider that this does not have to be a make-or-break issue. One does not necessarily have to surrender loyalty to a religion or even their belief in a god in order to acknowledge the evil within religion. If one chooses to believe in a god or gods, so be it. But how can anyone possibly justify that belief by claiming that her or his religion is beautiful? A casual glance at the past and present clearly shows that religions are terribly flawed in many ways. A nonbeliever might speculate that this is the inevitable result of human rather than divine origins. In any case, religion in its totality falls well short of anything we might justifiably call beautiful.

CHAPTER 35 BIBLIOGRAPHY AND RECOMMENDED READING

"Indian 'Witchcraft' Family Killed." *BBC News*, March 19, 2006. http://news
    .bbc.co.uk/2/hi/south_asia/4822750.stm.

Chapter 35

Some very smart people believe in my god.

Intellect distinguishes between the possible and the impossible; reason distinguishes between the sensible and the senseless. Even the possible can be senseless.

—Max Born

It was obvious early on during my interview with Jane Goodall that she was the real deal. The famous primatologist was sharp and thoughtful. She was a deep thinker and well versed on many subjects. As I expected, she was brilliant on apes and conservation, but no less so on the issue of poverty too. I loved every minute of the encounter. It was the kind of interview I live for. This was about more than just getting a good story. I was going to walk away from it smarter than I was when I sat down and maybe even a bit inspired, too.

Before Goodall's remarkable career spent observing wild chimpanzees in Africa, humans were thought of as the animal kingdom's only tool users. Goodall forced a rewrite of that definition when she saw chimps making and using tools in the wild. Today she is widely considered to be one of the great scientists of the twentieth century and one of the greatest female role models ever. Her contributions have made a huge impact on how we view ourselves, other animals, and our place in nature. She also believes in a god.

It would be ridiculous to suggest that Goodall's religious belief in a god somehow cancels out or diminishes her intelligence. She is, by pretty much any definition I can think of, a very smart person. I have interviewed numerous astronauts of the *Mercury, Gemini, Apollo*, and space shuttle programs and found all of them to be every bit as intelligent as one would expect of people who make their living riding rockets. Although religious belief did not come up in every interview, I would guess that most if not all of them believe in a god.

Despite the existence of smart believers such as Goodall, some atheists jump to the conclusion that people who believe in gods must necessarily be dumb. Come on, they say, only a fool would believe that there are invisible beings floating around in the sky watching us and granting our wishes. How could any intelligent person believe such ridiculous things?

Ridiculous or not, any nonbeliever who says that all or most believers are unintelligent sounds pretty dumb themselves. There are far too many exceptions to make the case that dumb people believe in gods and smart people do not. Believers already know this very well. They are aware that numerous engineers, lawyers, medical doctors, and Nobel Prize winners believe in gods. They know this because smart people are sitting next to them in their churches, mosques, and temples every weekend. While it may not be very smart to accept claims of a god's existence with no good evidence to back it up, it does not stop millions of highly intelligent people from believing in gods.

Some religious people go too far the other way, however, pointing to intelligent and highly educated believers as evidence that their god or gods must be real. This does not hold up as a good reason to believe in a god. People are complex. The human mind contains many rooms. One can be very smart in one sense and less so in another. Human minds—even exceptionally intelligent ones—seem to have the ability to compartmentalize irrational beliefs in ways that shield them from the kind of analysis and challenge that is used diligently with other matters. This is why there probably are many students today in prestigious law schools who think astrology is a valid predictor of the future and many students in top medical schools who believe in ghosts. These are not weak thinkers; they are inconsistent thinkers. Highly intelligent people who believe in a god seem to have erected some kind of wall inside their heads that shields belief in a god or gods from the intellectual force that they bring to bear on other matters.

Imagine a smart believer who is looking to buy a new house. One can safely assume that they would make an effort to look around each room, scan the walls for cracks, peek in the closets, and ask many questions. They would let loose plenty of analytical and skeptical fire-power before closing the deal. But one would think that purchasing a home would be much less important than deciding on whether or not to believe in a god or which god to believe in, especially given the possible eternal implications. More than likely, however, a typical home purchase is given far more thoughtful analysis than the selection of a god to worship. Do you think Jane Goodall applied the same rigorous thinking to select Jesus over Apollo that she did to her scientific field-work in Gombe? How many believers bother to research even a small fraction of the numerous religious options that are available? Why isn't there a demand for some form of a shopping guide for gods, similar to *Consumer Reports Magazine*? Most believers today, regardless of their religion, have never even heard of Insitor (Roman god of agriculture) or Hazi (Hittite mountain god). So how can they be sure they shouldn't be worshipping them? After all, there was a time when many very smart people believed they were real.

Why do the analytical skills and skepticism that most people utilize when buying a house, car, or laptop vanish when religion comes up? Why don't believers ask hard questions and refuse to accept hollow answers the way they do for almost everything else? Why can't fundamentalists seem to recognize the numerous errors and contradictions in their holy books? Obviously they are capable of seeing errors and contradictions because they are so good at identifying them in the books and claims of rival religions.

Finally, the fact that many smart people believe in gods doesn't help answer the question of whether or not gods are real. It clearly is not a good reason for anyone to believe in gods any more than the existence of smart atheists is a good reason to reject belief. The unlikely existence of gods has nothing to do with what kind of people do or do not believe in them. For example, I don't give great respect to scientists just because they are smart. I respect them because they base their conclusions on the scientific method and I know other scientists are checking their work.

Gods probably are not real because there is no good evidence to suggest that they are. This fact would not change even if every Mensa member were a believer who spoke in tongues and juggled rattlesnakes during Sunday church services. If everybody on earth with a doctoral degree believed that Mbongo, the African river god, was real it would not be enough to prove that he is. Only evidence and overwhelming arguments can do that. Never look up to people or follow passively in their wake when it comes to belief in gods. So what if some guy has an impressive degree, a fancy professional title, or an impressive vocabulary? That stuff doesn't do anything to strengthen claims that a god is real. Forget the quality of a given religion's membership rolls and ask for evidence. Always ask for evidence.

The same applies to atheists. No one should ever conclude that gods do not exist solely because some scientist or a philosopher said so. Ask them *why* they don't believe. Never make the mistake of thinking that we can simply poll the brightest people to determine if gods exist or not. Reality is not a popularity contest. Reality is what it is, regardless of who knows it.

CHAPTER 35 BIBLIOGRAPHY AND RECOMMENDED READING

Dawkins, Richard. *A Devil's Chaplain*. Boston: Houghton Mifflin, 2003.

Chapter 36

Ancient prophecies prove my god exists.

I have recently been examining all the known superstitions of the world, and do not find in our particular superstition one redeeming feature. They are all alike, founded upon fables and mythologies.
—Thomas Jefferson

He is everywhere, this god of the Jews, Christians, and Muslims. I discover an echo of Yahweh/God the Father/Allah around every corner in Jerusalem's Old City. Even the yellow stones around me seem soaked through with belief. I lean against a building and watch as a parade of Christians pass. Their leader plays a guitar while several others sing. Some of them are crying. They are retracing what they believe to be the path their messiah walked on the day of his execution two thousand years ago. According to the Bible, Jesus promised to return to his followers very soon. Twenty centuries later, however, they are still waiting.

A Jewish man walks by at a brisk pace. He has a baby in his arms and smiles as he passes. The automatic rifle slung over his back is a reminder of the fear and hatred that is never far away in the Holy Land. The Old City is divided into ethnic or religious "quarters." Integration is a concept that has not caught on here. Military checkpoints and terrorism warning posters sour a city that could have been an

251

inviting time capsule of human history. Jerusalem may be a sacred place. It may even be God's chosen place. But it is not a happy place.

Approaching the Noble Sanctuary, all I can think of is how peaceful and calm it looks. Of course, appearances can be deceiving. This place is a flashpoint of religious prejudice, hatred, and violence. There are some believers who gladly would kill or die either protecting or destroying it, depending on which version of the same god they are loyal to. The Dome of the Rock stands out with its shiny golden roof, glowing and rising above the stone city. This is arguably the most sacred piece of real estate on the planet. If any god has a specific address on earth, this must be it. It was here, say Muslims, where Muhammad rode a winged horse up to heaven to meet Allah. Many Muslims are convinced that the end of the world as we know it is coming soon and their messiah will visit the earth to finally show everyone that Islam is the one true religion. Jews and Christians, of course, are far too skeptical to believe that this will happen in this way. They are unconvinced, probably aware that in sixteen hundred years Muslims have failed to produce any convincing evidence to support this extraordinary prediction.

Many Jews see no beauty in the golden dome. They see only a misplaced structure built by misguided believers. For some it is a crude and horrible violation that must be destroyed before crucial prophecies can be fulfilled. This is where Yahweh wants his most important temple to stand, not this Dome of the Rock. Jews who believe in the prophecy wait for the day when they will be able to rebuild the temple and watch their god's plan unfold. When this happens, they say, the true messiah will finally come and it will be confirmed that they really are God's chosen people and they were correct to reject Christianity and Islam. Muslims and Christians are far too skeptical to believe that it will happen in this way, of course. They are unconvinced, probably because in thousands of years Jews have failed to produce any convincing evidence to support this extraordinary prediction.

Meanwhile, inside the nearby Church of the Holy Sepulcher, visiting Christians are praying, weeping, and posing for photographs. They have a prediction, too. Theirs is similar to the Jewish and Islamic prophecies except that their messiah, Jesus, has already been to earth once. Next time will be his second visit, they say. And it is going to happen any minute now. We are close, very close to the end of the world as we know it, some Christians say. Muslims and Jews are far too skeptical to believe that this is correct, of course. They are unconvinced, probably because in two thousand years Christians have failed to produce any convincing evidence to support this extraordinary prediction.

What is convenient about all of these messiah predictions is that he is always "coming" and never needs to actually get here for the prophecies to be accepted and defended as true generation after generation. It is difficult for a nonbeliever to understand how so many people across so many centuries can continue to be confident that they will see the messiah in their lifetime. How many more centuries must pass before believers start to doubt? How many more thousands of years must pass before we can all agree that these predictions are unlikely to ever come true?

Magical predictions of the end of the world are never far from one's mind in Jerusalem. Millions of people believe that Israel itself is the fulfillment of a prophecy. Many Jews and Christians say that their god created the nation of Israel, just like he promised he would long ago. "Fulfilled" prophecies such as this are a powerful motivation for many believers. They feel confident that their god is real because he made promises and kept them. For many believers, prophecy is the clincher, the decisive proof that their religion is true.

After a few days of exploring the Old City, I venture outside the walls to see more of Jerusalem. At the Israel Museum I find an impressive collection of art and ancient artifacts. There is no shortage of creativity or passion in this land, I think to myself. In a garden outside the museum, I meet and chat with a group of beautiful Israeli women. Their smiles and laughter make me feel welcome in this place that is so far from my part of the world. Later, I wander around Yad Vashem, a sprawling complex of museum exhibits, outdoor sculptures, archives, and memorials dedicated to teaching about and remembering the Holocaust. It is obvious that this young nation has a powerful sense of its history and that unity means a great deal to its people. Much of that unity, I suspect, is the result of past suffering and present dangers. Outside the Holocaust museum building, I see hundreds of Israeli soldiers stream out of buses. Apparently a visit to Yad Vashem is part of their duty. As they stack up their rifles on the lawn before entering the museum, I am stunned by how young they are. They are too young to be carrying guns and wearing military uniforms, I think. Far too young to hate or be hated. But here in the Middle East belief in a god has led to separation, fear, hate, and the inevitable violence those mistakes bring. Guns and young soldiers are necessary for survival. But why? Why have Jews, Christians, and Muslims found it so difficult to live in peace for the last several centuries? Is it because Yahweh/God the Father/Allah was not clear enough about how he wanted to be worshipped? Or maybe it was the fault of prophets who failed to communicate his messages properly. Regardless of the reason, the result has been a never-ending clash between believers who share both the same god and the same unwavering confidence that they know his will. Christians and Muslims slaughtered one another during the Crusades and now seem dangerously close to a rematch. Christians slaughtered Jews in Europe for centuries. And, of course, Jews and Muslims are at each other's throats in the Middle East. For my entire life I have heard about peace plans, cease fires, and peace summits for the Middle East. I believe that these kinds of efforts have always failed and always will fail because they never address the root problem of religion. The way to bring people together who are separated by belief in a god is to get them to take that belief a little less seriously. The people of the Middle East need doubt. They need skepticism. So long as warring sides are 100 percent certain that their belief is true, they are unlikely to ever yield.

Later that evening I end up at a shopping mall where I happily stumble upon a good bookstore, good food, and a movie theater. I like this place. It's almost enough to make me forget about all the problems and controversy that burden Israel. Almost.

Hatred. Settlements. Intifada. Walls. Tanks. Suicide bombers. Children throwing rocks. Segregation. Prejudice. Babies dying. And all the while, both sides point to the God of Abraham to justify their actions.

God is love? Through the eyes of a nonbeliever, all of this bears a remarkable resemblance to insanity.

Back on the streets of Old Jerusalem once again, I wonder how it is that I could be walking on "evidence" of a real god. I am in the nation that many Christians claim to be irrefutable proof that their god is real. The nation of Israel, they say, shows that the Bible correctly predicted the future in a way that only a god could. Therefore, they declare, the Jewish/Christian god must be real.

It is odd that so many believers are convinced that their god magically created the modern nation of Israel. There is, after all, a much simpler explanation available—one that does not require faith, magic, or a god. One only has to consider the fact that many Jews around the world emphasized and cherished a cultural and religious link to this region. Jews also have a long tradition of believing that this land was promised to them by their god. Many of them didn't just feel that it would be nice to live there; they believed they were *supposed* to live there. It was where their god meant for them to be. No doubt the intense persecution Jews suffered in Europe helped motivate the drive for a new nation. Jews dreamt of once again praying at the remains of the Jerusalem Temple, not as visitors but as residents. Some Jews did more than dream. They worked to make it happen. Theodor Herzl (1860–1904), for example, pushed so hard and so long for a Jewish homeland that today he is honored as the father of Zionism. (Zionism was the international movement for the establishment of a Jewish homeland.) Herzl believed that anti-Semitism was so bad and so incurable that the best hope for Jews was simply to leave Europe and other places where Christians continually discriminated against Jews and sometimes murdered them. The idea of a Jewish nation in Palestine fit well with the beliefs of many Christians too.

For many years Jewish people around the world, some of them

wealthy and influential, worked to realize their goal of creating a Jewish nation in the Middle East. The United States and some European nations were agreeable to the idea more than ever after the horrors of the Holocaust, and in 1948 the State of Israel was created. But how is this the obvious work of a god? How is it the magical fulfillment of a prophecy? Let's keep in mind that creating countries was nothing new to Western powers. After all, nations such as England, Germany, and the United States had redrawn national borders as they pleased and pushed people around many times before all over the world. So where exactly is the supernatural component in the creation of Israel? Why do believers imagine they see magic and gods in what appears to have been a completely human-engineered event?

Now, if the Knesset and other Israeli government buildings rose instantaneously from the ground, fully constructed and with a fresh coat of paint, *that* would be something to get excited about. Or even if Israeli flags had sprouted magically from the soil, that would be a good reason to suspect that this was the divine fulfillment of an ancient prophecy. But when the feat was accomplished by the United Nations, the governments of the United States and Great Britain, and many highly motivated Jewish people, it cannot reasonably be considered a magical feat. Maybe it was the work of a god but where is the evidence for such an amazing claim? United States president Harry Truman was a Christian and was well aware of the claim that God promised the Jews a homeland. This probably influenced his decision to officially recognize the new nation. There is no evidence at this time that a god cast a magical spell on Truman to make him support the creation of Israel.

I wonder how Herzl, the visionary of Zionism, would feel about Israel today. Undoubtedly he would be proud of the strength, productivity, and beauty of the nation and its people. But what would he say about the violence, the growing tension between secular and orthodox Jews, and the walls? Would he be heartbroken to see that still, in the twenty-first century, there is no universal peace between Jews, Christians, and Muslims? Would he reconsider any of his beliefs about

Zionism, religion, or his god? Or would he believe that this is precisely what his god wanted?

For me the bloody history and current conflicts between these three religions seem more likely to be the work of imperfect humans rather than an all-powerful, super-intelligent, and perfect god. Why would a real god who knows the future set such madness in motion? Anyone with a clear head and a good heart can see that hating Jews because they are Jews is immoral. But how many people also admit that it is wrong for some Jews to isolate themselves from the rest of humankind in the name of loyalty to a god? There are neighborhoods in Jerusalem that I was told not to walk in because the ultraorthodox Jews who live there would throw rocks at me because they don't tolerate "others." One morning at the Temple Wall, I was approached by a man wearing a little yarmulke and a big smile. I told him I was a visitor and he enthusiastically welcomed me to Jerusalem and wished for me to have a wonderful visit. For a moment I sensed that I might be making a new friend. But then he asked me if I was Jewish. When I told him I was not, his smile vanished and so did he. It was extraordinarily abrupt and rude. He was only interested in knowing me if I was Jewish. It was so shallow and shortsighted. Why should unproven gods influence who we talk to, who we befriend? Why should it matter if I don't belong to this god's tribe or that god's tribe? I am still a fellow human. Turning our backs on one another, whether it is for nationalism, race, or gods, is always bad for humanity in the long run. Maybe the answer is not to build new nations and erect new walls. Maybe the answer is to finally confront the problem of religious belief as a dangerously divisive poison in our species. Is any religion really so obviously true that it justifies separating people? Is any god so obviously real that killing people is justified? For all our evils, for all the killing we have done over land, resources, and gold, killing for invisible gods that may not even exist may be the most unforgivable crime of all.

Although I mentioned the Israel prophecy, there are, of course, many more. And they are not just found within Judaism, Islam, and

Christianity. Numerous religions over thousands of years have made a big deal out of their god or gods fulfilling predictions. But all of them are so vague, flexible, or unconfirmed by credible sources that one usually has to already be a believer to be impressed. I'm not Jewish or a Christian. Therefore, the creation of Israel does not convince me that their god is real. I simply think that it's far more likely that Jews wanted their own country so they lobbied for it, worked for it, and got it. I don't see a god in that process, whereas a Jew or Christian might. Don't prophecy-believers understand that if just one of their prophecies were unambiguous and confirmed by credible unbiased sources, it would convince virtually everyone in the world overnight? The fact that no prophecies from any religion have ever done this is telling. If just one religion had one clear prediction that could not be easily explained away, there would be a rush of people to join that religion. But it hasn't happened because no religion has such a prophecy.

The excitement about prophecies that we see in many diverse religions is likely a result of the fact that most people don't think critically. This is why Nostradamus still has fans in the twenty-first century. He never made an impressive prediction about anything that came true but he still shows up in books and on television today. This is also why astrology continues to be profitable, despite having no basis in reality. This is why people give their money to psychics despite the likelihood that they are frauds.

For those believers who are certain that some obscure prophecies really did come true, even that is not good enough. People who believe in gods have been making thousands of predictions for thousands of years. Isn't it likely that at least a few of them would come true just by luck alone? Even the bumbling psychics of today get a few things right every now and then. Besides, anyone can predict the future accurately. Try it yourself. Write down fifty predictions on fifty separate sheets of paper and then seal them all in individual envelopes, and don't open them until a year has passed. Assuming you are not the unluckiest person in the world, you will get at least a few of them correct. Here's the trick, only show your friends the ones you got right. A few of them will be convinced that you are a psychic or a religious prophet. They might even want to give you money.

To really excel at predicting the future, always be vague—very vague. For example, don't say, "A five-foot two-inch man named Wilber T. McFurter from Gifford, Florida, will be elected president of the United States within the next ten years." That is way too specific, too risky. No smart prophet would ever paint himself or herself into that corner. Instead, say: "A wealthy religious person of European descent will be elected president of the United States within the next fifty years."

Dan Barker, the man who went from Christian preacher to atheist, was deeply immersed in biblical prophecy claims during his days as a believer. It reinforced his conclusion about Jesus being a real god and he used prophecies to convince others that Christianity was true. When he allowed himself the freedom to think critically, however, it all fell apart. This was a man who studied the Bible from cover to cover. He learned it, loved it, preached it, and believed in it completely. But critical thinking popped the bubble. Today, Barker knows that there are no predictions made by the Bible that are so specific, accurate, and otherwise inexplicable that they can stand as evidence of a god's existence. Barker writes:

> Christians, if they want to be consistent, and if they desire to convince us unbelievers, should welcome a close examination of their holy scriptures. Perhaps the reason they avoid close scrutiny is that such inquiries only show that the claims of the fulfilled predictions are either gross exaggerations or downright lies. The refutation of prophecies can be arranged into five general categories: vagueness, forced fulfillments, post-dated predictions, nonprophecies and chance fulfillments.
>
> Some predictions are so vague or general that any number of situations might be made to fit. "For nation shall rise against nation, and kingdom against kingdom; and there shall be famines, and pestilences, and earthquakes, in divers places." (Matthew 24:7). There have been twenty different centuries since Matthew that could have

> qualified as fulfillment of that situation. Christians for two thousand years have consistently considered that the world is ending. The world is "always ending." The imprecision of this "prophecy" makes it impossible to nail down. (Barker 1992, 190)

What about Jesus? His appearance on Earth was "prophesized" and then he came, right? Well, not exactly. Where was it predicted and where was it fulfilled? It all happens in the Bible, one book. There are no historical records that verify the events of Jesus's life beyond the Bible. No other sources collaborate the story of his virgin birth and resurrection. The Bible is the only source we have for predictions of Jesus's life so it is not sensible that the same book can be cited as proof that the predictions it makes came true. Suppose I handed you a book and said it was obviously a true story because something is predicted in chapter 1 that later comes true in chapter 25. Based on that alone, would you be convinced that the book is factual? Of course you wouldn't. You would be more likely to conclude that the author wrote it that way in order to make the story work like she or he wanted it to.

Anyone who thinks it is reasonable to accept claims of predictions and fulfillments in the same book or story would have to swallow a whole lot more to be consistent, including the gods of ancient Greece. Ever heard of the Oracle at Delphi? A priestess accurately predicted future events many times, at least she did according to stories written more than two thousand years ago. By the standards of contemporary prophecy believers, then, she must have been magically tuned in to Mt. Olympus, which can only mean that the Greek gods are real.

For some reason, however, followers of one religion transform into hardcore skeptics when followers of other religions hit them with their prophecy claims. That's why Christians aren't converting over to Islam by the tens of millions when they hear about the Prophet Muhammad and Islamic predictions that the end is near and signs of it are all around us. This is why millions of Muslims aren't converting to Christianity, despite all of the "fulfilled" prophecies contained in the Bible and "clear signs" that Jesus is about to return.

Like most other atheists, I am not insane and I don't like pain. Believe me, I don't want to suffer in anyone's hell for all eternity. If there were just one precise and detailed prediction that came true and could only be explained as the work of a god, no matter if it were in the Bible, Koran, Torah, Bhagavad Gita, *Dianetics*, David Koresh's diary, and so on, I would not ignore or deny it. If gods are real and they want to impress all of us with their prophecies, then why don't they make the predictions obvious to everyone, including well-meaning skeptics? Imagine, for example, if a holy book was discovered in the 1990s and contained the following ancient prophecy confirmed to have been written down more than three thousand years ago:

> In a year to be called 1969 by the people of tomorrow, two men named Neil and Buzz will ascend to the Moon and walk upon its surface. A metallic bird named Eagle will serve as their chariot and they will do a thing called EVA while wearing white. Upon their heads will be large sturdy hats. Shields of gold will protect their eyes. The people of the Earth will cheer them from afar. Upon the return of the two men, plus one named Michael, many will shout the name *Apollo*. As the Lord saw their flag standing in the stillness of the lunar landscape, he did smile.

Now if a believer can show me a prophecy with that kind of detail, I'm on board with their religion. Sign me up. But such predictions simply do not exist. The ones we have are vague or too easily explained as events that could have occurred without the involvement of a god. To make matters worse, some believers defend the murky nature of prophecies. They say that their god wants it this way so that faith will be required of followers. If the god made it obvious, then it would be too easy to believe, they say. But why would a god only want gullible people to believe? Why would a god make his or her existence so mysterious and so unlikely as to trick those who think critically and ask questions? Why would a god give us powerful minds and then bar us from heaven if we use them?

CHAPTER 36 BIBLIOGRAPHY AND RECOMMENDED READING

Barker, Dan. *Losing Faith in Faith: From Preacher to Atheist*. Madison, WI: Freedom From Religion Foundation, 1992.

Callahan, Tim. *Bible Prophecy: Failure or Fulfillment?* Altadena, CA: Millennium Press, 1979.

Chapter 37

No one has ever disproved the existence of my god.

I can't prove that there are no fairies living in my backyard. Maybe they are there. They could be there. Why couldn't they be there? No matter how strongly I may doubt that tiny winged humanoid creatures are buzzing around in my garden, I can't prove that they aren't. I never see them when I look out the window or walk around in my yard but maybe that's because they see me first and hide. They could be highly evasive thanks to hummingbird-like wings that make them fast and agile. Perhaps they are so well camouflaged that I often look in their general direction but fail to recognize them because they blend in with the bushes and flowers. It is even possible that these fairies can read my mind and know when I am about to look in their direction. This advance-warning system allows them to fly away just before I spot them. Even if I set up a video camera in my yard to record images of them at night when I'm sleeping, it might not work because these fairies could have a magical force field that renders them undetectable to cameras and other electronic equipment. Even more frustrating is the possibility that they are invisible all the time. This would mean I have no chance of ever seeing them.

Despite my inability to disprove the existence of fairies in my backyard, I do not believe in them. It doesn't matter that I can't come up with any evidence or argument that conclusively proves fairies are not real. All that matters is that there is no positive evidence to support any claim that they are real. No evidence most likely means no fairies. No evidence definitely means no reason to believe in fairies.

One can, of course, replace "fairies" with elves, aliens, trolls, ghosts, angels, demons, genies, and, yes, even gods. How, for example, can I be sure that Ogiuwu, the god of death, does not live in my backyard alongside the fairies? I can't because I can't think of a way that would conclusively disprove the existence of an invisible god in my backyard. But does this mean that I am obligated to believe that Ogiuwu is really there? Just to be safe should I begin conducting human sacrifice rituals to appease him? People used to kill for Ogiuwu all the time. How can any Muslim, Jew, or Christian, for example, be sure that the Hindu snake god, Nagaraja, is not somewhere in their backyard? They can't be sure because it's an elusive god with the ability to become invisible. No one has ever disproved the existence of this god. So should Jews, Christians, and Muslims worship Nagaraja?

Many believers attempt to put the burden of proof on nonbelievers rather than on themselves when it comes to their god. They incorrectly assume that an atheist is responsible for proving that gods are make-believe. They fail to see that this is an impossible challenge given the broad descriptions of what gods are and what gods can do. A typical god is said to exist outside the limits of our natural world and beyond the laws of physics. How can such a being ever be completely ruled out by a species that lives in the natural world and under the laws of physics?

I suspect that the reason believers try to shift the burden of proof onto atheists is because they know they cannot prove the existence of their god. They hope to escape that basic responsibility by dumping it onto the nonbelievers. In fairness, however, the person making a claim about something is the one who must be responsible for backing it up. As an atheist I have no belief that gods are real. That is different from declaring that no gods exist. If that was my position then a believer would be correct to challenge me on it. No atheists can prove that gods do not exist because they are too elusive by definition. Most gods are supposed to be beyond detection by our five senses at least some of the time. Many gods are described as invisible and able to fly. Some know my thoughts and would be able to anticipate every step of my investigation if they wished to remain hidden. How can anyone ever prove that beings with such supernatural abilities do not exist? Even if one were able to see gods, looking under every rock and searching the bottom of every ocean would fall well short of a thorough search. Remember, many of these gods are supposed to be able to travel freely throughout the universe. Some atheists may disagree, but for these reasons I maintain that no one can say for certain that gods do not exist. The cosmos is too big and the definition of god is too loose to ever make such an absolute declaration. Maybe Sukra, Jesus, and Edeke really are out there somewhere. Of course, given the weakness of the arguments for any god, coupled with the absence of compelling evidence for any of them, it still seems far more likely that all gods are the creations of human imagination. It is true that no one has ever disproved the existence of the gods. Probably no one ever will, given the apparent impossibility of total verification. Anything goes when we are dealing with invisible beings, so a believer can always come up with an excuse for why neither fairy nor god left a footprint in the garden. It seems the best that a nonbeliever can safely say is that while gods may indeed exist there is no reason to believe that they do exist because no one has yet been able to prove it.

Do not forget that believers reject their own argument when the tables are turned. Believers do not think it is such a good idea to place the burden of proof on nonbelievers when they are the nonbeliever. Again, the key question is how many religious people would agree to believe in rival gods just because they can't prove that they do not exist?

Finally, this terrible idea that one should believe in something until it is disproved opens the door for a staggering number of silly things that would have to be believed. For example, the supernatural claims made for astrology, psychic readings, palm readings, the Bermuda Triangle, dowsing, levitation, ghosts, and Nostradamus have been demolished by skeptics repeatedly. But no skeptic has ever conclusively proved that these are impossible claims that can never be true under any conditions. So, should we believe all that stuff too?

CHAPTER 37 BIBLIOGRAPHY AND RECOMMENDED READING

Gardner, Martin. *New Age: Notes of a Fringe Watcher*. Amherst, NY: Prometheus Books, 1991. Great writing from a great skeptic.

Hines, Terence. *Pseudoscience and the Paranormal*. Amherst, NY: Prometheus Books, 2003.

Kelly, Lynne. *The Skeptic's Guide to the Paranormal*. New York: Thunder's Mouth Press, 2004. Informative survey of many paranormal claims.

Stenger, Victor J. *God: The Failed Hypothesis: How Science Shows That God Does Not Exist*. Amherst, NY: Prometheus Books, 2007.

Chapter 38

People have gone to heaven and returned.

A scrawny dog gnaws on a jagged arm bone with frightening intensity. Judging by the decay and the smell, the person has been dead for at least a few days. Walking up on a scene like this was not in my plans. Instantly I know that this is the single most horrible thing I have ever seen or will probably ever see in my life. Against my better instincts, the journalists' reflex kicks in and I drop to one knee so that I'm eye level with the dog for a better photo angle. Unfortunately, looking through my camera lens doesn't make it any less horrible.

The scenery certainly has changed for me, I think to myself. Just a couple of hours earlier I was looking up in awe at the Taj Mahal, one of India's many stunning experiences and my pick for the world's most beautiful building. Now, just an hour or so later, I am standing on the muddy bank of the Yamuna River watching a hungry dog eat a rotted human corpse. "Damn," I say to myself, "this must be why people take those fancy bus tours with cheerful guides." It's not so much the sight of this grisly feast that disturbs me as the sound. The constant cracking of that arm bone is unbearable. I swing wide around the dog and continue down the river. Overall I handled it pretty well, I'd say. I'm well aware that the value of travel comes from experiencing new things, even unpleasant scenes like a dog eating a dead person. Bad moments often make the best memories. I've seen and experienced many disturbing sights and events around the world that probably made me wiser, tougher, and a lot more grateful for my life. This one, however, I could have done without. I wish there was some way that I could unsee it, or at least unhear it. But I can't. This encounter with death is with me forever now.

The sun is low in the sky and shadows from the trees make it seem even later and darker but I keep moving. I just want to go a little farther. I'm not sure what I hope to find but the river is too interesting to turn back now. I come across a human skull, half buried in the mud. Most of the flesh is gone but, strangely, there is an eye in one of the sockets. After the dog incident, this is not so bad.

I walk another hundred meters or so and catch a glimpse of a large fire glowing in the dusk. Several people are moving around it, singing or chanting. I move in for a closer look, slow and quiet. From behind a tree I see that it is a Hindu cremation ceremony. It's the final page of the final chapter of someone's life. Believers would add that it is the beginning of something new. Branches are stacked up into a rectangular shape with the body lying on top. It's night now and the flames illuminate the corpse. The body is not in a coffin. There is a robe or cloth wrapped around him. I can see the head clearly in the flames. The people gathered around continue to sing and pray.

I keep still and silent. I don't want to disturb the ceremony but I'm fascinated by the sight of a human body being slowly consumed by fire right in front of me. I can see his flesh burning away. This man was once alive and now he is turning into smoke and ash right before my eyes. A man walks to the front of the body and extends what appears to be a long metal spoon into the fire. He pours something onto the dead man's head. The fire flares up dramatically in reaction to the liquid. I learn later that this was butter or oil. It's poured onto the head to raise the temperature and aid in cracking the skull. Believers say this allows the soul to escape the body. I watched closely but never saw a soul.

I had never been confronted with death like I was this day. A human's body was reduced to mere food for a wild dog. An anonymous skull was sinking slowly in the mud where it likely would be lost forever. And a man's body slowly melted into fire while those who loved him said good-bye. It was powerful stuff and remains fresh in my memories. Whenever I think of death, I inevitably recall that late afternoon walk in India. Not that I dwell on death. I don't think about it much. It's not a happy subject because death is so final and unforgiving. So much is lost when a human dies. All their accumulated knowledge, all their memories, and all their dreams vanish just like smoke in the evening breeze. Of course believers keep telling me that I am wrong to think like this. Death is not really death, they say. Death is not the end at all but a mere pause before the beginning of another existence. It might be heaven, hell, or reincarnation, but something definitely comes after death, they promise me.

To live beyond death sounds great. Who wouldn't want to believe in that? Well, I wouldn't. I reject the claims of heaven, hell, and reincarnation for the same reason that I reject the gods who are supposed to oversee these post-death transitions: there is a complete and total absence of credible evidence to support the claims. It is almost surely a false hope and it's a terribly destructive hope if it leads people to demand less of themselves in this life because they expect more after they die.

As a journalist I have enjoyed encounters with many fascinating individuals and heard many amazing stories. I interviewed a man who was in the Berlin bunker with Adolf Hitler during the final days of the Third Reich. I have interviewed famous soccer player Pelé, two heavyweight-boxing champions, a Nobel Peace Prize winner, and a man who had been to the bottom of the deepest ocean. I once fired questions at the "father of the H-Bomb" and I felt chills as a Jonestown survivor described her escape from religious madness. There is one interview, however, that stands apart from all the others. It's the one I conducted with a woman who died, spent a day in heaven, came back to life, and then returned to Earth.

Although I was skeptical of her story, all my questions were politely crafted and delivered with delicate care because there was the possibility that she sincerely believed she really had been to heaven. The woman made money by traveling around conducting faith healing sessions so it is possible that she was lying in order to help sell her services, but I chose to give her the benefit of the doubt. The woman described her bizarre journey in remarkable detail. She told me that the streets of heaven were paved with gold—literally. She told me about a magical fruit basket that was in a room she was taken to. The basket automatically replenished itself whenever fruit was taken and eaten. Jesus himself even visited her. She said that Jesus was an entrancing man with beautiful flowing hair and dazzling blue eyes. He told her that she must go back to Earth and do good work for him. Once she was back among the living, she says she discovered that she had been given the power to heal sick people.

Wow. After hearing such a powerful and important story, how could anyone not believe in her god? He must be real. Heaven must be real. This is an eyewitness account from someone who met him face-to-face in heaven. What more proof can one ask for? For starters, one can and should ask for a lot more than a mere story. The woman had no evidence to prove her claim. She didn't bring back a magic self-filling fruit bowl or a lock of Jesus's hair for DNA analysis. (Who knows? Maybe his DNA would have some sort of Bible code imprinted on it or something.) She couldn't even produce a gold flake from one of those shiny streets. As for her special ability to heal the sick, she had not bothered to subject herself to a double-blind test conducted by independent researchers. This might have been able to confirm that she is able to magically heal people. It could have ruled out chance, biased observations, and maybe the placebo effect. All she was able to do, however, was tell a story. No evidence, just words.

Never forget that anyone can say anything when no evidence is required to back it up. When it comes to telling stories, it is easy for people to lie, make honest mistakes about the facts, or to have even hallucinated or dreamed up the entire episode. Consider the countless millions of tales about gods, aliens, UFOs, ghosts, and so forth, none of which have any strong supporting evidence. Because of this lack of evidence, most of these stories are dismissed by most people. For example, most of us consider reports of Elvis sightings after his death in 1977 to be untrue because there was no evidence. There are just too many wild stories out there to safely accept all of them or even a small fraction of them without demanding evidence first. Otherwise, one's head might explode from the sheer volume of nonsense.

The late Carl Sagan promoted a simple but invaluable working philosophy in his outstanding book *The Demon-Haunted World.* Sagan encouraged people to see that extraordinary claims should always be backed up with extraordinary evidence. This requirement can make navigating through and around false stories much easier. For example, if your neighbor says she saw a butterfly in her backyard you might go ahead and accept it as most likely true based on her word alone. That's not an extraordinary claim. It might easily be true. However, if she claims that she saw a four-headed turquoise dragon in high heels, you probably should ask to see photos, footprint casts, and a stool sample before getting too excited. The more unusual and unlikely the story is, the more powerful the evidence needs to be. It's the only safe way to fly in this wacky world of ours. Keep this simple rule in mind and many stories, including those about trips to heaven and talking to gods, whither and die as nothing more than unproven tales. Sure, it is possible that some of them might be true, but which ones? How could you ever choose?

It is important to add that refusing to accept an extraordinary story about ghosts or gods from someone is not necessarily a negative judgment on the story or an insult to the storyteller. Anyone can get facts wrong. Smart people make mistakes recalling events all the time. Witnesses are notoriously unreliable in courtrooms. Memory is now understood to be more like a mental retelling of an event, rather than an accurate snapshot. Everyone is vulnerable to misinterpreting sensory input and even to experiencing hallucinations. It doesn't mean that the person making the claim is mentally incompetent or dishonest. Look at it like this: asking for evidence is just a smart way of doing business in life, nothing personal. It's not rude. It's safe. If you don't want to risk having a bunch of nonsense take up valuable real estate in your head, then consistently ask for evidence when confronted with unusual stories. Every tale that involves something outside the bounds of normal existence, such as magic or a god, should be approached like a used car for sale. Kick the tires, check the odometer, and look under the hood. Most importantly, always apply Sagan's rule: extraordinary claims require extraordinary evidence.

CHAPTER 38 BIBLIOGRAPHY AND RECOMMENDED READING

Eller, David. *Natural Atheism*. Parsippany, NJ: American Atheist Press, 2004.

Sagan, Carl. *The Demon-Haunted World: Science as a Candle in the Dark*. New York: Random House, 1995.

Chapter 39

Religion brings people together.

He that is not with me is against me.
—Jesus, Matthew 12:30

Kill those who join with other gods . . .
—Koran, Sura 9:5

Religion is intensely tribalistic. A devout Christian or
Muslim doesn't say one religion is as good as another.
—E. O. Wilson

One of the most unlikely justifications for belief is the claim that a god unites people. Some believers see unity within a religion as direct evidence for their god's existence. They also claim that belief in a god is able to make positive and lasting connections between people from different backgrounds.

This idea of unity proving the existence of gods is so obviously wrong that I was reluctant to include it in this book. Yes, religion might succeed at uniting people to a limited degree but it clearly does a far better job of dividing people. One would think that this would be clear to anyone, regardless if they believe in a god or not. I worry readers will see the inclusion of this reason for belief as an attempt to create a soft target for no other reason than to take a cheap shot at religion. However, I have found this idea to be surprisingly common among believers around the world and therefore felt obligated to include it.

Believe it or not, many people really do think that their god is real because their religion is so good at bringing people together. So, let's analyze this claim and see how well belief in gods has done in uniting humankind. It is important to make clear up front, however, that the question of whether or not religion promotes more unity or more division does not necessarily have any direct bearing on whether or not gods exist. Who knows? Maybe there is a real god who wants us to be divided and in constant conflict. In fact, many people do believe in just such a god. On the other hand, humans are social beings and naturally join together in tribes, villages, cities, and nations. So far as we can tell, however, our tendency toward some level of unity is natural, not supernatural. So the bottom line on this justification for belief is that it is not really proof of anything, even if it were true. Still, it is worth addressing because so many believers see "religious unity" as justification for belief.

There are nearly seven billion people alive around the world today. I would love to cite the number of religions that currently occupy the minds of some six billion of these people, but I cannot. No one can because the number of active religions is so high and so volatile that it is impossible to keep an accurate count. But even if that number were available it would not provide the whole picture. Many more religions have existed in the past than do today. So the total number of religions that have ever existed must be incredibly high, probably exceeding one million easily. This high number of religions is the first indication that belief divides for more than it unites.

In addressing the claim that religion brings people together, one could make the case that there is nothing on earth that humans disagree about more than religion. Nationalism might seem like a contender for the most divisive force of all, but there are barely more than two hundred nations. Anyway, despite the challenges of politics, nationalism, and international wars, nations still find a way to come together in the United Nations building and talk. Sometimes the UN even manages to bring about tangible and positive progress for the world. The world's religions have nothing comparable. No major religion today, for example, would likely be able to even agree on a representative if something like the UN existed for religions. Who, for example, would represent Christianity in a meaningful world forum? A Catholic? A Protestant? A Baptist? A Mormon? A Rastafarian? Somebody's feelings would be hurt. Who would represent Islam: Sunni or Shiite? What about Judaism? Should the single representative be Orthodox, Reform, Conservative, or Reconstructionist? Is there any doubt that holy wars would break out all over the world during the process of choosing a single representative for each world religion? And, no, there couldn't be a representative for each branch of each religion, not when Christianity alone has thousands of denominations. No meeting room could hold so many people for such a gathering.

Not even economics carves up the world as sharply and deeply as religion. Yes, the gulf between the rich and poor is monstrous, but a world population divided by economics into two, three, or four classes is far less divided than a population that is splintered by countless religions. It is likely that we will see the world's poor people and rich people unite before we see the world's believers unite.

Even the terribly destructive concept of race fails to match religion's mischief across the centuries. No matter how misinformed, deluded, or obsessed one may be about races as meaningful biological categories, the number of religions available to pit neighbor against neighbor is far greater than the number of traditional racial categories. Depending on how you define them, Christianity alone has thousands of variations active today. Most get along just fine, but not all. Christianity has a bloody history of internal conflict. But perhaps this should not be surprising to anyone given Jesus's own words as quoted in the Bible: "Do you suppose that I came to give peace on earth? I tell you, not at all, but rather division. For from now on five in one house will be divided: three against two, and two against three. Father will be divided against son and son against father, mother against daughter and daughter against mother, mother-in-law against her daughter-in-law and daughter-in-law against her mother-in-law" (Luke 12:51). This doesn't sound much like the unifying force for the world that many believers tell me it is. Yes, Christians are united in their belief that a man named Jesus was a god but this is just about the only thing the world's Christians agree on. To a non-Christian the differences between denominations might seem unimportant. Even some Christians probably think they do not matter. But this view comes from a lack of awareness about how seriously many Christians take their rituals and their interpretations of the Bible. Some Catholics, for example, tell me that Protestants will find themselves in a lot of trouble one day for abandoning the one true church and for not respecting the authority of the pope. Some Protestants, on the other hand, seem very confident that Catholics have made a tragic mistake by obeying popes and "worshipping idols." Meanwhile, the Eastern Orthodox version of Christianity thinks both the Catholics and the Protestants have plenty to be worried about. In public, many Christian leaders speak about the harmony and the common path they share with all forms of Christianity. Their warm words are attractive and portray a religion that seems more interested in unity than division. When speaking frankly to their own congregations, however, many preachers and church members can be quite open about how their specific brand of Christianity is the real truth and all others are a one-way ticket to hell. I have heard such comments myself loud and clear many times inside of churches.

Hinduism appears united to outsiders because it is one of the world's most flexible, open, and accommodating religions by far. Hindus have told me that everybody on earth is born a Hindu. That attitude may explain why practicing Hindus are not so concerned with converting everybody to their religion like many other religious people are. However, there is still plenty of division within Hinduism. There are the Veerashaivas, the Vaishnavites, neo-Hindus, the Shaivites, and the reform Hindus, for example. And they do not always get along.

As a result of the fighting in Iraq, more Westerners than ever are now aware that Islam is not one big happy family. The Shia and Sunni sects are deeply divided, for example, and the costs of that split have been high. Sometimes, in some places, they live together, intermarry, and overlook their religious differences. But not always. Many thousands of lives have been lost over the centuries directly due to prejudice and hatred between Sunni and Shia Muslims. Much like the split in Christianity between Catholicism, the Eastern Orthodox Church, and Protestantism, the Sunni–Shia divide seems to be a lot more about human politics and power struggles than any divine plan by a god.

Although there are some differences between the two groups, such as how most Sunnis wash their feet before prayer and many Shia feel that merely wiping them is sufficient, they still share the bond of Allah, the Koran, and Muhammad the Prophet. Shia and Sunni are not the only versions of Islam, by the way. There are Wahhabis, Sufis, Kahrijites, Ismailis, Nation of Islam, Ahmadi, and many more. An outsider might think that their beliefs in common would be enough to bring them together. Clearly it is not enough, however. Islam—like all religions—is so flexible, so easy to interpret in different ways, that it can transform a neighbor into an enemy with ease. This has been demonstrated repeatedly throughout history.

When Catholics and Protestants hurt and kill each other, and when Sunnis and Shia do the same, they may or may not have a god on their mind when they strike. What is undeniable, however, is that belief in a god is the crucial step that sets the stage for the bloodletting. Is religious belief the only reason we keep killing one another century after century? Of course not. Killing for a nation has been and continues to be popular too. But for that at least combatants almost always require a patch of land that actually exists for their motivation. Killing for race is fairly convenient as well because people can team up based on the exaggerated importance of superficial but observable physical characteristics and get on with the hating and the killing. Religion, however, provides the easiest route to violence of all. This is because nothing has to be real when it comes to belief in gods. There are no limits to the absurdity of religious motivations and justifications for war and murder. Someone with nothing more than a little bit of confidence and charisma merely has to say a god wants those people over there killed and some number of believers are likely to go along with it, so long as they have sufficient faith, of course.

Those who think belief unites more than divides only have to do the math. The Mormon religion, for example, is less than two hundred years old and has already divided into different sects, mostly over disagreements about polygamy. One wonders how long it will be before the young religion of Scientology suffers its own great schism.

One might have thought that Buddhism would avoid breaking up like other religions since its founder was supposed to have been just a man who was only interested in suggesting ways that people might better cope with suffering and desire. But it has. Not only has Buddhism split into many versions, it has also collected many gods along the way. This is despite its origin as an atheistic religion/philosophy with no god. The three primary versions of Buddhism are Theravada, Mahayana, and Vajrayana. Many more sects have branched off from them.

Judaism is a relatively small religion with only about fourteen million members. Nonetheless, it comes in many versions. A few of them are: Orthodox, Reform, Conservative, Hasidic, Traditional, Kabbalah, and Reconstruction. From an outsider's perspective, it appears that the only thing a religion requires to spawn new versions of itself is time. Bickering over invisible gods has led to the deaths of millions of people throughout history and people continue to suffer and die today. Some believers tell me this turmoil is because it is in our nature to rebel against a god or gods, or it is an inevitable by-product of free will. I disagree. I suspect that a more likely reason for so much arguing and fighting within religions is because there is no evidence for their most important claims. The absence of credible evidence means nobody ever really has to win or lose an argument. Disagreements between two parties are far more difficult to settle to everyone's satisfaction when neither side has a logical leg to stand on. For example, how can anyone ever objectively decide that a Lutheran is more correct in matters of faith than a Rastafarian? It can't be done. Who does Allah favor, Sunni or Shia? Who knows? Such a question can never be decided based on reason and evidence because the very existence of Allah has never even been established based on reason and evidence. All the monumental religious controversies that end up killing people exist solely in the minds of believers in the first place so rational, satisfying, and logical resolutions are virtually impossible.

A religion can bring some people together, but with a tragically high price. Each religion builds its base by pulling people away from the rest of humankind. Striving to create airtight subsets of our species is not productive or safe in the long run. Coming together as a species and recognizing our common future is probably the most important step we will—or will not—make this century. We have very serious challenges confronting us. Environmental problems are intensifying. Severe water shortages are projected for the Middle East. The ability of nations and small groups of people to make or obtain weapons of mass destruction is going to keep rising. The crisis of extreme poverty in the developing world still has not been solved. We need real unity, not the kind of shortsighted, limited, and corrosive unity that religions generate. We need a unity that is based on the reality of who we really are: one people sharing one planet. In the light of that truth, religions seem no better than false walls standing before progress, prosperity, and peace.

CHAPTER 39 BIBLIOGRAPHY AND RECOMMENDED READING

Hitchens, Christopher. *God Is Not Great: How Religion Poisons Everything.* New York: Twelve Books, 2007. Hitchens pulls no punches in letting readers know what he thinks about belief in gods.

Chapter 40

My god inspires people.

Believers often point to religion's ability to inspire wonderful things as evidence for the existence of their god or gods. They cite great art, music, and literature that may have a direct link to belief in a god. Of course an atheist might point out that dragons and ghosts have inspired art, music, and literature too but that doesn't prove those things are real. Still, there are some creations that seem almost too special to have come from the hands of mere mortals alone. When I saw the *Pieta* in the Vatican, for example, I was amazed by the detail. It is more than a statue of Jesus's limp body in Mary's lap. There is an undeniable warm glow that comes out of that cold marble. I can only wonder how an artist in his early twenties was able to discover that stirring image somewhere inside of lifeless rock. Some believers see a work of art like this and come to the conclusion that it could only have been inspired by their god. Only a real god could have guided the sculptor's hands, they say. But if Michelangelo's *Pieta* is evidence for the existence of Jesus, then what about all those glorious Roman gods who also stand frozen in stone around Rome? Some of their statues are extraordinary too. Do they prove the existence of Jupiter and Neptune? Cairo's Muhammad Ali Mosque is beautiful inside and out. Does its pleasing symmetry and imposing visual power prove the accuracy of the Koran? I saw fascinating spirit masks in Papua New Guinea made from wood, shells, and feathers. Some of them were entrancing, absolutely unforgettable works of art inspired by belief. But I didn't think they were proof of spirits.

Believers also frequently cite the accomplishments of religious people who impacted history in positive ways. This justification for belief has always been of interest to me because Mohandas Gandhi and Martin Luther King Jr. are high atop my personal list of heroes. Both men believed in a god or gods. And they almost certainly drew upon their beliefs for inspiration, courage, and strength when they faced powerful foes. Of course, given the private nature of one's thoughts, we can never be sure whether or not belief in a god really was their primary source of inspiration. However, I believe it is reasonable to accept that these two men were sincere about their religious beliefs and did indeed draw upon them during their battles for justice. I think it is fair for believers to connect the courage and achievements of Gandhi and King to their religions. And I don't believe it is justifiable for an atheist to belittle achievements that may have been inspired by belief in a god. However, the important question is how courageous behavior or noteworthy artistic creations can be directly connected to a god's existence. This is important because believers so often cite the accomplishments of religious people to suggest that their god helped significantly or actually did it. They see art and great achievements as proof that they believe in a god who really does exist. But is it really a god providing all this inspiration and assistance or could it be nothing more than *belief* in a god that does it? After all, sincerely believing that one is working toward a goal that will please a god can be a powerful motivation—whether or not the god is real.

Let's not forget that there are many nonmagical things that are capable of inspiring supreme efforts from people. Sports is an obvious example. World-class competition routinely inspires athletes to pull incredible performances from their bodies. Family love and romantic love inspire people to remarkable accomplishments all the time. For example, I'm confident that I could find the strength in me to lift a fairly heavy boulder if my daughter's leg was pinned under it. Nothing more than human ambition and ego can motivate and energize people, enabling them to achieve difficult feats from earning a college degree to climbing Mount Everest. Most troubling for those who see special accomplishments as evidence for their god, however, is the fact that many different gods are credited with inspiring people. According to the believers' descriptions of these gods, they cannot all be real. Somebody is wrong. Throughout history many people have been inspired by their gods, real or not, to achieve great deeds, evil deeds, and seemingly impossible deeds. But note that, except for the rarest of conversion stories, it is always *their* god, the one they believed in who helped. We don't see Christians claiming to have been inspired by Vishnu to paint a masterpiece. We don't find many Muslims crediting Jesus for inspiring them to write beautiful poetry. This common practice of crediting gods for special accomplishments within many very different religions derails the idea that divine inspiration proves any particular god is real because all cases can't be authentic. For example, the god who inspired Joseph Smith to start the Mormon Church does not sound like the same god who inspired Muhammad to start Islam, although technically they would have to be because Allah and the god of the Bible are the same god. However, Islam and Mormonism disagree on so many basic claims that it is difficult to imagine how both founders were truly inspired and guided by a real god. So what is going on here? Both Muhammad and Smith did nothing less than launch new religions that have not only survived but flourished. Islam has more than a billion followers today. Mormonism is less than two hundred years old and already has more than ten million followers. It is likely, of course, that these men really were deeply inspired to have put in the effort necessary to create new belief systems. But inspired by what? It would seem that at least one of these men did what they did on their own, inspired by nothing more than belief, perhaps, because the god who spoke to Muhammad and the god who spoke to Joseph Smith are too big to live in the same universe. They can't both be real, thus proving that impressive feats can be accomplished without a god.

Any believer who maintains that real gods are necessary to explain the inspired works of art that are connected to their religion must explain how it is that so many other religions, now and in the past, managed to produce impressive works of art too. No one religion can justifiably claim artistic superiority. A couple of hours spent strolling through the Metropolitan Museum of Art easily confirms that. The fact that great art has come out of so many diverse belief systems, as well as from artists who did not believe at all, shows that gods are not required for human creativity to produce spectacular results.

I spent a full day in the Egyptian Museum in Cairo and left feeling that I could spend a week more. While browsing through the incredible abundance of archaeological riches there, I thought to myself that the artists who created the alabaster statues, the spectacular golden mask of Tutankhamen, and case after case of elaborate jewelry must have been extremely talented and also deeply inspired. I could not imagine anyone producing such beauty in a casual or disconnected manner. They must have held many of those objects with love and reverence, I imagined. Many of the artists must have cared deeply about what they were creating. However, the fact that ancient Egyptian culture produced stunning works of art—much of it inspired by religious belief undoubtedly—is not a good enough reason to conclude that pharaohs were gods, as believers once claimed.

When I saw the Emerald Buddha and the giant Reclining Buddha in Thailand, I admit I was overwhelmed by their irresistible beauty. But it was not enough to convince me that Buddhism's claims of supernatural reincarnation are valid. I was a willing prisoner in Egypt's Karnak Temple for an entire day. The place was so fascinating to me that I couldn't have left before sundown if I tried. It's the world's largest religious structure and, despite its immense age, still manages to stun visitors with its art and architectural force. But I certainly did not walk away from Karnak believing that gods must have guided the builders' hands. I have visited beautiful Hindu temples in India, Nepal, and Fiji and was very impressed. The Great Pyramids of Giza are spectacular, too. But none of these are proof of gods in my opinion. Not even the Bodnath Stupa in Kathmandu or the temples of ancient Athens revealed to me the slightest hint that anything other than human creativity, passion, and sweat had built them. Perhaps I have too little faith in gods and too much faith in humans. I do admit, however, that many such sights are examples of religion's ability to stir emotions and inspire unique achievements. But there simply is no reason to jump to the extraordinary conclusion that gods were involved, not when we humans are capable of so much on our own. We can build pyramids. We can paint images that stir a million hearts. We can chisel smooth beauty from jagged rock. We really are that good. Those who are so eager to believe in gods might consider believing in the limitless creativity of women and men.

In the end, we are left with a choice. We can credit a broad spectrum of unproven gods for all great religious art and achievement, from the wooden spirit mask carved by a Sepik River tribesman to the Parthenon designed and built by the Greeks, or we can credit the people who we know actually did the work with mortal hands.

CHAPTER 40 BIBLIOGRAPHY AND RECOMMENDED READING

30,000 Years of Art: The Story of Human Creativity across Time and Space. London: Phaidon Press, 2007.

Burn, Barbara, ed., *Masterpieces of the Metropolitan Museum of Art.* New York: Metropolitan Museum of Art, 1993.

Chapter 41

Science can't explain everything.

All our science, measured against reality, is primitive and childlike—and yet it is the most precious thing we have.

—Albert Einstein

Ask a biologist how life began on Earth and you are likely to hear something about organic molecules hooking up some four billion years ago and charging down the road to life as we know it. The scientist might even bring up panspermia or exogenesis, the idea that the first life may have come to Earth from space, perhaps by hitching a ride on a meteor. Sooner or later, however, the scientist is sure to admit that nobody really knows how life began on our planet. At this time the evidence is just not there. Unfortunately, it happened so long ago that conclusive evidence for how it happened may never be discovered. Although there is now a good overall picture of how life evolved on our planet, scientists have failed so far to figure out the great mystery of life's origin.

What about the entire universe? How did it start? Science offers a fascinating partial answer with the big bang theory but many unanswered questions remain. As with the origin of life on Earth, it is possible that science will never be able to fully explain how the universe started. Maybe it was just too long ago and the crucial evidence for a complete picture will never be found.

What about life in space? Is there life on other planets? Do other civilizations exist in our galaxy or in other galaxies? Again, scientists have some interesting ideas and opinions on the subject but, for now, they just don't know.

What happens to us when we die? If you ask a typical biologist, she likely will give you some bland talk about thoughts ceasing to exist and atoms dispersing. Ultimately, however, she probably will admit that nobody really knows for sure if anything else happens.

Why can't science answer so many big questions? Religions certainly are not shy about offering their answers confidently and directly. Does this mean that religion is better than science? Some believers say it does. They point to science's failure to explain important mysteries and call it one more reason to be confident that their religion is true because their god answers every question thoroughly and definitively.

There are significant problems with this popular idea. First of all, it does not logically follow that a god must exist just because scientists haven't figured everything out. However, many believers do see science's weakness as their gods' strength, so let's look at why science seems to be so far behind in the eyes of many believers. The reason there are so many gaping holes in science's attempt to explain everything in the universe while religions enjoy an apparent mastery of the topic is because science and religion operate in very different ways. Scientists are confident enough in themselves and their profession to admit ignorance. Proper science does not claim to know anything with certainty unless there is plenty of evidence behind it, and, even then, all conclusions are fair game for revision *forever*. No discovery, no theory, no fact in science is beyond correction. It is remarkable that most scientists get along as well as they do considering that a quick way to advance one's career is to tear apart a colleague's work. Nothing in science is off-limits if it is shown to be wrong. This willingness to admit errors and to accept blanks in our knowledge is what makes science so productive. It's why science is by far the most reliable method we have for figuring things out about our world and our universe. Gaps in our scientific knowledge are not shortcomings or failures. They are shining examples of why science is better than religion. Science can't answer everything because science doesn't cheat by providing answers without evidence.

Religions have a very different way of doing business. Most of them operate on faith, which means declaring things to be true without evidence to support the claim. Most religions also demand extreme loyalty to authority figures and to ancient writings. Calls for evidence and open debate are usually discouraged, if not outright forbidden. By operating like this, it is relatively easy for religions to get away with making extraordinary claims they can't prove.

It's safe to assume that many of today's scientific facts are wrong. Scientists know that errors have been made and that corrections will need to be made when somebody gets it right. They accept this as standard procedure. This culture of checking and changing constantly nudges us toward greater understanding of the universe and everything in it. It obviously works because it keeps producing more answers and better answers. If an unknown scientist who works at a tiny university on one side of the world can prove that the revered theory of a famous scientist on the other side of the world is wrong, then that theory gets tossed out. It doesn't matter who graduated from the most prestigious school or who has more awards. In science, evidence triumphs. Clearly this is the best way.

Since the publication of his book *The God Delusion*, Richard Dawkins may have become the world's most prominent out-of-the-closet atheist. Many believers don't like him because they think he is too aggressive, too dismissive of religion, and maybe a little too smart for his own good. Having read many of his books and interviews, I feel I have at least some sense of who he is and how he thinks. Despite the fact that he is an evolutionary biologist and well-known for his nonbelief in gods, I am confident that if he were presented with overwhelming evidence for the existence of gods and a ten-thousand-year-old Earth on which life does not evolve, he would accept it and admit that he was wrong about his atheism and his life's work. Dawkins has shown himself to be a good scientist, and good scientists care first and foremost about getting it right. I don't think he disbelieves in gods simply because he wants to. I think he, like most atheists, probably cannot believe in a god because he has never heard a convincing reason for why he should.

The unfortunate creation–evolution conflict is a good example of how science can work for anyone. Many believers have been misled to think that evolution is some kind of evil plot by the scientific community to draw believers away from the gods. But this conspiracy is very unlikely when just one scientist—even a fundamentalist Christian, Muslim, or Jewish scientist—could possibly produce a research paper that conclusively shows that evolution does not occur and destroy a widely respected theory. This scientist would clinch a Nobel Prize, make headlines around the world, get a million-dollar book deal, and become a hero to billions of believers. Why hasn't this happened? All it would take is one scientist to blow the whistle on the lie of evolution.

It reveals a lot about creationism and intelligent design when their leading advocates choose to fight battles in the news media and in schoolboard meetings rather than inside laboratories and on the pages of science journals. Science changes when it is wrong. It has done so countless times and will do so many more times to come. If just one believer could produce verifiable evidence for the existence of a god, there is no doubt that science would accept it. Scientists are not likely to run away from a real god. They would charge straight at it to learn more. A new branch of science called "godology" probably would be created and the process of learning more about the newly discovered deity would begin. That god simply would be added to the long list of human discoveries. But science will not pretend to answer questions before the evidence is on the table.

Some believers criticize science for leaving them cold and empty. Compared to religion science is unsatisfying, they say. But people who condemn science in this way fail to understand that it was never designed to serve as some kind of heart-warming life philosophy. Science helps to reveal life, the world, and the universe for what they are—good, bad, beautiful, and ugly. Science is a not a feel-good religion. It is not a system that is designed to cater to everyone's emotional needs.

Who knows, over the next several thousand years or so, maybe science will be able to answer every question, but that day is a long way off or it may never come. In the meantime, there is nothing wrong with scientists shrugging their shoulders and saying, "beats me" when confronted with questions they cannot answer. They should be applauded for their honesty, not condemned for it. Admitting ignorance is not a confession of weakness. There is no shame in it and it certainly is no reason for people to abandon science for religion. The fact that scientists freely admit their ignorance should reassure us. And religious leaders who rarely if ever admit their ignorance should raise concern.

Science is not a belief system. As inspirational and exciting as it can be, science cannot consistently provide warm and fuzzy feelings. Beyond the joy that comes from understanding, perhaps it was never meant to make us happy. It is not a security blanket or a reassuring parental figure. Many times science takes us down dark paths of knowledge and gives us answers we would rather not hear: A massive asteroid will threaten to strike our planet one day; supervolcanoes will erupt sooner or later; the Sun will die, and so forth. Science brings us scary knowledge such as these as often as it brightens our days with positive discoveries. The scientific method brought us the polio vaccine and the hydrogen bomb. For better or worse, science is the best way to try and understand the universe and ourselves. That's it. No one with good sense ever claimed that science was a consistent source of soul food for the weary and peace of mind for the anxious.

When believers complain that science leaves them hungry because it hasn't yet answered many big questions such as where we come from or where we are going, they are only expressing a natural and reasonable frustration. I, too, want to know exactly how the universe began, how life started on Earth, and what, if anything, happens when we die. No one is more curious than I am about such things. But it is best to be mature enough to accept that we may never know everything. One does not have to let go of reason and respect for science in order to cope with mystery. It's okay to be ignorant of some things. It's also honest.

Believers who feel that their belief system is superior to science in answering questions might ask themselves if they really think their religion plays fair. After all, religions make the biggest claims with the least evidence. This is the generation that will witness the return of Jesus. Wow, that's amazing! But wait, where's the evidence for that? I can go to heaven when I die? Great, I want in on that! But wait, where is the proof? Your god made the world? How do you know?

Another point for believers to keep in mind is that religions don't really answer anything anyway. Few believers think about this but it's true. Religions don't explain *how* life started on earth. Religions only claim to know *who* started life on Earth. Religions do not answer *how* the universe began. They only claim to know *who* started the universe. Religions do not explain *how* our consciousness survives in the form of a soul after we die. They just claim that there is an afterlife. These are not answers. Imagine if cosmologists said, "The big bang definitely started the universe," and didn't bother with presenting any evidence or a detailed theory. Wouldn't that be a pretty shallow explanation? Would anyone take them seriously?

Rather than turn away from science in search of more reassuring and confident answers to our origins and ultimate fate, I urge believers to make conditional peace with ignorance. You don't have to like it but you can accept not knowing. Ignorance gets a bad rap. So what if we don't have all the answers? Admitting ignorance shows that we are honest and unwilling to go to absurd lengths in order to create the illusion of knowing everything. Ignorance of the big questions is not as bad as you may have been led to believe. Scientists face it every day and use it for inspiration to keep seeking answers. So should we all.

CHAPTER 41 BIBLIOGRAPHY AND RECOMMENDED READING

Dawkins, Richard. *River Out of Eden: A Darwinian View of Life*. New York: Basic Books, 1995.

————. *Unweaving the Rainbow: Science, Delusion, and the Appetite for Wonder*. Boston/New York: Houghton Mifflin, 1998.

————. *The God Delusion*. New York: Houghton Mifflin, 2006.

Kurtz, Paul, ed., *Science and Religion: Are They Compatible?* Amherst, NY: Prometheus Books, 2003. An excellent book that should interest both nonbelievers and believers.

Randi, James. *Flim-Flam! Psychics, ESP, Unicorns, and Other Delusions*. Amherst, NY: Prometheus Books, 1982.

Sagan, Carl. *Billions and Billions*. New York: Random House, 1997. More fascinating thoughts from the late Carl Sagan.

Chapter 42

Society would fall apart without religion.

Despite the universal belief that religion makes people "good," it's obvious that it makes some people commit heinous acts.

—James A. Haught

I have heard the claim that religion is good for a society or nation more times than I could possibly count. It's one of the most popular justifications for belief. Most believers of virtually every religion I have ever encountered anywhere in the world say that society "needs" religion. It's simple: the more people who believe in a god and worship that god, the better off a country will be. More religion means more happiness, more security, and more prosperity. Just because many believers repeat this idea over and over, however, doesn't make it true.

The claim that belief in a god or gods is necessary for a nation's well-being may seem sensible to believers but it ignores the reality of our world. More belief definitely does not guarantee positive results. If anything, just the opposite is true. An objective look reveals that belief in a god seems to have a negative impact on societies. It might be a coincidence, but that's what the data show. Harsh as it may sound to believers, religion appears to retard social progress and facilitate barbaric behavior. There are many examples of this, both in the past and in the present. I would not go so far as to claim that this proves religion is bad or even the primary cause of a given nation's problems. There probably are many other factors one can blame a society's problems on other than religion. But the clear negative relationship between belief in gods and a society's overall condition strongly refutes the claim that religion is a key ingredient for social success.

Believers who call upon this idea to defend their belief in a god need to recognize how belief really plays out around the world when it flourishes and shapes a society. Sociologist Phil Zuckerman has researched how belief impacts the quality of life in societies. His work confirms that belief in gods falls far short of guaranteeing good things for a nation and its people. "If this often-touted religious theory were correct—that a turning away from God is at the root of all societal ills—then we would expect to find the least religious nations on earth to be bastions of crime, poverty and disease and most religious countries to be models of societal health," writes Zuckerman. "A comparison of highly irreligious countries with highly religious countries, however, reveals a very different state of affairs. In reality, the most secular countries—those with the highest proportion of atheists and agnostics—are among the most stable, peaceful, free, wealthy, and healthy societies. And the most religious nations—wherein worship of God is in abundance—are among the most unstable, violent, oppressive, poor and destitute" (Zuckerman 2006).

Zuckerman's findings about societies and belief have nothing to do with personal opinions or prejudice against religious belief. His data, drawn from objective and respectable sources, shows a pattern that anyone can see. Despite all claims to the contrary, belief in gods does not create or maintain superior societies. The pattern seen in our world is clear: the more belief and the more intense the belief, the more violence, more oppression, and more economic failure. Less belief and less intense belief mean more peace, more tolerance, and more economic success. One can look at modern immigration trends as well. The major flow of people is away from more-religious societies toward less-religious societies. Why is this? If more belief is better and if gods protect societies that worship the most, then shouldn't people be moving in the other direction? I do not want to overstate this or antagonize believers, but belief in gods really does seem like a social toxin based on the current state of the world. The more of it there is, the sicker the society. So many times during my travels around the world I noticed that intensely religious societies were more stressful for me. As a solo traveler concerned with staying safe and healthy, I found that the more in-your-face religious belief was, the more on the edge I was because of security and health concerns. Conversely, visiting countries that were relatively free from the overbearing presence of religion were safe and enjoyable, like a walk in the park.

The following are a few of the key points from Zuckerman's research that believers should be aware of:

- The 2004 United Nations' Human Development Report ranked 177 countries on a "Human Development Index," by measuring such indicators of societal health as life expectancy, adult literacy, per-capita income, educational attainment, and so forth. According to this report, the five top nations were Norway, Sweden, Australia, Canada, and the Netherlands. All had notably high degrees of organic atheism. The bottom fifty countries lacked statistically significant levels of organic atheism. ("Organic atheism" refers to atheism in societies were there is sufficient freedom for citizens to openly state their lack of belief without fear of persecution.)
- The United Nations Report on the World Social Situation (2003) found that, of the forty poorest nations on Earth (measured by the percentage of population that lives on less than one dollar a day), all but Vietnam were highly religious nations with statistically minimal or insignificant levels of atheism.
- A study reported in the *Journal of Law and Economics* (2002), looked at thirty-eight non-African nations and found that the ten with the highest homicide rates were highly religious, with min-

imal or statistically insignificant levels of organic atheism. Conversely, of the ten nations with the lowest homicide rates, all but Ireland were secular nations with high levels of atheism.

- Of the thirty-five nations with the highest levels of youth-illiteracy rates all were highly religious, with statistically insignificant levels of organic atheism. This is according to the United Nations Report on the World Social Situation (2003).

- The most religious nations on earth—particularly those in Africa—have the worst rates of AIDS and HIV infection. Conversely, the highly irreligious nations of Western Europe, such as those of Scandinavia—where public sex education is supported and birth control is widely accessible—fared the best, experiencing among the lowest rates of AIDS and HIV infection in the world.

- Nations with a high degree of organic atheism are the most equitable to women, while highly religious nations are among the most oppressive. According to the 2004 Human Development Report's "Gender Empowerment Measure," the ten nations with the highest degrees of gender equality were all strongly organic-atheistic nations with significantly high percentages of nonbelief. Conversely, the bottom ten were all highly religious nations without any statistically significant percentages of atheists. Countries such as Sweden, Denmark, and the Netherlands, with the most female members of parliament, tend to have high degrees of organic atheism, and countries such as Pakistan, Nigeria, and Iran, with the fewest female members in parliament, tended to be highly religious. (Zuckerman 2006)

Is it fair to pin all of this on belief in gods? What about a nation's historical problems that don't have anything to do with religion? What about economic exploitation by other nations, wars, environmental disadvantages, political oppression, racism, corruption? Of course there are many factors that drag some societies down and keep them there. The point here, however, is that belief in gods is supposed to solve serious social problems and provide a better life for people. This is the claim so many believers make. More religion is better, they say. Clearly, however, it is not.

Zuckerman adds: "Religion is clearly not the simple and single path to righteous societies that religious fundamentalists seem to think it is. Belief in God may provide comfort to the individual believer, but, at the societal level, its results do not compare at all favorably with that of the more secular societies. When seeking a more civil, just, safe, humane, and healthy society, one is more likely to find it among those nations ranking low in religious faith—contrary to the preaching of religious folks" (Zuckerman 2006).

Author Sam Harris shows in his book *Letter to a Christian Nation* that this pattern can hold true even within highly religious societies:

> The United States is unique among wealthy democracies in its [high] level of religious adherence; it is also uniquely beleaguered by high rates of homicide, abortion, teen pregnancy, sexually transmitted disease, and infant mortality. The same comparison holds true within the United States itself: Southern and Midwestern states, characterized by the highest levels of religious literalism, are especially plagued by the above indicators of societal dysfunction, while the comparatively secular states of the Northeast conform to European norms. (Harris 2006, 44)

America's political landscape shows more of the same. "Red states" that are dominated by conservative Christians do not fare well in measures of bad behavior. Harris reports that 76 percent of the twenty-five most dangerous cities in America are found in red states. The twelve states with the most reported burglaries are red, and seventeen of the twenty-two states with the highest murder rates are also red. "Of course, correlation data of this sort do not resolve questions of causality—belief in God may lead to societal dysfunction; societal dysfunction may foster a belief in God; each factor may enable the other; or both may spring from some deeper source of mischief. Leaving aside the issue of cause and effect, however, these statistics prove that atheism is compatible with the basic aspirations of a civil society; they also prove, conclusively, that widespread belief in God does not ensure a society's health" (Harris 2006, 45).

A common catchphrase is that a society is judged best by how it treats it prisoners. I believe how a society treats its children is an even better measure. In 2007 UNICEF published *An Overview of Child Well-Being in Rich Countries*. The report analyzed and ranked the world's wealthiest nations by how well they protected, educated, vaccinated, and nurtured their children. As you can probably predict by now, nations with high levels of atheism (Netherlands, Sweden, Denmark, Finland) ranked higher than nations that are far more religious (Ireland, Greece, Poland, United States). If belief in a god and the sincere worship of that god bring "blessings" upon a nation, then shouldn't we at least be able to see this payoff in the condition of that nation's children? Surely a protective god or gods would look out for the basic needs of children within those societies that are more dedicated to belief and worship. Apparently not.

Any believer who claims that religion is necessary for a nations's social well-being needs to explain why nearly every measure of social well-being point to exactly the opposite conclusion. Why do the most religious societies have the most problems? Why do societies with the highest ratios of atheists have the least problems? This is a very important question that believers are obligated to think about if not answer. Jesus has not delivered widespread good health and comfort to Christian-dominated Haiti, Cape Verde, or Bolivia. Allah has not delivered security and justice to the faithful women of Afghanistan, Saudi Arabia, or Yemen. Likewise, Ganesha and Vishnu have not provided India with a solution to poverty and illiteracy. I suspect, of course, that the serious problems some countries face have nothing to do with gods because gods are most likely not real. However, it seems reasonable to suspect that taking belief in gods too seriously can distract governments and citizens from earthly concerns such as healthcare, crime prevention, education, and economic development. This lack of focus on what really matters can have a severe impact on a society by slowing progress, if not derailing it completely.

CHAPTER 42 BIBLIOGRAPHY AND RECOMMENDED READING

Harris, Sam. *Letter to a Christian Nation.* New York: Alfred A. Knopf, 2006.

An Overview of Child Well-Being in Rich Countries. UNICEF report, 2007. http://www.unicef-icdc.org/publications/pdf/rc7_eng.pdf.

Zuckerman, Phil. "Is Faith Good for Us?" *Free Inquiry* 26, no. 5 (August/ September 2006). http://www.secularhumanism.org/index.php?section =library&page=pzuckerman_26_5.

Chapter 43

My religion is so old, it must be true.

It's never too late to learn.

—Proverb

Many believers point to the age of their religion as some sort of evidence for their god's existence. A lie or a mistake, they declare, could not have endured for so long. So many people could not be so naive that they would worship a made-up god generation after generation, they say. This is another justification for belief that I have found to be common within many different religions.

The fact that this claim is so common is another indication of just how little people know about religions other than their own. Perhaps from the very limited perspective of a society in relative isolation where a single religion dominates, one can see how this view might seem to make a little bit of sense. However, if one simply looks at religious belief, both globally and historically, it is immediately obvious that the "my religion is old and therefore true" claim doesn't hold up at all.

Believers would never go down this path if they thought about it a little more and did the tiniest bit of research on what the people over in the next valley are up to because there are many very old religions still hanging around today. If age mattered, some of today's most popular religions would be in trouble. For example, Christians, Muslims,

Mormons, Scientologists, and followers of other relatively young religions might have to switch allegiances and start praying to Poseidon and Athena because the much older religion of the ancient Greeks is still in business.

Christianity is by far the most popular belief system in Greece today and many years have passed since Zeus and his crew enjoyed top billing. Nevertheless, the old pagan gods refuse to die. In 2006, for example, an Athens court ended a ban against worshipping the ancient gods. "What we want, now, is for the government to fully recognize our religion," said Zeus-believer Vasillis Tsantilas. "We will petition the Greek parliament, and the EU if that fails, for access to worship in places like the Acropolis, for permission to have our own cemeteries and, where necessary, to re-bury the [ancient] bones of the dead" (Smith 2006).

Does the fact that some Greek citizens are still worshipping ancient gods in the twenty-first century prove that these gods are real? Clearly Zeus is showing impressive stamina to still be attracting new worshippers. Does the measure of time make claims of his existence legitimate? I don't think so, but if you make the argument for one god, especially a younger god such as Jesus, then why can't you make the same argument for Apollo? Isis was an ancient Egyptian goddess but, after more than three thousand years, she's still in play. Some "new age" believers today look to Isis for guidance, protection, and comfort. Is this evidence of her existence?

Hinduism is so old that it can take on anybody's religion in the age race. This ancient and still-popular belief system should trouble non-Hindu believers who see a connection between age and truth. Hinduism has nearly one billion followers today, making it the third-largest religion in the world behind Christianity and Islam. It also might be the oldest of today's "great religions." One can't be sure, however, because Hinduism is so old that nobody even knows when it started. Without a doubt it is much older than Christianity (2,000 years), Buddhism (2,400 years), and Islam (1,400 years), however. Judaism is very old as well, stretching back at least a few thousand years, but Hinduism probably can match if not beat that. So does this mean that the Veda and Torah are more likely to be true than the New Testament, the Koran, or the Book of Mormon? "Hinduism is the most ancient religion on planet Earth today," declares an article in *Hinduism Today*. "No other religion, living or extinct, even approximates the distance in time Hinduism has traveled. The earliest known discovered evidence of the Hindu religion—temples, fire pits, ceremonial baths, Siva Lingams, dancing Siva-like figures, Sakti figures, yogi statues and seals—from the Saivite Indus Valley empire in Northwest India, is over 60 centuries old. That is 200 generations of human souls, a continuity of historical religion that is twice that of any other faith" (*Hinduism Today* 1988).

Hindus are very proud of their religion's age. While traveling throughout India I spoke with many Hindus about their religion and several of them were very quick to tell me that it is the oldest on Earth. No other comes close, they declared. It was an obvious source of pride and validation for them. There is no clear picture of Hinduism's ancient origins and I am sure there are many rival believers who would argue that their religion is just as old or older. Nevertheless, Hinduism is tough to beat.

So, does the fact that some Greeks are still worshipping Aphrodite, Hera, and Hermes prove that a bunch of gods are up on a mountain somewhere peering down at us right now? Of course it doesn't. But how could the religious beliefs of ancient Greece endure for so long if they were not true? It is because religious claims do not live or die based on whether or not they are accurate. The duration of a belief is influenced by far more down-to-earth factors, such as who wins the wars and who gains political and economic superiority. It also depends heavily on which religion can adapt to changing times and which religion does a better job of selling itself to each new generation. And don't forget that virtually no believers make the effort to study a broad range of religious options before settling on the one they judge to be the most reasonable and accurate. The primary reason that beliefs endure is because parents teach them to their children. This simple method of perpetuating belief works and it sufficiently explains how a religion can survive for thousands of years. Intrinsic truth does not necessarily have anything to do with it.

Still, some believers question why so many religions have faded away while others, such as Christianity or Islam, have become so popular. The duration of more successful religions might be explained in many ways. Maybe they have staying power because they are flexible and evolve in ways that help maintain the interest of believers century after century, while more rigid belief systems come and go like fads. Christianity is a good example of this. With many thousands of versions available today, Christians have a wide variety of options to suit their tastes. One Christian can be a monk and live a life totally immersed in the religion. Another Christian might never enter a church or never once pray aloud in the company of others. Perhaps some religions have survived simply because their followers tended to be smarter, kinder, meaner, more compassionate, more evil, better at cooperating, more aggressive, more passive, more imperialistic, or maybe just lucky. Perhaps it comes down to which religion has the superior military behind it. It all depends on what attribute is advantageous at a given time.

Most Hindus claim that many gods exist and most Jews claim that only one god exists. Both Hinduism and Judaism have shown impressive endurance so far, stretching back a few thousand years or more. They have overcome invasions and fierce competition from rival religions. But they cannot both be true if only for their contradictory claims about the number of gods. At least one must be wrong because the math just doesn't work any other way. This shows that time offers nothing conclusive about truth when it comes to belief in the gods.

Finally, what about animism? Still very popular around the world, animism is the belief that spirits or gods inhabit just about everything in nature. It is not a highly structured religion like Islam or Christianity but it should not be ignored when millions of people embrace it. Animism likely predates all other known religions, even Hinduism and Judaism. One can easily imagine some version of it being the first form of religious belief practiced by our prehistoric ancestors. If animism reaches back fifty thousand to one hundred thousand years or more—and it probably does—how can today's believers who place a premium on age dismiss it as untrue?

CHAPTER 43 BIBLIOGRAPHY AND RECOMMENDED READING

Haught, James A. *2000 Years of Disbelief.* Amherst, NY: Prometheus Books, 1996.

Sagan, Carl. *The Varieties of Scientific Experience.* New York: Penguin Press, 2006.

Smart, Ninian. *The World's Religions.* New York: Cambridge University Press, 1998.

Smith, Helena. "Greek Gods Prepare for Comeback." *Guardian*, May 5, 2006. http://www.guardian.co.uk/world/2006/may/05/greece.

"Windows to Timeless Truths." *Hinduism Today*, June 1988. http://www.hinduism today.com/archives/1988/06/1988-06-07.shtml.

Chapter 44

Someone I trust told me that my god is real.

Only you can make your mind up!
You're the one and only one!

—Dr. Seuss

This is a tough one. Suggesting that gods are almost certainly not real is not as simple as pointing to the absence of evidence and leaving it at that. It also means getting around the sticky issue of personal loyalties. The most important people in a believer's life, usually parents, were probably the ones who introduced the god or gods in the first place. Many believers have strong emotional ties to both the magical being and the real live people who taught and encouraged the belief. This mix of loyalties can be a powerful obstacle to thinking freely and questioning the existence of a god. For some, admitting that a god is not real can feel like betraying mom and dad.

Religious belief comes to most people very early in life. If it didn't, there is a good chance that all religions might fade away within a couple of generations. Consider how easy it is for a child to believe just about anything. When I was around four or five years old, for example, I believed in Santa Claus. I thought he really existed. I imagine that it didn't take much work for my parents to get me to believe in him. I loved my parents and they told me he was real, so I believed. It was as simple as that. But I am an adult now and if someone approached me with a wild claim about a man flying around the world in a sleigh delivering presents, I would not be convinced so easily. Belief in a god seems to follow a similar process. Some trusted authority figure, usually a parent, tells a young child that a god or gods are real and that's that. It's presented in a matter-of-fact manner with no mention of doubt or rival gods. End of discussion and the child believes. What is a four-year-old supposed to do, challenge the parent to a philosophical debate? Is a five-year-old likely to research classic religious claims and skeptical rebuttals? No, the belief usually settles in unopposed without resistance. After all, mom and dad would not say it if it weren't true, thinks the child.

In most cases, parents never tell the child that there are many thousands of gods who people have claimed to be real throughout history. They also fail to mention that there are thousands of religions active today and most of them make contradictory claims so many of them must be wrong. And they are sure to leave out the part about no religion having any strong evidence to back up its claims. The parent just declares that their god is the real one and the child should believe it, too. The child agrees, of course, and that's that. Given this process, it's no wonder that most people are believers today. And it's no surprise that virtually every believer believes in the same god that her or his parents believe in.

Most Christians today were born into societies where Christianity is the dominant belief system. Most Muslims today were born into societies where Islam is the dominant belief system. Most animists were born into societies where animism is the dominant belief system. And most Hindus were born into societies where Hinduism is the dominant belief system. This pattern shows that there is little or no thinking taking place when it comes to the selection of a god to believe in. It's all about what one is told to believe as a child. There are exceptions, but in the vast majority of cases, adult believers are clinging to what they were told as children by someone they trusted. Belief in a god comes to them as part of the parental package of love, guidance, protection, and wisdom. Believing in a parent's god becomes a significant part of the childhood experience. For some, it becomes extremely important, maybe even the most important part of their identity. To doubt one's god might be interpreted as disloyalty to parents. I think many nonbelievers fail to appreciate the complex emotions that can be tied up in belief. Believing in a god is not just about analyzing evidence and debating the concept of faith. Many times it also is about having to admit that a beloved parent probably was wrong.

Everyone should know that being led to an incorrect belief by parents does not necessarily mean that one was raised by bad parents or parents who were unintelligent. Mothers and fathers pass on belief in their god because they think it is true, not because they intend to trick children into believing things that are not true. After all, the parents likely were indoctrinated in the same way by their own parents. This chain of belief transfer from parent to child stretches back a long way but one should not have to feel bad or disloyal for breaking the chain. Most parents want what is best for their children so they wouldn't want their daughters and sons to give time, energy, and money to something that was not real.

The hard truth is that parents, no matter how loving, can be totally wrong about gods. Hindu parents do not love their children any less than Christian parents do. Jewish parents do not love their children any less than Muslim parents do. Animist parents love their children as much as Greek Orthodox parents do. Most parents who knew that their religion was wrong probably would not pass it on to their children. However, most of the loving parents on Earth today are teaching their children to believe in gods that are not real because all religions cannot be true. Therefore, many well-meaning mothers and fathers are introducing their children to fictional characters and telling them that they are real. Think about that, hundreds of millions of parents are encouraging or forcing their children to spend countless hours of their childhoods worshipping, studying, praying to, and fearing gods that do not exist. In most cases, the loving parents who do this would not if they suspected that their god or gods probably were make-believe.

Therefore, believers who dare to doubt do not have to feel that they are betraying their parents. Good parents do not want their children to believe in lies or mistakes. They want the best for their children, and most parents probably would agree that having a sharp mind that is uncluttered by made-up gods is best. So when a believer doubts and questions their god, they are not necessarily going against the wishes of the parents who originally encouraged the belief. By thinking and being honest, the son or daughter may be doing precisely what a loving parent would want them to do.

People do not necessarily have to tell anyone what they do or do not believe if they don't want to. If the topic of doubting gods is too sensitive for the people you care about, or if it may lead to discrimination or execution as it still does in some societies today, then skip it at the dinner table and talk about the weather instead. But never shut down your mind for the sake of anyone. Your mind is yours, or at least it should be. An incredibly long line of your ancestors were strong enough, smart enough, and attractive enough to keep your genes moving forward to the next generation. They delivered to you a human brain, a spectacular and powerful gift that deserves your appreciation. Don't disrespect all the hard work and good luck that led to you by wasting your ability to think.

Figuring out that gods are probably human creations does not necessarily have to turn one's life upside down. Ex-believers do not have to join an atheist club and start debating every creationist they can find. Ex-believers do not have to stop being around friends who are believers. Most of my friends believe in gods and I don't like them any less for it. Ex-believers do not even have to stop going to churches, mosques, or temples. If you like going there because you love the people, the stories, the music, the songs, the food, the sense of belonging, or any other reason, then keep going. Religion is not only about believing in unproven gods. The unquestionably real aspects of religions, such as the rituals, are a large part of human tradition. All people, believers or not, have a right to these things if they wish to participate in them.

I've been a nonbeliever for many years now but I still enjoy some religious things. Even though I think all gods probably are not real I can still enjoy being in some places of worship occasionally. I'm human and it's in my blood. I'm capable of *feeling* those songs and prayers. I see no reason to deny who I am, where I come from, and what I am a part of. Right now, there are several gospel songs on my iPod, for example. I don't believe that the songs reflect much that is accurate about the universe but I still like them because they make me feel good. I'm glad that I was able to become an atheist without developing contempt for religion. After the September 11 attacks on the World Trade Center, I came close. Fortunately, I realized that total condemnation was not intellectually justifiable. While I never hesitate to criticize the bad in religion, I have not lost sight of the good. Wouldn't it be great for the world if every believer made the decision to keep the positive and harmless aspects of their religions while rejecting the negative?

A growing number of Jewish people seem to be doing just that. Called "cultural Jews," they are atheists who still identify strongly with their Jewish religion and ancestry. Many of them attend temple regularly and observe Jewish holidays. Believing in a god is not necessary for them to enjoy their religion. It is the best of both worlds. People can be true to their mind and live in the real world while still experiencing a connection to their religious traditions. Perhaps one day we will see millions of "cultural Christians" and "cultural Muslims" enjoying their religious traditions without taking any of it too seriously.

Come to think of it, I suppose I could be considered a "cultural Christian." As I mentioned previously, I like a lot of gospel music, especially the old stuff, but it goes further than that. I love many classic films with strong religious themes such as *Ben-Hur* and *The Ten Commandments*. I consider them to be pure fiction rather than the docudramas some believers think they are, but I still enjoy them. I am also probably more gung ho about baby Jesus's birthday than most Christians are. When Christmas rolls around each year, I boom "Away in the Manger" in my car. I watch *It's a Wonderful Life* to see that lovable angel Clarence work his miracle on George Bailey one more time. And I refuse to take down the Christmas tree until well into January. None of this feels hypocritical to me. These things are a part of my cultural traditions, so I own them every bit as much as any devout believer does.

The important point here is that, by embracing reason and skepticism, believers do not have to feel disloyal to anyone should they come to the conclusion that their god is not real. They also do not have to give up everything they like about their religion if they don't want to. Who ever said that religion belongs to believers anyway? Religious *belief* may belong to the believers but religion belongs to all who want it.

CHAPTER 44 BIBLIOGRAPHY AND RECOMMENDED READING

Harpur, James. *The Atlas of Sacred Places: Meeting Points of Heaven and Earth*. New York: Henry Holt and Company, 1994.

Chapter 45

Atheism is a negative and empty philosophy.

I cannot be angry at God, in whom I do not believe.
—Simone de Beauvoir

My atheism describes what other people believe and how other people think; my atheism says nothing about what I believe and how I think.
—Cliff Walker

Some people attempt to defend their belief in a god by attacking the alternative. Nonbelief is a tragedy for an individual, they claim. By turning away from gods, atheists condemn themselves to a cold, bitter, and lonely life. If atheism offers nothing for one's life, say these believers, then obviously it is a negative and empty philosophy that should be avoided at all costs. In light of all this, is skepticism worth the risk? Could it be better to just believe and never question anything?

With nonsensical ideas like this floating around, it's no wonder so many people never find the courage to honestly analyze their beliefs. The claim that atheists are empty inside because they don't have a god in their life is laughable from the nonbeliever's perspective, but what about happiness? Maybe the atheist really is humankind's ultimate loser, forever languishing outside of the true human experience, never a legitimate member of the team, resigned to exist as nothing more

315

than a lump of flesh that won't be missed by the cosmos when death comes around.

So, is atheism really such a negative experience? It's a fair question. It is also a very relevant question because many religious people justify their confidence in a god's existence by imagining that there is a sort of horrible living death one must endure should they ever lose their religion. Fortunately for atheists, however, believers are completely wrong about this.

Few groups of people in the world are as misunderstood and misrepresented as nonbelievers. Although atheism does not necessarily mean anything more than the absence of belief in a god, many believers eagerly pack that term with as many negative connotations as they can. These believers typically think that atheists are immoral, mean, bitter, untrustworthy, and unhappy misfits. If atheism is a negative and empty lifestyle, then atheists must be negative and empty people, they conclude. This is a common sentiment. More than a few believers have directly or indirectly told me that they feel sorry for me because I don't believe in a god. It's a fact that many believers think atheists are victims. Rick Warren, Christian preacher and author of best-selling *The Purpose Driven Life*, says he has never met an atheist who wasn't angry (Meacham 2007). Warren needs to get out more. Apparently he hasn't met any of the millions of atheists spread across the world who are happy and far too busy living their lives to spend time grinding their teeth over religion. I'm definitely not angry and I'm pretty sure that most atheists aren't either. Between 46 and 85 percent of Sweden's population are nonbelievers. Do Warren and other like-minded believers really think that half or more of Sweden's population is angry? Many believers are so convinced that atheists are a bunch of deranged rebels who flew religion's coop purely out of anger and arrogance that they never seem to consider the possibility that most atheists just might be normal people who simply recognized that there is no good evidence or arguments for the existence of gods. Becoming an atheist can be a calm and peaceful process, and probably is for most people. Certainly anger and misery are not prerequisites for moving beyond belief.

Many believers also think that atheists are by definition bad people because anyone who could turn their back on a god cannot possibly be of good character. This is why most believers in America, for example, tell pollsters they would never vote for an atheist candidate. And this is why blatant prejudice against nonbelievers is not restricted to extremists on the fringes of religion. For example, when George H. W. Bush was campaigning for the US presidency in the 1980s he admitted to a reporter that he had doubts about whether or not American atheists could be considered citizens or patriots. Think about that, here we have a man who went on to become president and he openly suggested that atheists were some kind of inferior Americans.

Why do believers develop these negative feelings about people who don't believe in a god? Most believers are more negative toward atheists than they are followers of rival religions that strongly contradict theirs. Somehow a typical believer is more comfortable with someone who says, "I think my god is real and yours is not," than they are with someone who says, "I think it's likely that no gods are real." I suspect this is because the existence of atheists is disorienting for many believers. They might silently wonder how religion and their god can be so important when people who are kind, sane, and intelligent are able to live happy lives without religion or gods. Those who believe in other gods can be explained away as well-meaning people who were fooled by false prophets. "At least they believe in something," says the believer. But the smiling, open-minded atheist is a contradiction to everything they have been told. Hundreds of millions of atheists who have looked for gods and found only empty air destroy the believer's fantasy of an obvious need for religion.

Generalizing about atheists is almost always a mistake. Yes, atheists may be overrepresented among highly educated people and underrepresented among inmates on death row. Yes, they are prominent among elite American scientists and scarce within terrorist organizations. Beyond that, however, not much is safe to assume about the world's atheists. There is even significant variation on their position about the existence of gods. For example, some atheists say they are absolutely certain that gods do not exist. They "know" it in a way that is similar to people who "know" that gods are real. Other atheists freely admit that they can't say for certain that all gods do not exist but simply don't believe in any of them. And some atheists don't care about gods one way or the other. They can't, or don't want to, devote the time to think about it. They just know that they aren't convinced that any gods are real. Few believers seem to be aware of it, but atheism is not a club with a list of membership requirements. It's not a religion that demands leaps of faith, a dress code, or allegiance to a leader. It is not a shadowy organization with rules, traditions, and a secret handshake. Atheism is the absence of belief, nothing more. What does or does not fill that void, if there is a void, is up to the individual atheist.

Despite their diversity, there may be some trends among nonbelievers worth noting. A 2005 Gallup International study called "Voice of the People" surveyed fifty thousand people in more than sixty-five countries and found that people with secondary or high-level education are less religious than people with no education or only a basic education. While this is interesting, I would caution against reading too much into that, however. Nonbelievers may be overrepresented among better-educated people only because higher education increases the chances of being exposed to alternative ideas about gods. It does not necessarily have anything to do with innate intelligence. Some religious claims may seem stupid but it does not necessarily mean that all people who believe them are stupid. The same goes for atheists. Some nonbelievers may have sidestepped irrational belief, not because they are brilliant thinkers, but only because they were fortunate enough to hear key criticisms or stumble upon enlightening books.

So, are atheists these angry misfits believers say they are? Sure, some of them are, but too many atheists are warm, happy people to ever make that accusation stick. People do not need to believe that Allah, Jesus, or Luna are real in order to have a little pep in their step. There is plenty of inspiration, contentment, meaning, and happiness to be found in the real world too. Millions of cheerful, optimistic, and energetic atheists prove it every day.

One should always be careful about generalizing too much about atheists, however. It's no less risky than generalizing about believers. Imagine trying to meaningfully describe all the world's believers in just a few words. It can't be done safely. Across the human population, there are many differences among those who believe in a god. "Believer" does not necessarily mean anything other than one who believes in a god or gods, just as atheism does not necessarily mean anything other than one who does not believe in a god.

By the way, believers who read so much negativity into atheism might consider the fact that every baby in the world is an atheist— even babies born into very religious families. It's true. No one is born believing in Allah, Jesus, or He Zur, the ancient Egyptian baboon god. Despite the various religious labels adults instantly impose on their babies, adults have to introduce gods into their minds when they are sufficiently developed to accept them. Prejudiced believers might remember this when they talk about how horrible atheists are. We all start out in life as atheists. Some of us finish life that way, too.

Some believers are more forgiving of agnostics than atheists. Some view agnostics as only momentarily lost or confused, and likely to eventually find a god. While it's nice to sit on fences sometimes, I suggest avoiding the whole agnosticism trip. It might seem appealing in a middle-of-the-road sort of way but agnosticism is not what most people think it is. There are different varieties of agnosticism but the popular version of it takes the odd position that gods are unknowable. Some people are attracted to it because it feels like a polite compromise between the too-soft believers and the too-hard atheists. But agnosticism does not take a position on belief or nonbelief at all. It addresses a different question and says nothing about belief itself. When someone tells me they are agnostic, I reply, "Fine, so are you an atheist or a believer?" Theoretically, one can be an agnostic and believe in a god just as one can be an agnostic and be an atheist. Agnosticism is a side road that leads nowhere. How can agnostics claim that gods are unknowable, anyway? What evidence do agnostics have that leads them to know that Jesus and Vishnu won't appear in Time Square next New Year's Eve? They would be knowable then, wouldn't they? How do agnostics know that archaeologists won't unearth the fossilized cranium of Medusa next week? Unknowable? Says who? NASA launches probes all the time. Maybe one of them will get lucky and land on Mars—the god not the planet. Our species is still too new to the game of exploration to declare anything unknowable just yet. The popular version of agnosticism just feels like a cop-out. I say belief is like being pregnant. You either are a believer or you are not a believer. My advice would be to pass agnosticism and proceed directly to atheism.

Believers who may be tempted to doubt should know that there is nothing to fear about atheism. Yes, religious people over the centuries have turned "atheist," "infidel," and "nonbeliever" into bad words but that's their hang-up and their mistake. It's not the fault of nonbelievers that they have been incorrectly defined by people with clear biases. Atheists in free countries have not come anywhere near compiling a list of crimes comparable to believers. From the conquistadors to the scourge of religious terrorism and molestation of children by holy men, believers have done far more to justify a bad reputation than atheists have.

Apart from the problem of believers' prejudice, however, atheism is nothing to lose sleep over. Many atheists are good people who raise bright children, rake the leaves in their yards, and open doors for strangers. One does not need to believe in gods to be a decent human being. Fear of becoming a godless zombie with a chilled heart certainly is no reason to cling to belief in a god or gods when one may be having doubts. Besides, most people don't have to make a decision about belief anyway. The mind usually makes it for you, if it is allowed to run free. A believer once asked me why I would ever choose to be an atheist. I answered that I had decided it made more sense. But that was not an entirely accurate answer. Later I thought about it and realized that I never actually *chose* atheism. I doubt that anyone makes the choice to not believe in gods. It is not a conscious decision in the way one chooses what shirt to wear in the morning. I think nonbelief just sort of happens for most atheists. It's like an involuntary reflex of the mind that kicks in when a sufficient threshold of skepticism and honest analysis is crossed. But it may come rapidly or slowly. The change from belief to nonbelief might be a sudden flash or a gradual realization with no recognizable moment of transition. However, I cannot imagine a believer simply waking up one morning and *deciding* that they would no longer believe in gods. It seems to me that, for those who sincerely believe, there must first be a process. There needs to be an erosion or demolition of all the empty arguments and false evidence that previously supported belief in the person's mind. One cannot just dismiss in an instant all those reasons for belief when they have worked so well for many years. Strong ideas have to confront weak ideas. It takes time.

The reverse of this is true as well. For example, I could not simply choose to believe in Allah, Apollo, or Jesus at this point in my life. The facts and ideas in my head simply do not support it so I cannot sincerely believe. There is no way of getting around the conclusions in my mind that led me to reject gods as real. I could say I believe that Tutankhamen is a god who still lives in some other dimension, but I would be lying. I don't really believe that. I could try very hard to believe in gods but, without some evidence or at least a few strong arguments to convince me, it would just be acting. The believer should take from this that atheism is not a conscious act of turning away from all gods. It is simply the final destination for those who think. Nonbelievers do not *choose* atheism. They arrive at it by thinking.

If you are a believer and one day find that somehow you have transformed into an atheist, you will be pleased to discover that the sky does not fall down on your head and demons will not jump inside you. If you still want to pray, you can. (The success rate of your prayers is unlikely to change.) And you will be in no more danger of being struck by lightning than you were when you believed in a god. However, you might notice a new sense of liberation. If you were deeply religious before, you might even discover that you have more time to devote to family and friends. Maybe you will have more energy for positive activities that enrich your life and make you happy. And with no more of that afterlife stuff as a distraction or excuse, you might even discover a newfound desire to get busy making the world better for yourself and everyone else right here and now.

It simply is untrue that life is necessarily empty and meaningless without some god flying around in your head. If you are fortunate enough not to be one of the millions of people who suffer in severe poverty or the horrors of some war, life can be a fantastic ride with or without gods. Belief is just one of many factors that influence the quality of life. Furthermore, it is impossible to measure how much of an impact belief has on someone's life. For example, is a happy believer who has a good education, a satisfying job, and a love-filled family happy because she or he believes in a god, or because of those other factors? Who can tell? Even the believers cannot know for sure.

There are, of course, many cultural variations, but from what I have seen, most believers are not much different than atheists when it comes to thoughts about death. Both don't like thinking about it very much and both try to avoid it at all costs. Most believers supposedly are convinced that there is something much better waiting for them when they die. Strangely, however, they look both ways before crossing streets, take medication, undergo surgeries, and even pray desperate prayers in the hopes of avoiding death when they are in trouble. If I truly believed that I would enter into some sort of amazing paradise when I died, I'm not sure I would worry as much about skin cancer or binging on cream-filled doughnuts. If I knew, I mean *really knew*, that I would go to heaven when I died, I could not possibly appreciate this life as much as I currently do. My time on earth would be diminished, subconsciously at least. There might be something more after death, but my hunch is that this is all we get. It's one of the reasons I tell my children and my wife that I love them every time I see them. It's one of the reasons I rarely fail to notice birds soaring above my head and green grass beneath my feet. It's probably one of the reasons why I have had an extremely happy life so far. I acknowledge death for what it is—death. Therefore I am highly motivated to be fully alive while I am alive.

Despite what believers think, it could be that atheism steers some people in precisely the opposite direction of an empty and meaningless life. Many atheists tend to confront reality like grown-ups. Not having gods to fear, look to for guidance, or shift responsibility to for the problems of the world makes one a lot more likely to care about changing things for the better. If I had been an atheist slave in the 1800s, for example, I would not have been content to shrug my shoulders and wait for better days in heaven. I think I would have done anything to escape or rebel because I would have believed that my life was too precious to waste in chains. When I think about the millions of children who die in poverty each year, I do not have the luxury of accepting it as the will of a god who allows horrible things to occur. I can't be content in the belief that those dead children will find peace and comfort in some god's heaven. As an atheist my only options are to be a heartless bastard and ignore their cries, or to try and save a few of them. As an atheist, I have to confront reality as I find it.

It really can be a wonderful life without gods. No matter what believers may say to the contrary, gods are not necessary for one to find happiness and purpose in this world. Family, friends, accomplishments, helping others, and the acts of creating and discovering are all sources of infinite joy and they do not depend on the existence of magical beings. Wise choices, hard work, being born somewhere other than an impoverished hellhole, good health, and a little good luck can add up to a fine existence for just about anyone. There are no guarantees in life, of course, but one can stack the odds favorably simply by playing the game wisely.

In a sense, believers are correct about what atheism fails to give. It offers no philosophy of life or sense of purpose. But they point to this as if it is a strike against atheism. Clearly they have misunderstood atheism to be a religion or some codified way of life. But the simple truth is that atheists are nothing more than people without belief. What they wish to be or do beyond that is determined by their own desires, ambition, and courage. Atheists are free to choose.

CHAPTER 45 BIBLIOGRAPHY AND RECOMMENDED READING

Meacham, Jon. "The God Debate." *Newsweek*, April 9, 2007. http://www.msnbc .msn.com/id/17889148/site/newsweek/print/1/displaymode/1098/.

Chapter 46

Believing in a god doesn't hurt anyone.

*With or without religion, you would have good
people doing good things and evil people doing evil
things. But for good people to do evil things, that
takes religion.*

—Steven Weinberg

Much to my surprise, I have discovered that many believers
think that believing in a god is perfectly safe. What could
possibly go wrong? Religion is a peaceful and positive activity, they
tell me with a straight face. Yes, this unlikely justification for belief is
more common than one might imagine. I have heard it from numerous
believers in a variety of religions.

So, where does one begin to challenge the claim that believing in
gods is a harmless hobby? How about any history book or any newspaper? There certainly is plenty of evidence available that links belief
in gods to people being harmed. Maybe this is the problem. Perhaps
violence rooted in religious belief is so common that few people notice
it for what it is anymore. When Shiite and Sunni Muslims slaughter
each other, it's not religious violence; it's "sectarian" violence. When
a Christian murders an abortion doctor or a Muslim blows up a
building, it's not religious terrorism; it's just terrorism. When believers
block the progress of medical science at the expense of suffering
people, it's not a problem generated by religion; it's "bioethics."

Following the media's lead, most people have taken up the habit of calling many of those who commit violence in the name of their religion "extremists" or "fanatics." While these popular labels may or may not be accurate, the rarely spoken description that is most accurate is "believer." Remove belief in gods from the minds of these killers and many of them might at least think twice about throwing away their own lives and other people's lives. But few people today point the finger at religion even when religion is obviously a factor.

Why is this strange defense of religious belief so common? Why do so many people say that belief in gods is harmless, when clearly it is so harmful? I wonder if perhaps it is because believers mean to refer only to themselves. Perhaps they intend to say that *their* personal belief is not leading them to hurt or kill others, that *their* belief in isolation is harmless. But even this much-reduced claim may not be true.

Author Sam Harris charges in his book *The End of Faith* that even the peaceful believers of the world are accomplices to evil. These people, Harris believes, form the necessary foundation that inspires and protects religious murderers. The men who flew planes into the World Trade Center, for example, did not spring from thin air. They were the products of the world's second-most popular religion. He makes a good point. I remember after the September 11 attacks that there was no meaningful public debate about the validity of Islam or religion in general. Instead, there was a strong effort by many people, including many Christians, to make the hijackers seem like they had come from another planet and had nothing to do with Islam.

The slight variation of "*my* personal belief is harmless" certainly has a better chance of being correct than the general statement that so often comes out of the mouths of believers. But, no, I have paid attention and the intent is clear. When believers declare that belief in a god is harmless, they are not just defending what is going on in their heads. They are defending religion in the broadest sense (or at least their specific brand of religion in the broadest sense). And this is very odd. If anything should be clear to us by now, after so many centuries of spilled blood, it is that religion is a source of tremendous prejudice, hatred, division, violence, and murder. It also slows scientific progress in ways that harm and kill additional millions and contribute to the suffering of millions more. Although it is not as dramatic as a sword or suicide bomber, religion as an obstacle to science, particularly medical science, probably has cost more lives than all wars combined. Just consider, for example, that early scientists and doctors in Europe could not even study dead bodies to learn more about human anatomy without stirring up dangerous religious objections that could land them in jail or worse. Many of the newer medications and procedures that are standard in hospitals around the world today, for example, might have been developed and made available much earlier if religions had not opposed so many avenues of research throughout history. The problem continues today with believers slowing stem-cell research.

Many believers are so committed to promoting the claim that religion is the source of everything good, that they have blinded themselves to the reality of today and of the last ten thousand years. Religion can be very bad. There, I said it. But why is that such a bold and daring statement to so many people? Isn't it obvious? To deny that very bad things come from believing in gods is to deny what we see all around us. Belief has led millions of people to hate and kill. Belief has robbed millions of people of their intellectual potential. Belief has enslaved millions of women. Belief has caused immeasurable suffering. These are facts, not opinions.

To state the obvious, that religion can be bad, is not to say that nothing good comes from religion. Of course many positive things have a direct link to belief in gods. But even the good we find in religion is not enough to justify the bad. First of all, I think enough of my fellow humans to believe that they have the potential to be good and to do good without having to believe that a god is watching over their shoulders. It is also important to make clear that I am not making a case against the existence of gods based on the horrible behavior that religious belief so often inspires. Bad religious people do not disprove the existence of gods any more than good religious people prove that gods are real. The harm religious belief inflicts on individuals and societies has always been obvious to me, but apparently that is not the case for everyone. So let's review a few ways in which belief in a god can cause harm. The book *Holy Hatred*, by James Haught, is an excellent, although depressing, review of some of the routine madness belief brings. Haught, a West Virginia newspaper editor, keeps his eyes on the news of the world so he is well aware of the havoc and horror generated by belief in gods. I was once a world news editor and relate to his experience at scanning daily wire reports. Part of my morning ritual was to browse through the Associated Press service that my newspaper subscribes to. Virtually every day I would find reports and/or photos of some religion-oriented horror that had occurred in the last twenty-four hours somewhere in the world. Perhaps because of our jobs Haught and I are just more informed than most believers about what goes on in the name of religion. If so, trust us, it's bad.

Religion has divided, deluded, and driven people to murder one another since the dawn of civilization. Now, in the twenty-first century, belief continues to incite many people to butcher their neighbors. I wish that every person who holds the notion that belief in gods is harmless would read Haught's book. Here are just a few lowlights of religious madness included in *Holy Hatred*:

- India (1992): approximately two thousand Hindus and Muslims are killed in riots over a site where Hindus believe Lord Rama was born nine hundred thousand years ago. Meanwhile, massacres occur in Kashmir related to a sacred relic—a hair from Muhammad's beard.
- The United States (1993): a Christian woman shoots an abortion clinic doctor and calls it "the most holy, the most righteous thing I've ever done." Another Christian who kills a clinic doctor is called "a hero" by a Christian magazine.
- Somalia (1993): Islamic leaders sentence five women to be stoned to death for adultery. Worshippers kill the women after evening prayers. Cheering onlookers videotape the execution.

- Israel (1994): a Jewish doctor with a machine gun opens fire on worshippers in a mosque, killing thirty Muslims. (Haught 1994)

Sadly, such acts are all too common. Belief in gods seems to me like a loaded gun left on the table. Most people would never pick it up and pull the trigger; but too many do. Although well-meaning believers would say that religious tolerance is the solution for all this violence, I can't imagine how. Read the uncompromising sacred writings of the world's major religions. Listen to the divisive words of prominent religious leaders. The "great religions" are incompatible worldviews. The more devout Hindus, Muslims, Jews, and Christians, for example, will never get along, fully integrate, and live in peace so long as they continue to take their beliefs seriously.

Haught's book also offers a glance back at several historical tragedies tied to belief. As with the news of today, there is no shortage of god-related massacres and wars over the last several centuries. Hopefully most people are aware of the Crusades, the Inquisition, and the witch burnings in Europe, but how many know about the Taiping Rebellion in China during the 1800s? It's a total blank in the minds of most Westerners. This is odd since it ranks as one of the bloodiest wars in all of history and the man who started it, Hung Hsiu-ch'üan, was a Christian who fought in the name of Jesus.

Hsiu-ch'üan claimed that Jesus visited him and, as a result, he became a highly motivated Christian. He studied under an American missionary to learn more about Christianity and then vowed to spread the religion across China. One of the goals of his war was to rid the nation of false gods and idols so that Christianity could flourish. The death toll of Hsiu-ch'üan's Asian crusade is shocking. This war in China, fought for Jesus, claimed an estimated twenty million lives. For comparison's sake, approximately nineteen million people were killed in World War I. Why have so few Christians heard of the Taiping Rebellion? Again, to be clear, citing mass deaths that were related to belief in Jesus does not condemn Christianity in general nor should anyone think it disproves the existence of Jesus. But it does show that religions, including Christianity, have the potential to cause extreme violence.

Many peaceful Muslims who condemn the murder of innocent people by Islamic terrorists seem to be unaware of just how supportive their belief system is of such behavior. The Koran, for example, contains lines that seem to condone, if not require, murder. Fortunately, most Muslims ignore these instructions. The problem, however, is that some Muslims do take it as they read it. As for Jews, their own stories in the Torah, if even half true, reveal a bloody past that includes massacres, rape, and slavery committed on behalf of their god or with his approval. Many of the laws listed in the Torah continue to be a source of and fuel for dangerous prejudice today.

Religion may be good for the world in some ways. But no matter what believers may claim, it can also lead to terrible harm.

CHAPTER 46 BIBLIOGRAPHY AND RECOMMENDED READING

Harris, Sam. *The End of Faith: Religion, Terror, and the Future of Reason.* New York: W. W. Norton & Company, 2004.

Haught, James. *Holy Hatred.* Amherst, NY: Prometheus Books, 1994.

Seuss, Dr. *The Sneetches and Other Stories.* New York: Random House, 1989. It may be a children's story but the tale of the irrational Sneetches and their obsession with labels offers a lesson for grownups too.

Chapter 47

The earth is perfectly tuned to support life.

"**M**y god *must* exist," declares the believer, "because the earth is put together in just the right way and positioned in space at just the right angle and distance from the Sun to provide the perfect home for us. Our world is too accommodating and too special to be an accident. Just imagine, if our planet was slightly different, we couldn't survive."

There's more. Some believers point to Jupiter's suspiciously convenient placement. With its immense gravity, our solar system's biggest planet has served as a sort of protective vacuum cleaner by sucking up or diverting many giant meteors and asteroids that might otherwise have hit us. Finally, believers ask us to simply look around the universe. Earth is a unique, warm, and watery outpost of life in cold, silent space. "It is obvious," say believers, "that my god made this planet exactly the way it is for us."

This line of reasoning seems to make perfect sense and it feels like a convincing argument, if not outright proof, for a god's existence. But it only works if one knows nothing about life on Earth. If the millions of species currently alive had popped into existence exactly as we find them today, then, yes, it would be justified to suspect that this planet is just way too perfect of a match for their needs to be anything other than a god's creation. However, evolution does a very good job of explaining why we find oxygen-breathing animals living on a planet with lots of oxygen. It explains why sun-dependent plants are living on a sunny planet. And it explains why creatures with fins and gills are swimming around on a planet that has lots of water. The interaction between this planet's environment and the life on it, over billions of years, has resulted in a workable fit—although a less-than-perfect fit, as an extinction rate of more than 98 percent shows.

Believers who gravitate toward this idea of the earth being a precision-crafted utopia for humans are making a completely understandable mistake given what they probably don't know about nature. Through no fault of their own, most people are never taught very much about evolution in school. So, it is to be expected that they wouldn't immediately understand how we ended up with needs and abilities that match the environment and the resources around us. Take away that four billion years of evolution and the only logical answer is that this planet must have been custom-made for people, ferns, and ants. But we can't ignore or deny those four billion years of evolution. They really happened. Life really did evolve, regardless of what TV preachers and the Taliban say. One cannot understand life on Earth without understanding evolution. It's as simple as that.

To say our planet was designed, created, and fine-tuned just so that we could live on it gets it precisely backward. What we have is life that has been fine-tuned to live on Earth. And it was evolution that did the tuning. Yes, we are fortunate that the earth does not have an atmosphere like Saturn's or follow the orbital course of Venus. If it did we could not function. We could not survive. But that's okay because we would never be. "We" would have either evolved to be something very different or we simply would not have existed at all. Given our current physical makeup, we need a planet with gravity like Earth's, an atmosphere like Earth's, and natural resources like Earth's. Why? The reason we have these requirements is because we are the current embodiment of evolutionary history on Earth (along with several million other species alive today). We fit on this world because we evolved on this world.

The book *Rare Earth: Why Complex Life Is Uncommon in the Universe* (Ward and Brownlee 2003) probably makes the best argument for our planet being a unique nest for intelligent life. Ward and Brownlee admit that there is a good chance that simple microbial life is common throughout the universe but they believe complex intelligent life is probably only found on Earth. This sounds suspiciously like pre-Copernicus thinking to me. It's as if they are saying that while the earth may not be the center of the universe, humans are the center of life in the universe. It seems like yet another effort, either conscious or subconscious, to reassure us that we are something special and important in a big, dark, and scary universe. I am not suggesting that the authors necessarily meant for there to be a subtle pro-god message in their book but many believers certainly have gobbled up their words to use as ammunition for the claim that their god made the earth just for us. The two authors support their case for a unique earth by citing numerous challenges life had to overcome in order to produce a highly intelligent species. They certainly are correct about this. It has been tough going for life here and it's still tough going considering the high extinction rate. But Ward and Brownlee overreach when they suggest that we know enough about the possible varieties of life in the universe to impose limitations on it. I have in my personal library, for example, a four-and-a-half-pound book called *The Variety of Life* by Colin Tudge. This hefty 685-page survey of life is impressive but it only scratches the surface. An estimated ten to one hundred million species are alive on Earth today. But we just reached the milestone of identifying the one-millionth species in 2007. Space exploration aside, scientists discover strange new life-forms right here at home all the time. For example, some rock-eating microbes have been found that don't need sunlight or oxygen to live. It seems to me that we have a lot more to learn about life here on Earth before we can justify limiting the potential for life—including intelligent life—everywhere in the universe.

It is misleading to list factors that enabled intelligent life to rise on Earth, as some believers do, and then declare it impossible for such complex circumstances to ever occur on another planet in just the same way. Of course it is unlikely or impossible if you are looking for a repeat of exactly what happened here. Even with billions of chances for earthlike conditions to be found on other planets throughout the universe, it is virtually impossible that life would evolve in the same way it has here. There are too many factors, too many possible tangents. Those who say that intelligent life is unlikely to exist anywhere other than earth reveal what I think of as an expanded version of ethnocentrism (bias for one's culture). In this case people are showing bias for humankind. How can anyone reasonably suggest that intelligent life must be similar to us and live in conditions similar to our planet in order to exist? So far, we only know about life on one planet, the earth, and we don't even know everything about that. We cannot assume that intelligent life elsewhere requires a planet with a certain amount of water, the right amount of hydrogen, a specific level of heat, and a limited amount of radiation. At this very early point in our exploration of space and with only the example of our own planet's life to study so far, there is no good reason to argue that intelligent life must be rare in the universe. There are billions of planets, billions of years to play with, and we have no direct knowledge of what extraterrestrial life may be like if it does exist. We cannot apply the specific success story of one species on one planet to the entire universe and use it to determine that we must be alone because intelligent life is just too fickle and demanding. Who knows? Intelligent life in a neighboring star system might *require* a strong and steady dose of gamma radiation in order to live. Water might be poison for the intelligent life over in the next galaxy. We can't eliminate possibilities yet. The most sensible position, therefore, is that at this time we do not know if Earth is a unique home to intelligent life or not. It is simply too early to draw conclusions. Imagine how much more we will know about the universe a thousand years from now. Maybe we really are special and maybe our world really is the unique creation of a god, but we have a lot of work to do before arriving at that profound conclusion.

The claim that the earth was made for us reminds me of a bizarre presentation I once saw on a religious television program. "Behold, the atheist's nightmare!" declared believer Ray Comfort, a host of the show. Comfort explained that the banana was perfectly designed to suit human needs and therefore had to have been made by his god for our use. The banana's easy-peel skin and curved structure that fits so well into the human hand proves it was intelligently designed for us, he said.

But hold on, just because something may be a good fit is no reason to necessarily conclude that it was magically created with that purpose in mind. This applies to both planets and bananas. The earth may be a good fit for much of the life on it today but this is not a reason to believe it was created by a god. We need something more than a comfortable fit to prove that, especially when we have an alternative explanation that is supported by strong evidence.

Has Comfort considered a scientific explanation? Maybe the primate hand evolved to grip tree branches and the result was a hand that is complex, flexible, and able to grip many different objects effectively. The human hand is able to grip a rattlesnake quite well too. Did Comfort's god design them for us to hold, too? Comfort, a creationist, sees the banana the same way he sees the earth. He thinks that they both were made by a god for our use. I think we evolved to live on the earth and our hands evolved to grip many things, including bananas. The problem for Comfort is that there is no evidence to support his claim of a magical creation for either the earth or the banana. Evidence for my claim, however, can be seen in thousands of museums and laboratories around the world.

I wish I had a TV show like Comfort because where I live we have the atheists' secret weapon lying around on the ground everywhere. I would love to stare into the camera lens, dramatically raise my glorious coconut high in the air like King Arthur's Excalibur, and say: "Behold, the believer's worst nightmare!" I could explain to my audience that the coconut, a popular human food, clearly was designed by unintelligent and indifferent evolution with absolutely no sympathy for the limitations of the human hand. I could smugly challenge believers to try opening coconuts with their bare hands. Yes, if Ray Comfort's banana proves a god is real, then my coconut proves evolution is real.

The earth is a wonderful planet that provides an ideal home for us. (Except for the frequent earthquakes, hurricanes, tornadoes, floods, and plagues of course.) But we still know so little about the universe at this time that we must hold off on judgments as to whether intelligent life only rose on Earth. If it turns out it did, then we may consider ourselves fortunate indeed. But it still wouldn't be enough to conclude that a god was behind our existence. Unusual things do happen. Rare events are not impossible events. Believers, more than anyone, should agree with that.

CHAPTER 47 BIBLIOGRAPHY AND RECOMMENDED READING

Darling, David. *Life Everywhere*. New York: Basic Books, 2001. This is a fascinating survey of what Darling calls "the maverick science of astrobiology." It presents a convincing rebuttal to the Rare Earth hypothesis that claims intelligent life is probably an Earth-only phenomenon.

Dawkins, Richard. *The Ancestor's Tale: A Pilgrimage to the Dawn of Evolution*. Boston/New York: Houghton Mifflin, 2004. An outstanding journey through time and a fun way to learn about evolution and life on Earth.

Tudge, Colin. *The Variety of Life*. New York: Oxford University Press, 2002.

Ward, Peter, and Donald Brownlee. *Rare Earth: Why Complex Life Is Uncommon in the Universe*. New York: Springer, 2003.

Chapter 48

Believing is natural so my god must be real.

The unexamined life is not worth living.

—Socrates

Many believers point to the popularity of belief in gods itself as proof that gods are real. Look at humankind, look at history, they say. Take note of how many people believe. Probably every society that has ever existed has had at least some people who believed in a god. Obviously this means there must be something to it. Belief could not be so common and so enduring if gods were not real, say believers. Or could it?

This is another common justification for belief that seems to make sense until it collides with a few facts. Yes, belief in gods has been around a long time and remains popular today. But this does not support any one particular religion's claims. If anything, the historic and global breakdown of who believes what strongly suggests that gods are not real. The existence of so many diverse religions is primarily a reason to suspect that humans have a strong inclination and talent for inventing gods.

Virtually all past and present religions do not complement or support one another. There is no common god among all the religions of the past or present. The only similarity is the belief in something or someone who is supernatural. These thousands of very different religions contradict each other so thoroughly that they cancel out each other's credibility. For example, ancient Romans believing in Neptune two thousand years ago do not provide support for Mormons today who believe that Joseph Smith had a conversation with an angel in the 1800s. How does the traditional religion of the Hopi people provide ammunition to modern Christians who seek to prove that Jesus is a god? A fondness for religions proves nothing about whether or not the objects of so much belief and worship exist.

Some people say believing in their god is natural and therefore their god must be real. But how "natural" is religious belief really? If by "natural" they mean belief that a god exists is a standard component of a healthy human being, then one would think it would blossom on its own and require little upkeep or encouragement. This is not what we see, however, as significant time and energy is required to instruct a person on which god to believe in and how to properly worship that god. This is why Hindu parents must instruct their children that many gods are real and Muslim parents must instruct their children that only one god is real. One would think that if belief were natural, placed in us by a god, then it should come a little more easily. Consider how much money and labor the world's religions spend recruiting and maintaining their members. Many religious organizations employ tactics that to some nonbelievers, at least, seem transparently devious. Speaking for the gods, religious leaders promise elaborate rewards to followers such as financial success in this life and access to heaven. Many religions also use fear as a motivator to keep people believing. The threat of hell or an unfortunate reincarnation, for example, are not taken lightly by many hundreds of millions of believers today. If belief in a god is natural, then why is there a need for prophets and preachers to continually push the lure of pleasure and the fear of punishment? Why is there this need to constantly sell belief? Shouldn't any valid religion that is derived from a real god be able to sell itself? If Jesus is really a god and Christianity is both true and natural, then why the need for missionaries, Gideon Bibles in hotel rooms, gospel rock concerts, and twenty-four-hour Christian TV channels? If Islam is true and it is natural for all humans to believe in Allah, then why hasn't Islam won over the world yet? It has been around for more than a thousand years and 80 percent of the world's population still does not believe it.

Imagine if there was only one religion instead of the many thousands that humans have claimed to be true at one time or another over the last one hundred thousand years. If this were the case, if the vast majority of people on Earth only believed in one specific god and no one had ever claimed the existence of any other gods in history, then the "belief is natural" claim would be more intriguing. It would, after all, be difficult to explain how people in North America, Europe, South America, Asia, Africa, Australia, and all the islands of the world came up with the same unique god. Seeing Pakistanis and Icelanders, Mexicans, and Fijians all performing the exact same rituals and praying to the same god, despite relative isolation over the last several thousand years, would be compelling to say the least. But this is not the world we see. Humans have never been united in belief at any time in history. Never. Our species has never agreed on who the gods are or how to worship them. And this disharmony is not a case of splitting hairs. We are talking absolutely irreconcilable differences here. Jehovah's Witnesses, for example, will never see to eye-to-eye with Hindus unless one of them jettisons virtually all of their core beliefs.

More trouble for the "belief is natural" justification is the existence of so many nonbelievers. Even if we omit all people who live in oppressive societies with government-encouraged atheism, we end up with a large number of people who freely opt not to believe in gods. These people, grouped together as nonbelievers, nonreligous, atheists, agnostics, brights, and free thinkers, come from diverse places and diverse backgrounds. But they all came to the same conclusion: that there is no justification for belief in any of the gods proposed by religions. Estimates for the number of free people who live without belief range from five hundred to seven hundred fifty million (*Cambridge Companion* 2007, 61). This is a huge number. So big, in fact, that it represents the fourth-largest block of people in the world, behind only

340   50 REASONS PEOPLE GIVE FOR BELIEVING IN A GOD

Christians (2.1 billion), Muslims (1.3 billion), and Hindus (900 million). This probably surprises many people because nonbelievers tend
to fly under the radar. They are not united in the way religious people
are so they don't get the attention their numbers would suggest they
deserve. There is also the factor of "closet atheists," those who choose
to keep their atheism a secret because they fear persecution or rejection from family, friends, schoolmates, colleagues, or bosses. Judging
by the numbers, most believers probably have an atheist for a
coworker, friend, or family member.

In the United States, for example, there are about as many nonreligious citizens as there are African Americans or gays. But those two
groups, despite their own acceptance problems, have more political
clout and receive more media attention than nonreligious Americans
do. Furthermore, nonreligious Americans outnumber ethnic Jews and
Mormons but, again, have such a lower profile that few people are
aware of it.

An interesting investigation is ongoing about the possible natural
roots of religion in the human mind and DNA. Some researchers think
that we may be biologically "hardwired" for religion. They suggest
that our brains are structured in a way that makes religious belief not
only possible but virtually inevitable, no matter how much it may contradict reason. If this turns out to be true, there are two ways to look at
it. Nonbelievers might latch onto it as a natural explanation for the
otherwise difficult-to-explain popularity of religion. But believers can
point to it as evidence that their gods are real. Our brains are built to
believe in a god because our creator wanted us to believe in him or her,
they will say. Of course believers will need to explain why their real
god programmed the human species in such a way that leads so many
people to believe in the "wrong" gods.

Religious belief might have had a functional value somewhere
along the line in our evolutionary past and therefore might have been
selected for. Maybe tribes that believed in gods were more unified and
able to organize themselves better than tribes that did not. Maybe
belief encouraged more communication, which led to faster cultural

and technological development. Maybe tribes who fought for imagined gods fought harder than tribes who lacked that motivation. There are many possibilities that could explain how we ended up being a species that naturally believes in gods, if that is what we are.

Sociologist Phil Zuckerman doesn't buy the "belief is natural" idea. He points to the large number of nonbelievers in the world and asks how belief can be a standard component of the modern human when as many as seven hundred fifty million people don't believe. Zuckerman writes in *The Cambridge Companion to Atheism*:

> With between 500 million and 750 million nontheists living on this planet today, any suggestion that belief in God is natural, inborn, or a result of how our brains are wired becomes difficult to sustain. Second, innate/neural theories of belief in God cannot explain the dramatically different rates of belief among similar countries. Consider Britain (31%–44% atheist) compared with Ireland (4%–5% atheist), the Czech Republic (54%–61%) compared with Poland (3%–6% atheist), and South Korea (30%–52% atheist) compared with the Philippines (less than 1% atheist). It is simply unsustainable to argue that these glaring differences in rates of atheism among these nations is due to different biological, neurological or other such brain-related properties. Rather, the differences are better explained by taking into account historical, cultural, economic, political and sociological factors. (Zuckerman 2006)

So, is belief in a god an instinctive impulse that most people can't resist? Is it a cultural phenomenon that only survives because it is taught to each succeeding generation? Are we hardwired to see gods in the sky and hear their voices, whether they exist or not? Is belief in gods as much a part of being human as language and music? The answer, of course, is that we don't know. Maybe there is a religion gene that drives most of us to believe in gods. But while this is a fascinating question, one well worth seeking an answer to, it is not likely to prove that gods are real. At most a belief gene will only demonstrate that our species has the innate tendency to believe. So what?

Remember, we seem to have an innate tendency to imagine monsters, too, but that does not mean Godzilla is real.

The fact that there is no agreement among the world's believers—and never has been—tells us that the popularity of belief offers no help to claims of a particular god's existence. Competing and contradictory claims for thousands of gods by billions of people throughout history only says one thing: we are capable of believing just about anything.

CHAPTER 48 BIBLIOGRAPHY AND RECOMMENDED READING

Martin, Michael, ed., *The Cambridge Companion to Atheism*. Cambridge: Cambridge University Press, 2007. An excellent collection of articles and essays on nonbelief.

Zuckerman, Phil. "Atheism: Contemporary Rates and Patterns." In *The Cambridge Companion to Atheism*, edited by Michael Martin, 47–65. Cambridge: Cambridge University Press, 2005.

Chapter 49

The end is near.

The hour of judgment is nigh . . .
—Koran, 54:1

The end of all things is at hand.
—1 Peter 4:7

*Religion was the creation of fear. Knowledge
destroys fear. Without fear, religion can't survive.*
—Michael Moorcock

W hy did I bother to write this book? Why are you bothering to read it? After all, the world is going to end soon. So, shouldn't we both do more important things with our time, like praying or digging a backyard bunker? Why not just crawl back into bed and await the apocalypse? After all, believers of numerous religions keep saying that obvious signs of the end are all around us. Earthquakes, tsunamis, hurricanes, poverty, war, terrorism, and even decadent Hollywood are all proof of the fast-approaching end.

Then again, maybe we shouldn't worry too much about the end of the world. Maybe we would all be better off if we live life under the assumption that the world won't end anytime soon. After all, countless believers have been wrong 100 percent of the time so far. Predicting the end has been a standard component of so many religions for so long that it's time to ask: When will it be enough? When can we agree that these claims of a god ending the world as we know it are not worth listening to anymore? People who claim this stuff never have good evidence or sensible arguments and, most important, they are always wrong. Why should we listen to the current round of warnings when believers have been crying wolf since the Bronze Age and probably long before? Of course, such reckless optimism for world's immediate future puts me at odds with hundreds of millions of believers who are convinced that a horrible—yet somehow wonderful—destruction is imminent.

Not only do many believers anticipate the end of the world as we know it, but they are happy about it. Some people actually think it will be great when blood runs in the streets and the skies are ablaze from nuclear explosions because it will mean that their god is fulfilling the master plan. I suspect they look forward to having a big "I told you so!" moment, too. Many believers have no idea how creepy and deranged all of this sounds to an atheist. I, for example, tend to think that mass death and destruction are bad things. So it's tough for me to understand how so many believers of various religions can get all giddy over an event in which billions of people will die agonizing deaths. But somehow they do. This stuff really excites them. If you doubt it, visit the popular Rapture Ready Web site, and be sure to check out the daily rundown of the world's worst news. Every natural disaster, every war, and every report of a disease outbreak in the developing world is considered exciting evidence in support of their god's fast-approaching day of reckoning. The site also includes a "Rapture Index" that claims to gauge how close we are to the return of Jesus. It is based on subjective numbers that are assigned to measure the level of activity in a variety of categories, including: false Christs, Satanism, financial unrest, earthquakes, and the Antichrist. The numbers are added up and tracked, making this a sort of Dow Jones Industrial Average for people who are heavily invested in the supernatural world. Too bad this Web site wasn't around when the Black Death killed more than a third of Europe's population seven hundred years ago or when Hitler was on the march in 1940. The Rapture Index would have gone through the roof.

The primary message of the Rapture Ready site is that you do not want to miss out on the rapture, an early departure for the approved believers. All nonbelievers and "wrong" believers who are left behind will be in for some tough times with plenty of nuclear war, diseases, riots, famine, and anarchy to cope with. An article on the Rapture Ready Web site called "Scary Scary Stuff" offers the following comment: "The Bible doesn't say exactly what percent of the world's population will perish, but it's clear from Scripture that the death rate will be very high. If you add up the judgments described in the Book of Revelation, at least two-thirds of the population will be wiped out" (Rapture Ready, 2007). How nice.

Skeptics, of course, point to the complete absence of any evidence for this stuff and the completely unproven connection between natural disasters and the return of a god. But I am also amazed that so many of these believers don't seem disturbed or curious about a god who would do this. This scenario of a violent end to all we know seems so unnecessary and evil. Why would a god have to scorch the earth and kill billions of people just because they worshipped on the wrong side of the tracks or were too skeptical to believe? I don't know about you, but if I was running the universe I am sure I could come up with a much nicer final act for humankind. At the very least I would leave out famine and war. I would probably have to go ahead and spare the children pestilence as well. But, for some reason, many believers do not recognize the obviously immoral act of causing or allowing the destruction of billions of children, women, and men.

Although the idea of a supernatural doomsday has inspired many movies and many more laughs, some believers are very serious about their end-of-the-world predictions. Many of them sincerely believe that this is the last generation, that their god is about to turn the world upside down, save the people he likes, and punish the nonbelievers. Well-meaning infidels like me will die a horrible death and then be tossed into some cruel pit to suffer forever. At least that's what some believers tell me will happen when their god's love reigns on Earth. Obviously, I hope they are wrong about all this. Then again, if there is a judgment day, maybe an omniscient god or gods would know my mind and see that I have only been honest to the reality before my eyes. I'm unwilling to pretend to believe in gods that seem to be nothing more than the creations of human imagination. Maybe upon reflection the gods would blame themselves for being so elusive and see fit to forgive me. Who knows? They might even praise all atheists for their intellectual honesty and brave skepticism. Wouldn't it be funny if a god punished everyone who had eagerly embraced the idea of billions of people dying when the world ended, and then rewarded all those who had the moral sense to criticize it?

Many believers have tried to scare me into believing in their god with detailed descriptions of their end-of-the-world senarios. When they do this, I usually ask them why it is that they are not afraid of the doomsday prophecies that come from other religions. Why, for example, aren't Christians terrified about the Islamic prophecy of the end of the world? Why aren't they afraid that they will suffer a horrible death and end up in the Islamic hell? After all, some Muslims say there are clear signs all around us that the end is near. However, despite using nearly identical arguments, Christians and Muslims casually reject each other's predictions and don't fear the other's doomsday. If they were to use that same skepticism and analysis on their own religion's claims, they would discover that there is no apocalypse to fear at all.

Believers who are confident about the end of the world being close often use this danger to justify their belief. They cite it as a motivation to believe and worship as passionately as possible. But perhaps if it can be shown that there is nothing to these claims, then maybe, just maybe, some believers will be more likely to question the existence of their gods. Once Armageddon's gun is no longer aimed at their heads, they might be likely to think a little more clearly about their gods.

What is weird about these prophets of doom is that they could be right. No, there is no reason to suspect that they are correct about the destruction of civilization by gods and magic, because no believer in the last several thousand years has ever produced any convincing evidence to support such a claim. What is true, however, is that there are very real dangers to global civilization. One does not need a divine revelation to know this. We are now or may one day soon be under serious threats from nuclear war, unstoppable germs, artificial intelligence gone berserk, environmental collapse, nanobots run amok, an asteroid on the way, supervolcanoes, huge methane burps from the seafloor, and so forth. Just become a regular reader of *New Scientist*, *Scientific American*, and *National Geographic* magazines and you will learn that there are no long-term guarantees for life on this planet. There are a wide variety of frightening scenarios that can bring about our end—no gods required. Strangely, I have found most believers to be much less interested in global destruction from human or natural sources as they are with their gods' doomsday.

There are two simple reasons why no one should worry about gods destroying the world or killing most of the people on Earth today, tomorrow, next year, or ever. First, there is no evidence that any supernatural disaster is coming, soon or ever. No evidence. Second, the line of people who have made these claims is very long, stretching back many centuries, and they have been wrong every time. *Every time.*

When people make the claim that believing in a god is urgent because the clock is ticking and doomsday is almost here, they need to provide a good reason why anyone should accept this as a credible danger. Saying it's so doesn't make it so. Many people around the world today fear the "evil eye." But I am not afraid of it because there is no evidence that a brief stare from someone can curse me or cause me to have a bad day. I don't believe it because, in thousands of years, no one has ever been able to show that the evil eye is anything more than a made-up belief. I view religious doomsday claims the same way. I refuse to lose sleep over the unproven possibility of a god ending the world. Until someone comes up with evidence, or at least one good argument for believing it, I won't worry and neither should you.

If someone wants to believe in a god, fine. I just hope they don't do so because they fear doomsday. It is the world's most enduring empty threat and after all these years no one should fall for it anymore.

CHAPTER 49 BIBLIOGRAPHY AND RECOMMENDED READING

Gorenberg, Gershom. *The End of Days: Fundamentalism and the Struggle for the Temple Mount.* New York: Oxford University Press, 2000. An enlightening—and frightening—study of people who believe the apocalypse is near.

Halsell, Grace. *Forcing God's Hand: Why Millions Pray for a Quick Rapture—and Destruction of Planet Earth.* Beltsville, MD: Amana Publications, 1999.

McGuire, Bill. *A Guide to the End of the World: Everything You Never Wanted to Know.* New York: Oxford University Press, 2002. If you insist on worrying about the end of the world, then at least do it sensibly. This book, written by a scientist, explains realistic threats that face our planet.

"Scary Scary Stuff." Rapture Ready Web site, May 2007. http://raptureready.com/ rap21.html.

Chapter 50

I am afraid of not believing.

Some believers accuse skeptics of having nothing left but a dull, cold scientific world. I am left with only art, music, literature, theater, the magnificence of nature, mathematics, the human spirit, sex, the cosmos, friendship, history, science, imagination, dreams, oceans, mountains, love and the wonder of birth. That'll do me.

—Lynne Kelly

No believers have ever admitted to me that they are afraid of letting go of their belief in a god. But many times I have walked away from conversations convinced that they were. It is understandable why many people might be reluctant, even afraid, to allow their minds the freedom to challenge belief in a god. It can't be easy for everyone to question the existence of a god who is seen as the ultimate force of good as well as a powerful protector in a dangerous world. For some believers it may feel like a terrible betrayal of family and friends to question the existence of a god. Another reason believers may shy away from skepticism and analysis is fear of punishment from an angry god. Religious leaders may have told them that a horrible fate awaits if they ever turn away from their god. Some of these leaders claim that those who stop believing in their god won't even have to wait until the afterlife to suffer but will be punished in this life with ill health, family troubles, employment problems, or worse. Christian television preacher Pat Robertson, for example, is well known for repeatedly warning people who are not religious enough for his taste. Several times he has said that his god will teach them a lesson the hard way, with a hurricane, earthquake, or some other divine slap-down. While atheists may laugh off such threats, many believers do not.

Another intimidating obstacle for believers who might otherwise consider rethinking the reality of their god or gods is the negative impact becoming an atheist can have on their personal lives. Friends and family relationships may change as a result. Sadly, sometimes relationships end when two people no longer have a god in common. It's not a difficult transition for all, however. Many atheists have the good fortune to have family members who love them unconditionally and friends who may be believers but are also sophisticated enough to respect one's right to think for themselves. Some of these atheists may not fully appreciate how difficult and scary it can be for a believer in more difficult circumstances to openly admit that they no longer think gods are real. It can be a rough ride for some people and no atheist should ever take a believer's fears lightly. Some religions discourage or even forbid associating with atheists. For example, some followers of Christianity, Islam, and Judaism are guilty of this and make no apologies for it. It's beyond me how they get away with it in the twenty-first century in supposedly developed societies where other such forms of prejudice are strongly condemned. Clearly, there can be a very real threat of banishment from one's social network or family when belief in gods stops making sense. For this reason, I would never suggest that a believer underestimate potential problems. Family and friends matter. Jobs matter. Safety matters. However, thinking for yourself and respecting yourself matter too.

Believers also may tend to avoid questioning the existence of gods because they fear the possibility of having to admit they were wrong. But this is not a big deal because everybody is wrong about many things over the course of their lives. There is no shame in being flat-out wrong, especially when it comes to religious belief, considering how it is pushed on most people in childhood when they may have been too vulnerable and trusting to challenge it. No one should ever feel guilty about having believed in a god, no matter how silly it may seem in retrospect. For most of us, it's part of being human and growing up in human culture. I don't feel ashamed because I prayed to a god when I was ten years old. That's what I was told to do by people I trusted, people who were smarter than me, so I did it. Today I view it as a rite of passage or part of a progression that I can be proud of. I trusted, I believed, I thought, and now I don't believe.

The only shame a believer feels should come from refusing to think critically. There is no excuse for refusing to analyze claims and ask hard questions. This can go on within your private thoughts where there is no danger of repercussions from the outside world. We may or may not be naturally inclined to believe in gods but we are definitely curious by nature. Deny this human trait and you deny who you are. In my view, questioning a god's existence is not necessarily a betrayal of that god anyway. If you believe your god made you—as well as that big brain in your skull—then why would this god be upset if you used it to challenge the most important claim of all? This god you believe in made you a member of a thinking species. So think! Why would a god have bothered creating these powerful, analytical human brains in the first place if we were never meant to use them to their full potential? If your god is real, then chances are you will be commended, not condemned, for putting that finely crafted brain to work. If your god is not real, however, then there is nothing to worry about. And if you fear that your god is the type to get angry over sincere human curiosity and honest inquiry, then maybe it's time for you to shop around for a more mature god. There are, after all, thousands to choose from.

Believers should not be troubled by the false assumption that one can either be a happy believer or a bitter, militant atheist who is committed to fighting religion. I'm an atheist and I am certainly far from bitter and militant. I think I'm a positive and optimistic person. And despite the terribly obnoxious behavior of some believers, I would never support the banning of religion or discrimination against believers solely for what they think. I believe freedom of thought should be a basic human right. Yes, I think it would be good for the world if reason, free thought, and science became so popular and widely respected that belief in gods faded away. But I would never support imposing atheism by bullying or by law.

I wish that I could offer my own life as a shining example of how one can go from devout believer to atheist and end up happy, but I cannot because I don't feel that I was ever fully convinced that gods were real. Even as a child when my sweet mother dragged me to church on Sundays, I questioned and I doubted. I sincerely searched for a god to believe in as a young adult but came up empty again. I have traveled widely and visited the world's most sacred places. I touched holy ground, rubbed blessed stones, inhaled incense, listened to chants, and even sang and prayed with believers. Faith healers have placed their hands on my body and I touched the sacred rock above Adam's supposed resting place. I believe that I have searched for the gods more sincerely and more thoroughly than most people who have ever lived. But for all my travels and efforts I found only believers and no gods.

I probably have been an atheist my entire life, even as a child, but was so busy trying to believe that I never noticed. I once worried that not believing in any of these gods my fellow humans offered would make me a bad person or hinder my life in some way. But I know now that one can have a wonderful life without believing in gods. I am still as passionately curious about my world and my universe as I was when I was a little boy. I could live for a thousand years and never run out of things to do. But what about true believers? Can one believe in a god deeply and still have happiness and fulfillment when that belief goes away? Dan Barker, the Christian preacher who became an atheist, says yes. Perhaps his journey provides a better example than mine for believers.

> The reason I am happy is because I choose to be happy. For me, happiness is primarily a state of mind and since I now control my own

mind, I also control my own happiness. I am no puppet of a higher mind, no slave to eternity. I never knew real joy before I regained possession of my own mind. (Barker 1992, 228)

There is joy in rationality, happiness in clarity of mind. Free thought is thrilling and fulfilling—absolutely essential to mental health and happiness. You cannot freely give or receive love until you first love yourself; and you cannot love yourself if your only claim to worth comes as an undeserved gift from a "merciful" dictator.

I have lived the Christian life. I prefer now to live my own life. (Barker 1992, 230)

Barker is directing these statements to Christianity, his former religion, but the message applies to all beliefs. There really is joy to be found in living one's life free from an intimidating god who, after all, was probably only imaginary anyway.

Finally, believers can be reassured that they will not be swallowed up by a gaping hole in the earth if they take the plunge into reason and come up for air over on the side of atheism. Many millions of atheists today are living happy, positive lives. They are doctors, teachers, police officers, firefighters, construction workers, soldiers, peace activists, mommies, and daddies. They are much like anybody else. The only difference is that they don't look to gods for strength. Instead, they look within themselves or they reach out to family and friends. Atheists don't run crying to gods in times of crisis. They are more likely to lean on their fellow humans and appreciate them more for it. There is nothing to support the believers' charge that atheists lead sad lives that are somehow diminished by the absence of gods. I think the opposite might be true. If anything, atheists are more likely to enjoy every minute of their precious lives. It may well be that atheists are in a better position to smell more flowers and hug their children a little tighter than those who believe they live in a god's shadow. Perhaps it is atheists who are more alive than anyone. But, then again, not believing is no guarantee of anything. A person who becomes an atheist may change a lot or change very little.

Believers can dismiss the idea that becoming an atheist separates them from everyone else. Atheists are more common than most people imagine, and most of them are probably far more boring and normal than anyone would suspect. The typical believer who becomes an atheist is likely to find that they are still the same person, at least initially. Becoming an atheist simply means you no longer believe gods are real. That's all there is to it. It is the universe around you that seems to change because you finally see it for what it really is: a big, beautiful, scary, and inspirational place. Atheism only opens your eyes and puts both your feet on the ground.

The rest is up to you.

CHAPTER 50 BIBLIOGRAPHY AND RECOMMENDED READING

Barker, Dan. *Losing Faith in Faith: From Preacher to Atheist*. Madison, WI: Freedom From Religion Foundation, 1992.

Free Inquiry. http://www.secularhumanism.org. An outstanding magazine that promotes critical thinking, skepticism, and humanism.

Kurtz, Paul. *Living without Religion: Eupraxsophy*. Amherst, NY: Prometheus Books, 1994. An excellent book capable of calming those who are worried about life with no gods.

Skeptical Inquirer. http://www.csicop.org/si. Another great periodical; challenges paranormal claims and pseudoscience.